Bigamy and Bloodshed

True Crime History

Bigamy and Bloodshed

The Scandal of Emma Molloy and
the Murder of Sarah Graham

Larry E. Wood

The Kent State University Press

KENT, OHIO

© 2019 by The Kent State University Press, Kent, Ohio 44242
All rights reserved
Library of Congress Catalog Number 2019014335
ISBN 978-1-60635-385-1
Manufactured in the United States of America

Library of Congress Cataloging-in-Publication Data
Names: Wood, Larry (Larry E.), author.
Title: Bigamy and bloodshed : the scandal of Emma Molloy and the murder of Sarah
        Graham / Larry E. Wood.
Description: Kent, Ohio : Kent State University Press, [2019] | Series: True crime
        history | Includes bibliographical references and index.
Identifiers: LCCN 2019014335 | ISBN 9781606353851 (pbk.)
Subjects: LCSH: Graham, George, -1886. | Molloy, Emma, 1839-1907. | Murder--
        Missouri--Case studies. | Polygamy--Missouri. | Lynching--Missouri.
Classification: LCC HV6533.M8 W66 2019 | DDC 364.152/3092--dc23
LC record available at https://lccn.loc.gov/2019014335

23 22 21 20 19   5 4 3 2 1

Contents

Preface

I FIRST became familiar with the Sarah Graham murder case around 2000 as I was perusing Jonathan Fairbanks and Clyde Edwin Tuck's *Past and Present of Greene County, Missouri,* published in 1915. I was struck by the authors' recollection of the preliminary hearing for two of the defendants in the case as "the most spectacular court procedure in the entire life of the county," and the more I researched the case, the more intrigued I became.

The case had a cast of characters ready made for a real-life drama. A smooth-talking man with a troubled past who had been twice married to his first wife, the mother of his children. A second wife, a chaste young woman naive in the ways of the world, but completely devoted to her roguish husband. Most intriguing, one of America's most famous temperance revivalists embroiled in scandal and accused of hypocrisy by her enemies in the press and the liquor industry. And, finally, a mob of vigilantes bent on dispensing rough justice, Missouri style. The case made headlines across the country, with the *New York Times* calling Sarah's murder "one of the most shocking crimes ever committed in the West."

In 2004, I wrote an article about the Sarah Graham murder case for the now defunct *Ozarks Mountaineer,* and I thought at the time I'd probably never write about it again. But something kept bringing me back to it. I included a chapter about it, similar to the magazine article, in my 2009 book, *Ozarks Gunfights and Other Notorious Incidents,* and the Sarah Graham case again made up a chapter in my book, *Wicked Springfield,* published in 2012.

But I still wasn't ready to let it go. I went on to other projects, but something kept drawing me back to the Sarah Graham murder story. It had all the elements of a compelling tale of true crime, and I knew there was a lot more to it than I had been able to chronicle in a twenty-five-hundred-word magazine article or one relatively short chapter of a book. I decided the Sarah Graham murder story deserved a complete telling. I hope readers agree.

Acknowledgments

I OWE A debt of gratitude to a number of people who contributed to my research for this book. First, I'd like to thank the reference department of the Joplin Public Library, in particular Jason Sullivan and Patty Crane, for filling my numerous interlibrary loan requests. Nellie Hoskins of the Galena (Kansas) Public Library also filled several interlibrary loan requests for me, and Patti Street at the adjacent Galena Archival Library was very helpful as well.

I spent a good deal of time at the Greene County Records and Archives, where Connie Yen and Steve Haberman greatly facilitated my search of Greene County Court Records pertaining to the Sarah Graham case.

I would like to thank Mary Alice Pacey of the Washington County Historical Society for showing me around Washington and for allowing me to copy her collection of Washington County newspapers clippings and transcriptions pertaining to the Graham case.

I appreciate the help of the Illinois State Archives in locating and forwarding George Graham's Illinois prison record. Matt Holdzkom of the Indiana Historical Society and Michael Vetman of the Indiana State Archives filled similar requests in a very timely fashion.

Rhonda Purvis of the Christian County Circuit Clerk's office was very helpful in locating Christian County Circuit Court records pertaining to Emma Molloy, and library specialist Brandon Jason provided similar help at the Christian County Library.

I thank John Rutherford, local history associate at the Springfield-Greene County Library, and Ben Divin, digital imaging specialist at the same institution, for locating and providing me with two historic photos for use in this book.

I want to thank William Underwood, acquiring editor for the Kent State University Press, for his suggestions and prompt replies to my inquiries as I was writing this book. I also thank copy editor Valerie Ahwee for her thorough and professional edit of the manuscript and managing editor Mary Young for her attention to detail during the proofing stage.

Prologue

JOHN POTTER, Isaac Hise, and several other local men hitch up their teams and head out to the Emma Molloy farm three and a half miles northeast of Brookline on the Springfield road. The men are determined to search the Molloy premises to see whether they can find any sign of Sarah Graham, the missing woman everybody around Brookline has been talking about for the past several weeks. Ugly rumors have begun to circulate about what might have happened to her, and folks are up in arms over the possibility that she might have been killed.

An immigrant from Germany, the forty-eight-year-old Potter has lived in this area since before the Civil War, and he hasn't seen people so stirred up in a long time. Maybe not since the Battle of Wilson's Creek, five miles south of Brookline, claimed the lives of over five hundred men early in the war and gave the Confederacy temporary control of southwest Missouri.

Potter kept a store at Little York until 1871, when Brookline was established as a stop on the newly completed Frisco Railroad two miles to the east. Like most Little York residents, he packed up and moved to the new community, and he has served Brookline as both postmaster and storekeeper ever since. He was also the depot station agent for several years.[1]

Brookline enjoyed a brief boom as a lead mining camp during the mid-1870s, but most area residents farm the fertile soil of the surrounding prairie. They use the railroad stop at Brookline to ship their wheat and other produce, go to one of Brookline's three churches on Sunday, and otherwise go about their customary lives. Not much out of the ordinary has happened in Brookline since a tornado heavily damaged the place in 1883. The community bounced back and is now a bustling village of 150 residents, but Brookline is still a place where things like murders and missing-person mysteries just don't happen.

Not until now.

As both storekeeper and postmaster, Potter knows everybody in the Brookline area, and very little happens that he's not privy to. It was his role as postmaster that first drew him into the Sarah Graham case last October when he and his friend William O'Neal, the Brookline Township constable, started receiving letters from Sarah's father, Marquis Gorham, and other Gorham family members inquiring as to Sarah's whereabouts. In late September, Mrs. Graham left her Indiana home with plans to live with her husband, George, on the Molloy farm, but nobody back in Fort Wayne has heard a word from her since.

And everybody on the Molloy farm claims not to have seen her either.

But Potter has serious doubts about that. Every inquiry he and O'Neal have made has been deflected or rebuffed by George Graham or some of the rest of the outfit living on the Molloy farm.

There was the time last fall when Graham told Potter that Sarah's whereabouts was none of his business. Or the time in early January when Graham saw O'Neal in Brookline and assured him the only reason Sarah hadn't written her folks was because she had a sore hand, which was the phoniest excuse O'Neal and Potter had ever heard. Then, in mid-January, after O'Neal learned that Graham had remarried the previous summer, he went out to the Molloy farm to inquire again about Sarah's whereabouts, and the new wife, Cora Lee, wouldn't talk to him, telling him to come back when George was home.

And the highfalutin Emma Molloy hasn't helped matters either. Maybe judge James Baker and his teetotaling Springfield friends are under the mesmerizing spell of the famous temperance orator, but her so-called charm doesn't cut any mustard with Potter and the people around Brookline. Because they've seen nothing but her cheeky side. Like the time a month earlier when she came charging into Brookline in a huff, demanding to see a letter Graham's thirteen-year-old son Charlie had mailed to his relatives back in Indiana. Afraid Charlie was going to reveal something incriminating. Obviously hiding something. Trying to protect George Graham and her foster daughter, Cora Lee.

Some folks have even been gossiping about the attractive Mrs. Molloy getting too cuddly with the disreputable Graham, her own foster son-in-law. Like Mrs. Stokes, the woman who saw Mrs. Molloy and Graham strolling hand in hand in the field last summer, shortly after Judge Baker deposited them and the rest of their clan on the old Cooper farm.

Even after Graham got caught forging checks in January and was arrested later in the month as a bigamist, Cora Lee and Emma Molloy kept trying to hide something. Like the time in early February when Sarah's brother-in-law came from Indiana to look for the missing woman and Cora tried to keep Charlie and his seven-year-old brother, Roy, from talking to him.

But this time Potter and his friends mean to get to the bottom of Sarah Graham's mysterious disappearance, once and for all. They approach the Molloy home on the Springfield road at the south boundary of the farm. Entering the front gate, they pause near the house to announce their mission. Emerging from the house, Cora Lee seems upset, but she doesn't try to stop them. The men continue along a diagonal trail that cuts across the Molloy farm from the south property line to the east one and then head down into a low-lying area northeast of the house to an old abandoned well that they especially want to search. They've brought along a windlass for that purpose, to lower a man down into the shaft to see whether the missing woman lies dead at the bottom.

There is scarcely anybody on the farm to obstruct the men's effort. George Graham sits in a Springfield jail on the bigamy charge, and Emma Molloy is off on one of her evangelical crusades. Cora is too busy tending to Charlie and his younger brother, Roy, to interfere, trying to keep them at the house and away from the well while the men are working. Even now she seems to hide something, afraid of what the men might find. Or maybe afraid of what she knows they will find.

The men throw off the brush and boards covering the old well and lower a lantern into it, but it's hard to see beyond the cribbed, upper portion of the shaft. Isaac Hise volunteers to go down and explore its depths. Using the windlass, the other men gradually lower him into the well. At a depth of about fifteen feet, the cribbing ends, and the well narrows briefly to a rectangular limestone shaft wide enough to admit the passage of an

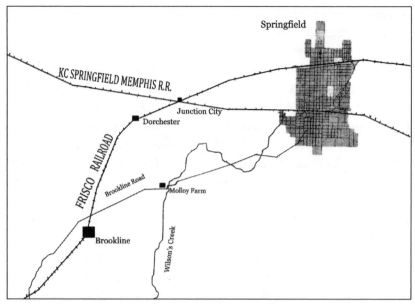

Map of southwest Greene County in the late 1800s, showing location of the Molloy farm in relation to Brookline, Dorchester, Nichols Junction (that is, Junction City), and Springfield (Composite drawing based on an 1884 topographic map of Greene County by the US Geological Survey and an 1876 atlas of Greene County)

adult male but with little room to spare. It then widens into a cave-like room. Hise gingerly makes his way through the narrow opening, and the men lower him carefully another thirty or forty feet to the cave bottom. The floor is damp but with little or no standing water. The room is about eight feet wide from east to west and about twenty feet long from north to south. The base of the cave slants steeply downward toward the north so that anything thrown into the shaft might roll in that direction. Hise steps over and holds up his lantern to peer into the darkness of the north chamber. There, lying on the floor, is a woman's nude, decomposed body.

Hise yells to his fellow workers up above, relaying the news of his discovery, and a buzz of excitement passes through the small crowd gathered round the well. Presently Cora Lee comes down the trail from the house, accompanied by Charlie, Roy, and two teenage girls. Cora pauses near the east gate beside A. J. McMurray, one of the men who has come to the farm to help search the premises. "Mr. McMurray," she asks with disbelief, "are you sure they have discovered the body of a woman in that well?" Assured that a woman's body has indeed been found, Cora says she doesn't want the children to see anything that is taken out of the well, and she starts shooing the boys back toward the house, leaving McMurray to wonder whether Cora's show of surprise is a sincere expression of disbelief or a phony put-on for his benefit.

John Potter, leaving the retrieval of the body to Hise and the other men, hops in his buggy and starts for Springfield to report the news to county authorities. Sarah Graham has been found! Oh, there will be an inquest to officially determine her identity, but Potter, like Hise and the other men back at the well, already knows in his heart who the woman is. And he's almost as sure who killed her: George Graham. The only real question is: *How much help did he have?*

1

The Agreeable, Intelligent, and Interesting Emma Molloy

EMMA MOLLOY was no stranger to trial and tribulation. She had dealt with heartache and loss from the time she was a little girl, and, after she became an outspoken and well-known advocate of temperance and women's rights, controversy walked beside her as a constant companion. But nothing could have prepared her for the ordeal she faced in Springfield, Missouri, in the late winter and spring of 1886.

Emma was born Emily F. Barrett on July 17, 1839, in South Bend, Indiana, the daughter of William Lovell Barrett and Harriett Newton Barrett. Of the three Barrett children, Emily, or Emma as she was later called, was the only one to survive infancy. Emma's mother died, too, when Emma was not yet two years old. Although Emma was not old enough to comprehend her loss except on an instinctual level, the premature death of her mother was but the first of many tragedies in her life.[1]

Left a motherless child, Emma was boarded out to other families for several years during early childhood while William Barrett went to Chicago to work. The absence of her mother and the temporary abandonment by her father left young Emma with feelings of loneliness and insecurity, but she also developed a strong sense of independence and self-reliance. She found warmth and affection in the home of George and Martha Bryson and in the home of their daughter and son-in-law, Amanda and Ruben Burroughs. George Bryson was a Methodist minister, and prayer and Bible study were a part of Emma's everyday life. She attended district schools as well as a small private school and was a bright student.[2]

In the early 1850s, Emma's father returned to South Bend with a new wife, Harriett Eaker Barrett. Emma's later writings suggest a difficult relationship with her stepmother, and she became increasingly determined to establish her independence. At the age of fifteen or sixteen, she left South Bend to teach at a rural one-room school several miles outside town. But she aspired to be a writer. Praised in school for her literary bent, she started submitting essays and poems for publication when she was just sixteen years old. Assuming the identity of an older woman and using a pseudonym, she scolded girls who socialized with no higher purpose in life than finding a man, criticized men who were untrue in romance, and denounced gossips who ruined reputations.[3] The latter theme was one she would find herself returning to throughout her life, sometimes in defense of her own reputation.

On April 8, 1858, at South Bend, when Emma was not yet nineteen, she married Louis A. Pradt, a printer from Wisconsin. She moved with Pradt to Wisconsin, but the couple relocated several times during the early years of their marriage. After a brief return to South Bend, they moved to Montgomery, Alabama, where both Emma and Louis had relatives. Writing to a cousin, Anna, from Montgomery in August 1860, Emma voiced her support for Southern Democrat presidential candidate John C. Breckinridge, suggesting that his election would be the only way to save the Union from dissolution. Emma praised Louis as a good husband and said she was happy.[4]

Her politics would change over the next several years. And the state of her marriage would change even more rapidly. Although Emma made no mention of Louis's excessive drinking in her letter to her cousin, her husband's taste for alcohol was already putting a strain on their marriage. For a young woman who'd grown up in the Methodist Church, listening to sermons against liquor, her husband's dissipation was very distressing.[5]

During another visit to South Bend, Emma gave birth to a daughter, Lottie, in early 1861. The Pradts then moved back to Wisconsin, settling in Madison, where a son, Allie, was born in early 1863. Later the same year, though, tragedy struck when Lottie died of diphtheria. The shock of the little girl's death caused Louis to sober up for a while, but then Allie died, too, in the summer of 1864, less than a year after his sister's death. Grief-stricken by the death of her children, Emma turned to her Christian faith for comfort, but she carried the loss with her for the rest of her life. Her husband, meanwhile, dealt with the tragedy by relapsing into habitual drunkenness.[6]

Louis's drinking strained not only the emotional well-being of the Pradts' marriage but also the couple's financial resources. To help make ends meet, the multitalented Emma sold some of her stories and poems, gave guitar lessons, and did other odd jobs, like taking in washing and sewing. But whatever efforts the couple made to salvage their marriage were in vain. In 1866, Emma took the bold step of leaving her husband and returning to South Bend. The next year, she filed for divorce in Dane County, Wisconsin, taking advantage of the state's liberal divorce law, which allowed for chronic drunkenness as a ground.[7]

Emma married Edward Molloy, editor of the *South Bend National Union,* on November 27, 1867, just two weeks after her divorce from Louis Pradt was final. The editor of the rival *St. Joseph Valley Register* dared to suggest that the couple might have taken a "honeymoon" before their marriage. Emma and her new husband had much in common, including the fact that Molloy was, like Emma, a strong advocate of temperance, and he promptly made her coeditor of his struggling Democratic weekly newspaper.[8]

The Molloys were active in the Editors and Publishers Association of Northern Indiana, and the organization's editors often traded gibes. The other editors tended at first to view Molloy's appointment of his wife as his editorial partner with amusement, but most quickly gained a measure of respect for her journalistic and business acumen. Largely through Emma's efforts, the Molloys' newspaper got out of debt and began to hold its own financially, and her fellow editors quickly recognized her writing ability. Commenting shortly after Mrs. Molloy assumed her duties as "editress" of the *National Union,* the *Goshen Democrat* allowed, "She wields a vigorous pen."[9]

In fact, the *Democrat,* under the editorship of W. A. Beane, had little but praise for Emma Molloy, referring to her at various times as "talented" and "lovely." But not all her colleagues in northern Indiana liked the idea of a woman in the newspaper business. In early March 1869, Beane praised Emma as an "accomplished" editor, "admirable writer," and "one of the best conversationalists of the day," and he concluded the piece by asking, "Who wouldn't have an editress to prepare the tender loins for his spinal columns?" The *Plymouth Republican* promptly replied in its next issue, "This is all very well but who would not rather have an editress prepare the tender loins for the stomach?"[10]

Long an advocate of women's rights, Mrs. Molloy reprinted essays by women's suffrage leaders like Elizabeth Cady Stanton and Susan B. Anthony in the *National Union,* and she soon began writing her own editorials in support of greater opportunities for women, including the right to vote. Both she and her husband denounced men who mistreated women, and she argued against restrictive divorce laws that forced women to stay in abusive relationships. In one essay, provocatively titled "Free Love," she declared that a woman should have as much right to free herself from a "besotted husband" as a man would in a similar situation, and she said that the current laws sanctioned "legal marital slavery." In another essay, she defended a local woman who had been denounced for having an abortion. Such views placed Emma in the vanguard of the women's rights movement in post–Civil War America. Although less well known than feminist pioneers like Elizabeth Cady Stanton and Susan B. Anthony, Emma was just as ardent in her insistence upon women's equality.[11]

Emma did not ignore the cause of temperance in her essays. She expressed alarm at the prevalence of drinking among young men and lamented the harm alcohol had done to former schoolmates and others she had known growing up.[12]

In the fall of 1869, Mrs. Molloy attended the Western Women's Suffrage Convention in Chicago, and early the following year she undertook a speaking tour on behalf of women's rights throughout northern Indiana. Public speaking by a woman was a radical step in 1870, but her speech titled "Woman" was generally well received all along the lecture circuit. Although the text of this early speech does not survive, Emma might have toned down her message in order to make it more palatable to a curious audience. After speaking to "highly pleased and interested audiences" at South Bend and La Porte, "the fair lecturer" spoke around February 1 at Elkhart, where she made a favorable impression partly because of the modesty of her demands and subtlety of her delivery. The editor of the *Elkhart Review* agreed with Mrs. Molloy that women were "capable of intellectual culture more profound than the latest fashions" and deserved a chance to occupy positions more exalted than "domestic drudges." He opined that if men would concede this, they would "hear less of 'women's rights'" and that "if the pioneers in the cause of woman would all make their appeals as modestly and logically as Mrs. Molloy . . . , we apprehend they would gain more converts."[13]

On February 10, Emma brought her speaking tour to Goshen, and she and her husband stopped in at the office of the *Goshen Times.* The Goshen newspaperman's jocular remark about the meeting in that day's issue of his newspaper suggests that Emma's speaking tour was seen at this point, like her groundbreaking editorship of the *National Union,* as an interesting novelty: "We received a call this morning from Mrs. Emma F. Molloy and her 'worse' half, (this is the way it will read in the days of 'Women's Rights')."[14]

In late August 1870, Emma gave birth to her and Ed's first and only child, a baby boy named Franklin. Emma continued lecturing and editing well into her pregnancy, earning a reputation for hard work and achievement in what were normally men's fields. D. T. Phillips and W. M. Nichols, new editors of the *Plymouth Republican,* credited the success of the Editorial Association of Northern Indiana convention held in South Bend in the spring of 1870 largely to "the exertions and influence of Mrs. Molloy." They praised her as "one of the very few women we have met . . . capable of raising and maintaining their minds above the one idea—a new bonnet and fashionable society—and devoting their talents and energies for the good of their sex and the benefit of mankind."[15]

Emma resumed activities soon after Frank was born. In the fall of 1870, when the boy was just a couple of months old, the Molloys took Frank with them on an excursion with the editorial association. Remarking on the occasion later, a fellow editor remembered Mrs. Molloy as "agreeable, intelligent and interesting in her manner."[16]

Although most of the members of the Editorial Association of Northern Indiana held Mrs. Molloy in high regard, she was not always received with the same level of acceptance elsewhere. When she and her husband attended a state editorial association meeting in Indianapolis about June 1, 1871, Emma was barred from the editors' banquet because she was a woman.[17]

By 1871, her lectures, too, began to meet more criticism than they had during her initial speaking tour the year before. That spring, she spoke in Rochester, Indiana, on "Marriage," defending the state's controversial divorce law, which had recently come under attack as too lenient. The editor of the *Rochester Union Spy* thought "the lecture itself was good in matter and manner," and he was impressed with the breadth of Mrs. Molloy's views and the "profundity of her reasoning." But he believed Indiana's lax divorce law, which allowed for immediate remarriage, led to marital infidelity, and he felt Mrs. Molloy's speech would have been better received if she were not such "an extremist."[18]

In early 1872, the Molloys moved to New York to edit the *Cortland Journal*, a Republican newspaper. Given their progressive views, their political conversion was overdue because the Republican Party was widely seen as more sympathetic to reformist causes like racial equality and women's rights than the Democratic Party. As she was wont to do throughout her life, Emma fell ill for an extended period shortly after her arrival in New York. By summertime, she had convalesced, and she and Ed disposed of the *Journal* and returned to Indiana, where they started another Republican paper, the *Elkhart Observer.* Susan B. Anthony's "An Address to the Women of America" was given two columns on the front page of the first issue.[19]

In Elkhart, Emma became active in the Women's Aid Society, which helped poor families. But her sense of mission and obligation went beyond merely helping from afar. About 1873, she took in a little orphan girl named Mary Frances Pogue, adopted her, and changed her name to Etta Molloy.[20]

Emma threw herself into her work as a writer and editor for the *Observer,* and she also took an active part in managing the paper. Just as she had done at South Bend, Emma continued to editorialize in favor of women's rights, as well as to reprint the writings of feminist leaders like Elizabeth Cady Stanton and Mary Livermore. One day in May 1873, Emma collapsed at the newspaper office and went into an extended series of convulsive spasms. Her fellow editors speculated that the seizure resulted from overwork, but, whatever the cause, she would continue to suffer similar attacks on a sporadic basis in later life.[21]

Still haunted by the deaths of her children from her first marriage, Emma took a passing interest at Elkhart in spiritualism, a system of religious belief in vogue during the mid- to late 1800s, which held that one could communicate with the spirits of the dead through mediums.[22]

But the issue that increasingly occupied her mind was the cause of temperance. In 1873, Emma urged vigorous enforcement of the Baxter law, a restrictive liquor regulation newly passed in Indiana. During the spring of 1874, she took up the mantle of the Women's Crusade, which had begun in neighboring Ohio the previous December and was sweeping across the Midwest. Frustrated with men's failure to make progress for the cause of temperance, women took to the streets to confront saloon keepers and liquor dealers directly, and they began publicly denouncing the evils of alcohol. Emma helped organize the Elkhart Crusade, and she began lecturing on behalf of temperance, giving her first Crusade speech in her hometown of South Bend in March.[23]

For women to take to the streets to confront saloon keepers was a bold step in 1874, and for a woman on her own to embrace the public limelight of the lecture circuit, as Emma had earlier done on behalf of women's rights and now for the cause of temperance, was an even bolder one. The temperance movement in America dated at least to the early 1800s, but prior to the Civil War its leaders were almost all men. Mothers were held up as paragons of virtue, protecting and sustaining the home, and the pathetic image of the drunkard's wife was used as a tool in the fight against intemperance, but women took almost no direct part in the movement. Their main role was to teach their children to abstain. For a woman to be directly involved in any social or political movement outside the home was considered radical and unladylike. Women's limited role in the temperance movement gradually began to change in the years immediately before and after the Civil War with the emergence of feminist leaders like Ms. Stanton and Ms. Anthony, but women taking prominent activist roles was still controversial and rare at the time of the Women's Crusade and into the 1880s. When James Hiatt published *The Ribbon Workers* in the late 1870s, for instance, only one of the sixteen temperance leaders he profiled prominently was a woman—Emma Molloy.[24]

By April 1874, Mrs. Molloy was already acquiring a regional reputation as an eloquent and powerful temperance lecturer, but her contention that the battle against drunkenness could ultimately be won only through legislative action and by empowering women with the vote aligned her with radical feminists and alienated many listeners. Emma, though, was not one to shrink in the face of opposition. When she was invited to speak at a Grange picnic in Goshen in early August 1874 and was interrupted by a drunken man who objected to her speaking, a vote was taken among the Grangers as to whether she should be allowed to give her speech. Although the men voted overwhelmingly to let her talk,

Engraving of Emma
Molloy (From *The
Ribbon Workers*)

she declined to do so to protest the fact that a vote had even been taken because a male speaker before her had been allowed to speak with no questions asked. A few weeks later, Emma carried on with a temperance lecture in Westville despite a loud uproar outside the meeting hall organized by two local saloon keepers.[25]

In late 1874, Emma attended an organizational meeting of the Indiana branch of the Women's Christian Temperance Union (WCTU), an association that grew out of the Women's Crusade. Temperance advocates had traditionally relied primarily on moral suasion, particularly the wifely and motherly influence of good Christian women, to advance their cause, and whether political involvement was necessary, as Emma and other radical reformers now suggested, was a divisive issue within the movement. In 1875, when Emma spoke to the WCTU state convention in Indianapolis, some of her listeners were taken aback when she declared that prayer was insufficient in combating intemperance, but the soaring power of her rhetoric had most of the audience breaking into applause by the time she ended her lecture. Comparing the fight against intemperance to the abolitionist struggle that had brought four million human beings to a new life of freedom, she concluded: "Today is again heard the tocsin of the lifeguards of the nation, ringing from shore to shore, echoing from the crags of the Alleghenys to the snow-capped peaks of the Sierra Nevadas. It whispers of a new star that has dawned, that shall by and by, like a diamond blazing in the dark, burn above our national capital, proclaiming that forty millions are born to a new life of sobriety and prosperity."[26]

Emma continued to write for the *Elkhart Observer*, but she spent much of her time on the road lecturing on behalf of temperance. During her travels, she met and became good friends with Jerome J. Talbott, a reformed alcoholic and head of the Indiana branch of the Independent Order of Good Templars, a fraternal organization devoted to temperance. In the wake of her less than enthusiastic endorsement by the Indiana WCTU, Emma started working for the Good Templars, organizing chapters throughout the state.[27]

In the spring of 1875, Emma was thirty-five years old. Her first two children had died in infancy, and her first marriage had been shattered by alcohol. She and Ed Molloy had much in common, but their marriage seemed to be one of convenience. Disillusioned, Emma adopted a stoic attitude toward life, as she revealed in a letter to her cousin Anna in April of that year:

> Have at last got my heart in my fist and am working for fame and money now. I've concluded it's no use, this side of Heaven, to expect to find our ideal dreams realized, and that life is a grand tragedy which, stripped of the tinsel, paint and footlights, is a very commonplace sort of matter after all. I've been on the mountain top of affection, but I find the flowers frozen there, so I've settled down in the valley, where the fires of desolation have seared and blackened everything. But my teeth are set hard to bear life—endure it because I have to.

In the same letter, she mentioned Talbott and hinted that she had warm, if not romantic, feelings toward him. Speaking of the organizers who arranged her and Talbott's lectures, she said, "Wish people had some sense about calling us together all the time."[28]

Emma's work for the Good Templars proved brief, however. The group was split over the issue of race, and both Emma Molloy and Jerome Tal-

Emma Molloy, circa
1876–77 (Courtesy of The
History Museum, South
Bend, Indiana)

bott aligned themselves with the breakaway faction that supported full inclusion of blacks. Talbott was disappointed in his attempt to bring the Indiana branch of Templars into the new organization, and Emma withdrew from active work for the lodge. In late 1875, she traveled to New York as an Indiana delegate to the Women's Suffrage Convention.[29]

In early 1876, Emma and her husband sold the *Observer* and returned to South Bend. In late May, Mrs. Molloy lectured on temperance in Massachusetts, "astonishing the Bostonians with her wonderous powers on the platform," according to the *Goshen Times*.[30]

Also during 1876, Emma began working in the Ribbon Movement, a temperance campaign sweeping across the country that urged alcoholics to wear a red or blue ribbon as a token of their pledge not to imbibe. Her speeches not only stirred drinkers to pin on the ribbon, but she also offered personal counseling and follow-up help to "her boys," as she called them, through support groups called Ribbon clubs.[31]

In mid-August 1876, Jerome Talbott came to the Molloys' home, ill and broken down after having recently fallen off the sobriety wagon. The Molloys tried to nurse him back to health, but he died in early September. During his illness and after his death, he was ridiculed as a hypocrite, but Emma rose to his defense.[32]

In 1877, when Emma traveled to Vermont for a series of lectures, she came under editorial fire back home after it was alleged that during one of her speeches, she had denounced the Episcopalian bishop of the Indiana diocese as a drunkard, even though he was a very moderate drinker. She was also criticized for maligning the memory of her first husband with a lie. Often in her lectures Emma invoked the pitiful image of herself as a drunkard's wife and led her audiences to believe that Louis Pradt had died of alcoholism while they were still married, but a Montpelier newspaper reported that Pradt, in fact, had died of consumption in Vermont shortly after he and Emma divorced. Mrs. Molloy's speaking tour of Vermont was aborted when she suffered another convulsive attack during one of the lectures.[33]

In early 1878, Emma returned to Massachusetts on behalf of the Ribbon Movement for an extended lecture tour that garnered an estimated one hundred thousand temperance pledges. During her stay in Massachusetts, she met and worked with other prominent reformers like Mary Livermore. About the time her speaking tour in the state ended, she was engaged to sail for England on behalf of temperance later that year. After a few months at home in Indiana, Emma went back to Boston for a gathering in her honor on the eve of her journey. When she reached London in early October, she was received enthusiastically, drawing about five thousand people to one of her first lectures there.[34]

Emma's temperance work in England was cut short after she fell and injured her back in December, and she returned to her home in South Bend to recuperate. She was back at work, though, by the late winter of 1879. After speaking to several groups around South Bend about her experiences in England, she returned to Massachusetts to campaign on behalf of the state WCTU. Women in Massachusetts had won the right to vote in school elections, and, during her lectures there, Emma often encouraged them to register. About the same time, she started writing about her London experiences in the *Morning and Day of Reform*, a temperance newspaper published by Henry Waldo Adams of New York, and she was soon named an associate editor. During 1879, Emma increasingly dosed her temperance lectures with a strong tincture of religion as she came to believe that religious faith was necessary to help pledge takers maintain their vows of abstinence. She began to assume the role of evangelist as well as temperance campaigner, and she was occasion-

NEW ENGLAND TEMPERANCE GATHERING.

Complimentary Farewell to the Indiana Temperance Missionary, Mrs Emma Molloy—Meeting at the Bowdoin Street Baptist Church.

Headline describing the farewell gathering in Boston for Emma Molloy on the eve of her trip to England (From the *Boston Post*)

ally invited to speak from the pulpit of churches, even though very few denominations ordained women at the time.[35]

In 1879, the national WCTU, with the election of Frances Willard as its president, adopted a more activist approach in the fight against intemperance, and Emma became more involved in the organization. She seemed to embody Willard's "do everything" philosophy, which encouraged members to engage in a broad range of social reforms. One of the areas of reform that Emma was particularly interested in was the improvement of prison conditions and the rehabilitation of ex-convicts, and she was appointed to the prison committee of the national WCTU. In February 1880, she helped organize the Ex-Convicts' Aid Society of Indiana and was named vice president of the organization at its meeting in Indianapolis.[36]

After Emma and her husband moved to La Porte in the spring of 1880, she often visited the Indiana State Prison North at nearby Michigan City to minister to the inmates. During one of her visits, she met George E. Graham of Fort Wayne and soon took a special interest in the prisoner. Emma had no doubt made her share of errors in judgment during her life, but adopting Graham as one of her "boys" would prove to be the biggest.[37]

2

George Graham, the Irrepressible

IF THE PEOPLE of Springfield had been more familiar with George E. Graham's long criminal history before he came to Missouri, they might not have been so eager to take his word over Emma Molloy's when they both became suspects in Sarah Graham's disappearance in early 1886. However, if Emma had known the full scope of Graham's career as a shyster and scoundrel, she might not have been so ready to take him under her wing to begin with.

Graham was born in 1851 in Allegheny City, Pennsylvania, and his mother died when he was an infant or young child. His father, James Graham, remarried in Ohio in 1856, and during the same year he brought the family to Fort Wayne, Indiana, where he was employed as a railroad engineer.[1]

Young Graham, according to his own story as told to the *Fort Wayne Daily Gazette,* first ran afoul of the law when he was just ten years old. Arrested for stealing from a Fort Wayne businessman, the lad, in consideration of his extreme youth, was given a light sentence of three hours in the county jail.[2]

If the shock time was meant to rehabilitate the youngster, it failed miserably. Less than four months later, James Graham, despairing of reforming his unruly son by milder means, sent George back to his birthplace of Allegheny City, where he was committed to the House of Refuge, a reform school for youthful delinquents. After just a few weeks, authorities at the House of Refuge sent young Graham back home on the grounds that an Indiana resident should not be housed in a Pennsylvania institution.[3]

Back in Fort Wayne sometime later, a teenaged George tried to appropriate a horse and sleigh from a local citizen but was captured before he could make his getaway. Intervening to save his son from state prison, James Graham again sent the boy to the House of Refuge, where he spent about two months.[4]

George then went to the Canton, Ohio, area, where he'd lived briefly as a child, and he promptly got into trouble there for stealing a horse and buggy from Peter Gribble. James Graham paid $500 to get his son out of this scrape.[5]

After his release, George "went through the town like a streak of lightning," stealing pocketbooks, jewelry, and sundry other items from young men and women of Canton. He then hightailed it for Kenton, Ohio, where he stole a carriage and a span of horses from a man named Weatherall. Graham took the team and rig to nearby Lima and sold them for $750. "With an audacity all his own," the thief came back to Kenton, where he was arrested, tried, and, for some reason, acquitted.[6]

At Hamlet, Indiana, soon afterward, George met and "ingratiated himself into the affections of a young female telegraph operator." He became engaged to marry the young woman, borrowed $400 and a gold watch and chain from her, "and left her to reflect on the degeneracy of man."[7]

Back home in early June 1870, Graham perpetuated "one of the boldest and most audacious robberies ever committed in Fort Wayne" when he entered the office of W. A. Roberts, an associate of James Graham in the railroad business, and carried off everything he could lay his hands on. He took off for Chicago, where he was quickly arrested on a larceny charge. Found guilty in July in a Cook County court, he was sentenced to a year in the penitentiary at Joliet. He was admitted to the prison on July 22 at the age of nineteen, and he was discharged on June 26, 1871, after having served almost his full term.[8]

After his release, Graham came back to Fort Wayne and worked steadily for several months, commanding a good salary as an employee of the Cincinnati, Richmond & Fort Wayne Railroad. His acquaintances supposed he had reformed, and in 1871 the twenty-year-old Graham became engaged to nineteen-year-old Sarah Gorham, daughter of Marquis and Eunice Gorham of Fort Wayne. According to the *Daily Gazette,*

Sarah was "an estimable young lady, who knew nothing of George's previous career." On the evening George and Sarah were to have been married,
George was arrested for stealing the carriage and horses that he drove to
her house with. However, "his usual luck attended him, and he not only
managed to go scot free, but to convince the young lady that the arrest
was only a part of a blackmailing scheme to extort money from him."[9]

George Graham and Sarah Gorham were, in fact, married in Fort
Wayne on December 18, 1871. Whether the caper described above happened at that time or on a previous date, causing the wedding ceremony
to be postponed, is not clear.[10]

Not long after the wedding, Graham convinced Bernard Carr of Val-
paraiso, Indiana, that it would be to the man's financial benefit to lend
him a carriage and span of horses to canvass Porter County as a "life insurance agent." Graham drove the team and vehicle to Wanatah, nine
miles away, and sold them for $600. "Here again," lamented the *Daily
Gazette*, "his almost Satanic luck was with him, for an *intelligent* jury said
he was 'not guilty.'"[11]

Back in Fort Wayne, Graham joined the Independent Order of Good
Templars, and he became one of the group's more eloquent speakers
in assailing the evils of intemperance. He was elected worthy financial
secretary, but, according to the *Daily Gazette*, he was soon arrested for
embezzling Templar money to fund his own alcohol habit. Formally indicted for forgery at the April 1872 term of criminal court, Graham was
subsequently tried, found guilty, and sentenced to two years in prison,
but he was discharged in September after a defense motion in arrest of
judgment was sustained.[12]

While the forgery case was still being decided, George borrowed a
horse and buggy from Jacob Young of Fort Wayne, supposedly to drive
to a funeral, but he was "next heard of at Warsaw going west" and was
intercepted and arrested at Inwood. Brought back to Fort Wayne, he
was tried in the summer of 1872 but was again acquitted.[13]

His next adventure, according to the *Daily Gazette*, "border[ed] on the
ludicrous." In the early fall of 1872, Graham borrowed a horse and buggy
in Fort Wayne, appropriated four pairs of handcuffs, and proceeded to
nearby Monroeville. There he registered as a US detective, arrested a man
for passing counterfeit money, and "had all the constables and marshals
in the place flying around to execute his commands." He borrowed an

overcoat and a number of other items, worth about seventy-five dollars in total, from the local prosecutor and took off for Dixon, five miles away, where he was intercepted on a telegram from the county sheriff and arrested under the recently enacted Baxter liquor law. Graham was indicted for larceny at the October term of court, but the case was continued.[14]

Many of the escapades chronicled above come from George Graham's own account of his life as related to the *Daily Gazette* after yet another arrest in the spring of 1873 for stealing a horse and buggy from a man named Robert Liggett. Some of the sketch, which the newspaper dubbed "Graham's Glories," was no doubt exaggerated because the reporter who interviewed Graham observed that he exhibited a "peculiar pride" in his "daring and successful exploits."[15]

However, some of the information contained in the story can be partially confirmed by other sources, notably Illinois prison records. In addition, the 1870 US census shows that a man named Peter Gribble did live in the Canton area at the time Graham said he stole a horse and buggy from him there. Fort Wayne newspapers confirm that Graham was arrested at least two different times in the summer of 1872 on separate charges of larceny and forgery, and they also show that, when he was arrested in the spring of 1873 for stealing the rig from Liggett, several prior cases were outstanding against him. So, it's safe to say that George Graham was already a desperado of some note by the spring of 1873 when he was but twenty-two years old.[16]

And he was just getting started.

Charged with grand larceny in the Liggett case, Graham appeared for trial in the Allen County Criminal Court at Fort Wayne on April 10, 1873. His lawyers argued insanity, and he was found not guilty, with the stipulation that the other cases outstanding against him would also not be prosecuted as long as he didn't get into further trouble. The *Daily Gazette*, in reporting the outcome, said, "Graham has been before the Criminal bar of this county a number of times for various offences, but notwithstanding the most direct and damaging evidence against him, he has always managed to get clear upon some technical quabble or other."[17]

"If he is mad," continued the *Daily Gazette*, "there is a singular method to his madness, and so far as we can observe, the only eccentricity observable in his conduct is that he is proud of his past career . . . and expresses no intention of doing better in the future."[18]

When a reporter interviewed Graham after his acquittal, he admitted that his uncanny luck would probably run out sooner or later and he would "'go over the road' to Michigan City some day" (the Indiana State Prison North was located at Michigan City).[19]

Showing some refinement and education, Graham expressed his thanks for the courteous treatment that all the officials of the jail had shown him during his recent incarceration. Despite Graham's show of sophistication, the newspaperman concluded, "Audacity and boldness seem to be the prominent characteristics of his organization."[20]

A few days after "Graham's Glories" appeared in the *Daily Gazette,* George wrote to the newspaper wishing to make one or two corrections to the story. While he conceded that the newspaper had written about him in a generally impartial manner and that most of the information in the account was true, he objected to the reporter's conclusion that he was proud of his misdeeds and had no intention of reforming. To the contrary, Graham said, "Nothing is farther from my mind than a repetition of these acts. . . . No one can more deeply than myself deplore the acts in which I have participated. That I intend to become a reformed man is, with me, a question settled beyond a doubt in the affirmative."[21]

The *Daily Gazette* editors, Robert McNiece and D. S. Alexander, concluded, "We hope that Mr. Graham is sincere in his good resolution, for with his natural ability, he should be able to do well in any occupation he may choose to follow."[22]

As it turned out, the ink had scarcely dried on the newspaper announcing Graham's intention to reform before he broke his "good resolution," and he ended up going "over the road" even sooner than he probably anticipated. On Saturday, April 25, three days after Graham's letter appeared in print, he "borrowed" a horse from Willard Vaughan, Marquis Gorham's brother-in-law, who lived about ten miles west of Fort Wayne, and rode into the city, where he was arrested the next day. Graham claimed he meant to return the animal, but he was lodged in jail in default of bond on a charge of horse stealing.[23]

At his trial on May 7, Graham again mounted an insanity defense, but this time he was found guilty and sentenced to five years in the penitentiary. He was also fined one hundred dollars and disenfranchised for ten years. He took the verdict with "the utmost nonchalance," the *Daily Gazette* reported, "merely tossing up his hat and remarking, 'I guess they have got me this time,' and bowing his way politely out of the courtroom."[24]

Acting as his own lawyer, Graham filed a motion for an arrest of judgment, but the motion was overruled on May 29, 1873. The next day, the county sheriff escorted Graham to the Indiana State Prison North at Michigan City, located on the shore of Lake Michigan 120 miles from Fort Wayne. Graham was received at the prison the same day. The registrar described him as five feet, six inches tall, with sandy hair and dark blue eyes. He was blind in his right eye, and his character was "temperate."[25]

In August, less than three months after George was sent to prison, Sarah Graham filed for divorce, citing abandonment and failure to provide for her and her infant son, Charlie. Commenting on the case at the time, the *Daily Gazette* observed, "George has not only been guilty of larceny, horse stealing, forgery, embezzlements, confidence games, obtaining money under false pretenses, assault and battery and other similar eccentricities, but has preached, delivered temperance lectures, studied law, been a telegraph operator and an engineer. He has been acquitted of numerous crimes, been declared insane by an Allen County jury, etc., but now languishes in the Michigan City Penitentiary." The divorce was granted, and Sarah received custody of the child.[26]

In October, a Fort Wayne reporter traveled to Michigan City to interview some of the inmates from the Fort Wayne area. He found George Graham running a brick kiln in the prison yard. Graham said he had an easy job and was satisfied being in prison. Asked whether he'd heard his wife had procured a divorce, Graham snapped, "Yes, but I don't care a damn. I can get along without a wife as long as I am in the penitentiary."[27]

In June 1874, Graham applied to Gov. Thomas A. Hendricks for a pardon. The quintessential jailhouse lawyer, Graham argued that "your petitioner" should have been allowed to testify on his own behalf and that the testimony of two additional doctors, who were ready to swear to his questionable sanity, should also have been permitted. The petition was quickly rejected because Graham provided only a synopsis of his trial from memory rather than a formal transcript of the proceeding.[28]

In early 1875, Graham still had charge of a kiln in the prison yard and was reported by his guards as being quiet and well behaved. In his spare time he was studying law, and he planned to return to Fort Wayne and hang out his shingle as an attorney upon his release. Calling him "George Graham, the irrepressible," the *Fort Wayne Sentinel* ventured to add that he would probably "devote especial attention to the criminal branch of the law, for which his past experience particularly qualifies him."[29]

Apparently one of the things Graham learned in his study of law was not to attempt to represent himself. In April 1875, he renewed his petition for a pardon through Fort Wayne attorney R. C. Bell, and this time the application was accompanied by a full transcript of Graham's trial and was endorsed by several Allen County officials. It, too, was nonetheless denied, with Hendricks responding to Bell's letter that he would not interfere.[30]

Graham was released from prison on Christmas Day 1877 at the expiration of his sentence, with time allowed for good behavior. The Ribbon Movement was in full swing, and George promptly took the pledge upon his return to Fort Wayne. In late December, he spoke at a local temperance meeting.[31]

In January 1878, he applied to Gov. James D. Williams for a remission of his remaining punishment. Although the Indiana State Prison North warden told the governor that he knew of no reason why Graham should be given clemency either inside or outside the penitentiary, the petition was granted, thereby restoring Graham's right to vote and canceling his hundred-dollar fine.[32]

In early 1878, Graham got a job selling insurance, and he resumed his work with the Good Templars, serving as the worthy right supporter in the local Amity Lodge, a group his father headed as the worthy chief Templar. George and Sarah reconciled and, over the strong objections of the Gorham family, remarried on April 16, 1878.[33]

In June the younger Graham was appointed deputy assessor for the Bloomingdale neighborhood of Fort Wayne, and by mid-November he had taken up the practice of law, as he'd vowed to do while he was in prison. Representing the defense in *Breese vs. Breese*, Graham kept "his end of the case up with a precision worthy of a veteran," observed the *Fort Wayne Sentinel*. Although the particulars of this case are unknown, it likely involved a dispute within the family of Timothy L. Breese, who was married to Sarah's sister Abbie. Remarking on the case at the time, the *Sentinel* said it was gratifying to see George Graham fulfilling "to the letter" the promises of reform he had made the previous winter at one of the temperance meetings.[34]

In early June 1879, Graham applied to the Allen County Commission as a candidate for constable. The next month, he was given a position of deputy constable, but even when he was working for the law, George

George Graham (Sketch from
*The Graham Tragedy and the
Molloy-Lee Examination*)

Graham couldn't seem to keep from breaking the law. Early that fall, he was accused of stealing a coat and some baggage while serving a warrant, but he managed to escape from that scrape unscathed. In the wee hours of the morning on October 12, though, he was arrested by a Fort Wayne officer for disorderly conduct involving two young women at a dance hall. Graham sued the *Fort Wayne Sentinel* over its coverage of the incident, claiming he'd gone to the dance hall to keep the peace in his official capacity as a constable and that the newspaper had libeled him.[35]

The *Sentinel*, commenting on the libel suit, said, "The mere thought the plaintiff had a character to be injured is an idea that would never have struck the average American citizen." Even though it was a frivolous lawsuit, the case would have to be heard, assuming Graham would "be sober long enough to give . . . his testimony." The *Sentinel* concluded, "It is a public disgrace that such a man should be allowed to occupy even such a humble office as constable." Despite his protestations of innocence in the dance hall affair, Graham ended up paying a five-dollar fine and dropping the libel suit.[36]

In late November, barely over a month after the dance hall incident, Graham got into a more serious difficulty when he forged a check on the account of a Fort Wayne firm and cashed it at another local business. He

was arrested on December 1 and jailed in default of bond. At his preliminary examination the next day, Graham "indulged in considerable con-
tempt of court." Later in December, he was formally indicted for forgery.
He was tried and found guilty on December 19, 1879, and was sentenced
to two years at his old "home" in the Indiana State Prison North. He was
transported to the Michigan City facility on December 22 and promptly
placed in the boot-and-shoe department to learn the shoemaker's trade.
George and Sarah's second child, Roy, was born shortly before George
returned to prison.[37]

In July 1880, Graham made the acquaintance of Emma Molloy during
one of her visits to the penitentiary on behalf of inmates and prison reform. The articulate, smooth-talking Graham made a favorable impression on Mrs. Molloy, who, as she later said, was always ready to help "the
outcast and the unfortunate." George Graham found a patron in Emma
Molloy, but if she had delved a little further into his background, even the
reform-minded Mrs. Molloy might have balked at taking on the role.[38]

3

Allowing an Ex-Convict to Manage Her Affairs

THOROUGHLY CONVINCED that the temperance movement could not achieve its goals through moral suasion alone, Emma began working increasingly for antiliquor laws in 1879. The Grand Temperance Council of Indiana was organized late that year to work for a prohibition amendment in the state, and several of Emma's friends from the temperance movement were among the leaders of the group. Emma worked tirelessly on behalf of both the prohibition amendment and a similar amendment to grant women's suffrage in the state. Reporting on an Indiana WCTU convention at New Albany in February 1880, one correspondent said, "Emma Molloy . . . occupied most of the time of the Convention in agitating the proposition for an amendment to the Constitution of the State providing for woman suffrage and for a prohibitory law."[1]

In October 1880, Emma went to Kansas at the invitation of Gov. John P. St. John, a strong temperance advocate, to work on behalf of a prohibition amendment to that state's constitution, which was under consideration. She spoke to large crowds in Leavenworth and Topeka and was credited with helping the amendment pass in November. It was the first statewide constitutional ban on alcohol in the United States.[2]

After a brief sojourn at home, Emma returned in early 1881 to Kansas, where she advocated for women's rights, preached temperance from the pulpit of several churches, and also spoke to both chambers of the state legislature at Topeka, urging strict enforcement of the prohibition law. Back home the same year, she resumed campaigning for Indiana's

amendments on prohibition and women's suffrage. Both won preliminary passage in 1881 but were later soundly defeated in the final votes.
Emma also continued writing and editing for the *Morning and Day of Reform*, and publisher Henry Waldo Adams moved its offices to La Porte.[3]

In the fall of 1881, Emma, whom one newspaper at the time called
"one of the most eloquent and interesting lady speakers in the country,"
traveled east for conventions of the National Prohibition Alliance in New
York and the national WCTU in Washington, DC. At the latter event,
Emma, frustrated with the lukewarm support of both major political parties for prohibitory laws, urged a third-party effort to "bury the two old
rotten parties beyond resurrection." Like a lot of temperance activists,
Emma had looked to the Republican Party for legislative backing in the
fight against alcohol, but she felt now that the GOP paid only lip service
to the cause and was, therefore, little different from the Democrats.[4]

Meanwhile, George Graham was released from the state prison at
Michigan City in mid-November 1881. Graham made his way to nearby
La Porte, where Mrs. Molloy paid his train fare to his hometown of
Fort Wayne. Shortly afterward, Graham came back to Mrs. Molloy at La
Porte, complaining that he was unable to find work. She recommended
him to Henry Waldo Adams, who hired him to work in the office of the
Morning and Day of Reform. He worked most of the winter, according
to Emma's later statement, and was "steady and faithful."[5]

In February 1882, Adams sold the *Morning and Day of Reform* to the
D. C. Cook Publishing Company of Chicago, and the paper was moved
to that city. Graham returned to Fort Wayne, where he secured employment around March 1 in the tool shop of the Pittsburg, Fort Wayne and
Chicago Railroad. He reportedly gave "good satisfaction," but his stay in
Fort Wayne proved brief, as he was summoned to Chicago to resume
his employment as a bookkeeper for the *Morning and Day of Reform.*[6]

At the time of Emma's 1878 trip to England, Ed Molloy had brought
his father and stepmother into his and Emma's home to live. Emma opposed such a move because Ed's stepmother was very critical of Emma's
way of life, particularly her friendship with temperance men. After a
couple of years of discord in the family, Ed finally asked the couple to
leave, but they came back in early 1882. Refusing now to live in the same
house with Ed and his parents, Emma filed for divorce, citing mental cruelty as the grounds. The decree was granted in April 1882, with
Emma winning custody of both Frank and Etta.[7]

Divorce in late-nineteenth-century America was rare. Only one divorce per every two thousand people was granted each year. By contrast, the rate was more than ten times that great a hundred years later. In 1882, when Emma dissolved her marriage, divorce was a glaring mark of disgrace, especially for women. Many people felt wives should abide by the biblical admonition to honor and obey their husbands, regardless of circumstances. For a woman to obtain a divorce on grounds other than physical abuse, adultery, or desertion was extremely rare, and for a woman to divorce more than once was almost unheard of.[8]

So, it's not surprising that newspapers throughout northern Indiana were more than willing to offer an opinion on the Molloy divorce. Most came out in support of their colleague, Ed Molloy, who was editor of the *La Porte Herald-Chronicle,* and blamed Mrs. Molloy for the breakup. The *Elkhart Monitor* surmised that she had devoted too much time to women's suffrage and temperance and too little to the household. Similarly, the *Fort Wayne Sentinel,* calling Emma a "strong-minded female," thought the problem was that she preferred "gadding about to a life of domesticity." Another editor cited the fact that Emma had been divorced previously as evidence that she was at least partly to blame in the present case, and another suggested that she not only was "too much on the go" but was probably chasing after a "fresh goose" as well. Even a few newspapers in Kansas, where Emma had recently lectured, got in on the gossip. The editor of the *Howard Journal* allowed that, having met both parties, "we are disposed to think Ed is rather fortunate than otherwise." One of the few observers who refused to get caught up in the rumor-mongering was the editor of the *La Porte Argus.* He concluded about the breakup, "Much is being said that has no foundation in fact," and he also suggested that the divorce was a matter that concerned "only those who are personally interested."[9]

About the time of the divorce, twenty-year-old Cora Lee and her younger sisters, Ida and Emma, came to live with Mrs. Molloy. The sisters and their parents, James and Amanda Lee, had lived in Indiana and southern Michigan when the girls were children. In 1872, when Cora was eleven years old, her father died, and the loss haunted her for years. Shortly after James Lee's death, Cora's mother moved to Missouri and remarried, leaving the girls in the hands of relatives in northern Indiana. In New Carlisle, where the Lee sisters lived for several years, Cora earned an impeccable reputation as a chaste and industrious young woman. In late 1881, Cora and her sisters set up housekeeping for themselves in La Porte, and Cora went into business as a seamstress. Mrs. Molloy made Cora's acquaintance in early 1882 when she engaged the young woman to do some sewing for her. Seeing that the sisters were struggling to make it on their own, she now took them into her home and gave them room and board in exchange for their helping with the housework, but she quickly came to look upon them as her foster daughters.[10]

In May 1882, the D. C. Cook Publishing Company moved the *Morning and Day of Reform* from Chicago to Elgin, Illinois, and George Graham moved with the newspaper. He wrote letters to his estranged wife, Sarah, asking to get back together with her, and Mrs. Molloy traveled to Fort Wayne to help convince Sarah to reconcile with her husband. Sarah and her kids joined George in Elgin in early July. Shortly afterward, Mrs. Molloy, who was still associate editor of the paper, sent her children, Frank and Etta, to Elgin to work in the newspaper office, and they boarded with the Grahams. Cora and her sisters also moved to Elgin. Cora and Sarah Graham opened a dressmaking shop there together, and Ida helped out in the newspaper office.[11]

Meanwhile, Mrs. Molloy returned to the lecture circuit on behalf of temperance. In mid-May she addressed the Indiana WCTU at Indianapolis, and immediately afterward she conducted a two-day temperance revival at Treaty, where she was a guest in the home of William and Edna Wohlgamuth. A few days after Mrs. Molloy left, Wohlgamuth, a temperance worker who'd first met Emma a couple of years earlier, left his wife, telling her that he loved Mrs. Molloy. When Wohlgamuth caught up with Emma on the lecture circuit and declared his love for her, she told him she did not share his passion and advised him to return to his wife, but the news that he had deserted his wife for Mrs. Molloy developed into a scandal, with Emma accused of being a home wrecker. The story, which one newspaper dubbed "Emma's Escapade," made headlines across Indiana. Mrs. Molloy telegraphed the officers of the Indiana Christian Temperance Union demanding an immediate inquiry into the matter, and the union leaders convened in Wabash on June 28, 1882. At the hearing, Wohlgamuth admitted that Emma had never shown him any particular attention or done anything to encourage his feelings toward her. Emma was completely exonerated in the matter, and Wohlgamuth was kicked out of the Temperance Union.[12]

During the Wohlgamuth scandal, at least one newspaper, in its attack on Emma Molloy, asked rhetorically why a man would want to leave his wife for a woman of Mrs. Molloy's "severe" features. In truth, Emma was still an attractive woman, although not the striking beauty she'd been in her younger years. After Emma was exonerated, the *Chicago Inter Ocean*, which first published the Wohlgamuth story, concluded philosophically, "All attractive women will tell Mrs. Molloy that it is impossible to prevent foolish men from falling in love, and that she need not assume responsibility for Wohlgamuth's wanderings."[13]

In the summer of 1882, Mrs. Molloy returned to Kansas to campaign for strict enforcement of the prohibition law she had helped get passed almost two years earlier. The law had theoretically taken effect in January 1881, but it was habitually disregarded in Leavenworth and other Kansas towns and continued to be a contentious issue. In November 1882, Mrs. Molloy joined her children in Elgin, with the whole family, including the Lee sisters, living together in a house about four or five blocks from the Graham residence. In March 1883, Ida Lee got married and moved out of the Molloy household.[14]

In the summer and fall of 1883, Mrs. Molloy campaigned throughout Ohio on behalf of a proposed prohibition amendment in that state. In the ballot later that fall, the amendment won a majority of votes cast on the issue but failed to get the necessary majority of total votes cast, since some people refrained from voting on the prohibition question.[15]

In late 1883, Mrs. Molloy traveled to present-day Oklahoma, where she held a number of very successful revival meetings among the Cherokee Indians in the Tahlequah area. After a brief return to Elgin about Christmastime, she went back to Tahlequah in January 1884, taking Cora Lee and her son, Frank, with her. Also accompanying her on at least one of her visits to Indian Territory was George Graham, who'd taken on the role of Mrs. Molloy's manager and agent. "Graham is a bright fellow," the *Fort Wayne Sentinel* commented at the time, "and about as nice and sweet a letter writer as can be found in the state. This is probably what caught Mrs. Maloy [sic], who is denounced by her enemies for allowing an ex-convict to manage her affairs."[16]

One of Mrs. Molloy's staunchest enemies and one of the people now criticizing her for hiring Graham as her manager was William Wohlgamuth. Not long after Mrs. Molloy rejected him and he was expelled from the Indiana Christian Temperance Union, Wohlgamuth had undertaken a letter-writing campaign against her, attempting to smear her character. Responding to one of Wohlgamuth's letters that appeared in the *Wabash Courier* about March 1, 1884, Emma said, "For two years the mails have carried to all parts of the country the vilest, most profane and obscene emanations from his pen, charging me with all sorts of crime. He has written to people of the highest respectability, my personal lady friends, the most vulgar letters, charging me with adultery with their husbands. . . . All this because I had no use for him as a lover." Mrs. Molloy concluded that, although many of her friends were worried about the attacks on her character, she was not because God would take care of her and her work.[17]

In early 1884, Mrs. Molloy left Oklahoma to conduct a series of temperance and religious meetings in Kansas, including an extended revival in the small town of Washington, where 265 people professed religion and 380 signed temperance pledges during her stay. In appreciation of her evangelistic effort, a number of local people subscribed a fund to build her a home in Washington on the condition that she relocate there, and she tentatively accepted the offer.[18]

Mrs. Molloy fell ill while in Washington from what was reported as spinal meningitis, but by early May she was well enough to travel back to Tahlequah. Mrs. Molloy was so esteemed among temperance workers and pastors proselytizing in the Indian Nation that her fellow Christians greeted her return almost like the second coming of a messiah.[19]

While she was in Oklahoma, Emma learned that the D. C. Cook Publishing Company had placed the *Morning and Day of Reform* up for sale. She scraped together enough money to purchase the newspaper, moved it to Washington, Kansas, and hired George Graham as its business manager. The newspaper office was on the second floor of a building across the street from the courthouse on the west side of the square.[20]

For the first month or two, the Molloy family, along with George Graham and his son Roy, boarded with Philip Darby, who also owned the building where the newspaper office was located, but they soon moved into a two-story house that the townspeople completed for Mrs. Molloy at the west edge of Washington. Shortly afterward, Sarah and Charlie Graham arrived from Elgin to join the household. The Grahams and the Molloy family, including Mrs. Molloy; her son, Frank; her adopted

daughter, Etta; and her foster daughters, Cora and Emma, all lived together in the same house.[21]

The *Morning and Day of Reform* fared well at first. Mrs. Molloy continued her temperance lecturing, and at every place she appeared, she

West side of Washington, Kansas, public square, where the second-floor offices
of the *Morning and Day of Reform* were located, as it appears today (Photo by
the author)

House in Washington where the Molloy and Graham families lived together, as
it appears today (Photo by the author)

picked up a number of new subscriptions for the newspaper, which had about eighteen thousand subscribers at its peak. After she spoke at Chetopa, Kansas, about June 1, 1884, the *Chetopa Advance* told its readers that the *Morning and Day of Reform* was "a most excellent temperance paper, and is only 50 cents a year, and would be a welcome visitor to every christian home in Kansas." Some observers, though, seemed resentful of Mrs. Molloy's success. The *Manhattan Mercury* in Manhattan, Kansas, speculated that "although a lone woman," she was "making more money than half a dozen ordinary men."[22]

In July, George Graham traveled back to Fort Wayne to attend his father's funeral. Upon his return to Kansas, Mrs. Molloy wrote a touching tribute to his deceased father that appeared in the *Morning and Day of Reform.*[23]

Gov. St. John, Mrs. Molloy's old friend from the Kansas amendment campaign of 1880, was nominated for president by the Prohibition Party at its Pittsburgh convention in July 1884, and Mrs. Molloy threw her support behind him, endorsing him in the *Morning and Day of Reform.* The decision alienated even many temperance advocates, who preferred working within the Republican Party as a more pragmatic approach than trying to establish a third party. They feared the "fanatical" Prohibition Party would only draw off support from the GOP and enable a Democratic victory.[24]

At first, Mrs. Molloy had published the *Morning and Day of Reform* in partnership with Samuel Clarke, publisher of the *Washington Post,* a local Democratic newspaper. However, Clarke severed the alliance about the time Mrs. Molloy announced her support for St. John, and the *Post* soon became one of her harshest critics.[25]

The Kansas state Prohibition Party convention two months after the national convention turned into a farce. First, anyone who did not support St. John for president was excluded from participation and then the remaining delegates split into two factions, one that wanted to select a slate of state candidates to run in Kansas alongside the national ticket and another, led by Mrs. Molloy, that opposed such a move and wanted instead to concentrate only on supporting the national ticket. Ridiculing the convention, the *Topeka Daily Commonwealth* called the event the "most funny and mixed affair that ever took place in Kansas."[26]

Even after the national WCTU convention in St. Louis, with Emma Molloy in attendance, endorsed St. John in early October, he remained a fringe candidate, but he drew enough votes in the November election to facilitate a narrow victory for Democratic candidate Grover Cleveland over Republican James G. Blaine. The outcome, the first time since before the Civil War that a Democrat had been elected president, was just what many Republicans had feared, and it further embittered them against the Prohibitionists, including Mrs. Molloy. Subscriptions to her *Morning and Day of Reform* dropped off dramatically to fewer than ten thousand, and by January 1885, the newspaper was "on its last legs." Mrs. Molloy moved the newspaper office out of the downtown building into her home, and she took to the revival circuit, using the offerings she collected from her evangelical meetings in a vain effort to prop up the struggling paper.[27]

During a revival in nearby Concordia, Kansas, Mrs. Molloy spoke to the local chapter of the Grand Army of the Republic (GAR, a fraternal organization for Union veterans), and she received seventy dollars in donations at the end of the meeting. Calling her "a wealthy Methodist minister," James M. Hagaman, editor of the *Concordia Blade*, criticized Mrs. Molloy for not returning most of the money for distribution to needy GAR members. The freethinking Hagaman found it insulting to liberals that Mrs. Molloy and her ilk insisted that temperance be tied to religion, and when she abruptly ended her revival in Concordia, Hagaman suggested that she was faking illness and that the real reason she left was to avoid his broadsides.[28]

Unlike the editor of the rival *Concordia Daily Times*, who found George Graham to be a "very pleasant gentleman," Hagaman also attacked Mrs. Molloy's manager as a scoundrel and a fraud. "If Rev. Mrs. Molloy does not want her reputation for respectability to suffer," said the *Blade*, "she had better sever her associations with George E. Graham."[29]

Hagaman was not the first person, nor would he be the last, to question Mrs. Molloy's association with George Graham.

4

Marriage at Highland Cottage

THE LIVING arrangement in Washington and George Graham's frequent absence placed a strain on the Graham marriage. George and Sarah got into an argument about January 1, 1885, and they decided to separate. Sarah and her boys went back to Fort Wayne to stay with her father. In March, Mrs. Molloy discontinued publication of the *Morning and Day of Reform* and sold the subscription list to a New York–based temperance journal, the *Voice*. After Mrs. Molloy's paper shut down, George Graham followed Sarah to Indiana, but he stayed with his stepmother, not with his wife.[1]

Graham returned to Washington in April, and he and Mrs. Molloy took a train together to Kansas City on May 1. When Graham went to the Union Depot Hotel and asked for separate rooms, the clerk told him the hotel did not have two single rooms but had a double room. Replying that such an arrangement would be fine if he was with his wife or his sister, Graham booked the one available room for Mrs. Molloy. He then went to a different hotel to spend the night, but the Union Depot Hotel clerk recorded both names as though the two stayed there together in the same room. Charles F. Barrett, who had succeeded Clarke as editor of the *Washington Post*, traveled to Kansas City the same day Graham and Mrs. Molloy did and learned of their supposed rendezvous. Like Clarke, Barrett was a confirmed adversary of the temperance lecturer, and upon his return home, he published an inflammatory accusation that Emma Molloy and George Graham had shared the same hotel room. A subsequent investigation discredited the allegation, but Mrs. Molloy's opponents were quick to latch on to the juicy bit of gossip and slow to let go of it.[2]

The next morning, May 2, Mrs. Molloy took the first train to Springfield, Missouri, where she had been engaged to hold a series of revival meetings, while George Graham returned once again to Indiana. The minor scandal stirred up by the sleeping arrangements in Kansas City would soon pale in comparison to what awaited Emma Molloy in Springfield.[3]

Founded in 1835, Springfield was the seat of Greene County, the largest town in southwest Missouri, and the hub of commerce for the entire region. The area was primarily settled by yeoman farmers, many of whom had migrated from the upper tier of Southern states like Tennessee and Kentucky. During the pre–Civil War years, Springfield was a rowdy, frontier town with a saloon on every street.[4]

Early in the war, a Confederate victory at the Battle of Wilson's Creek ten miles southwest of Springfield gave the South control of the town, but the Union soon took over and established Springfield as a district headquarters for the remainder of the war. Southern sentiment dominated in many rural areas of Missouri, a slaveholding Union state. However, Conservative Unionism held sway with most of the state's citizens, including a majority of those in Greene County and especially Springfield, meaning they were satisfied with staying in the Union, but they tended to oppose abolition.

At the close of the war, in July 1865, Wild Bill Hickok made a national name for himself when he gunned down Davis Tutt on the Springfield square in what is widely considered the first gunfight of the Wild West era. Telegraph service had come to Springfield near the beginning of the Civil War, and the railroad arrived in 1870, bringing the town closer to the outside world and to civilization. But fistfights and gunplay still erupted on the streets with some regularity. By 1885, when Emma Molloy arrived, Springfield was a bustling, growing town with a population of twelve thousand to fifteen thousand, but it still retained much of the flavor of its rough-and-tumble past. Coarse, tough characters still haunted the place, and even the permanent residents were a hardy lot.

Springfield was not new to temperance campaigns. About 1850, a local chapter of the Sons of Temperance, a nationwide brotherhood promoting temperance, got dram shops (that is, saloons) outlawed in Springfield, but the ordinance didn't stop the sale of liquor and was soon repealed.

A bird's-eye view of Springfield, Missouri, in 1872 (Courtesy of the Springfield-Greene County Library)

In 1856, the temperance advocates of Springfield, many of them women, persuaded the Missouri legislature to pass what was known as the Springfield liquor law, but again the rule was openly flouted until the Civil War, when it was displaced altogether. Periodic campaigns to stem the flow of liquor in Springfield resumed after the war. Most notable among these efforts was the Ribbon Movement of the late 1870s, the same campaign Emma Molloy was deeply involved in. During a ten-day period in late January and early February 1878, at the height of the Ribbon Movement in Springfield, approximately nineteen hundred men took abstinence pledges, but like the other temperance crusades before it, the ardor of the Ribbon Movement soon cooled. Now it was Emma Molloy's turn to have a go at the saloon keepers and whiskey swillers of Springfield.

After arriving in Springfield on May 2, Mrs. Molloy began almost immediately holding services at the First Congregational Church at the northeast corner of Jefferson and Locust. Reporting from North Spring-

Map of Midwest and Mid-South states, showing Springfield and other cities and towns pertinent to the Sarah Graham murder case (By the author)

field, a correspondent told the *St. Louis Post-Dispatch* on May 5 that Mrs. Molloy's revival services were already increasing in interest. In mid-May, "the noted evangelist," as the correspondent called her, was holding church services every afternoon and evening. On Sunday morning, May 24, she preached a GAR memorial sermon to a packed crowd of a thousand people at the local skating rink, the meeting having been moved there because the church could not accommodate the large numbers. The sermon was, according to the *Post-Dispatch* correspondent, one that would "not soon be forgotten," while a local newspaper, the *Springfield Daily Herald,* credited Mrs. Molloy's eloquent sermon with helping bring the rival towns of Springfield and North Springfield together. Mrs. Molloy closed her revival on Sunday evening, June 7, and was prostrated the following week with exhaustion and "congestion of the brain."[5]

Mrs. Molloy boarded with Rev. J. C. Plumb, minister of the Congregational Church, during her revival. Near the end of the meetings, Cora

Lee, who'd been in Nebraska visiting her sister, arrived and joined her foster mother at the Plumb residence.[6]

Mrs. Molloy had come to Springfield at the invitation of local temperance advocates, and one of them, judge James Baker, struck up a fast friendship with her almost as soon as she arrived. A former Missouri Supreme Court justice, Baker had been instrumental in bringing the railroad to Springfield and was one of the most prominent men in town. Like Emma, he had started out as a Democrat, switched allegiance to the Republican Party, and finally adopted the Prohibitionist cause.[7]

In the midst of Mrs. Molloy's revival, Baker offered to buy a farm in the Springfield area for Emma and her family and let her pay off the debt in installments. Mrs. Molloy accepted the offer, and Baker made arrangements to purchase the eighty-acre J. B. Cooper farm five miles southwest of town on the road to Brookline.[8]

While Mrs. Molloy's Springfield revival was under way, George Graham left Indiana and returned to Kansas. He wrote to Mrs. Molloy from Concordia seeking her help in finding employment, and he also wrote to Cora, declaring his love for her. A romance between George and Cora had been smoldering ever since Sarah Graham left Kansas several months earlier, and now it burst into the open. George "confessed" that Sarah had divorced him when he went to prison in 1873, and that the couple had, therefore, been living in sin at Elgin, Illinois, and Washington, Kansas. But George and Sarah's transgression also meant there was no legal impediment to a match between George and Cora, and he asked forgiveness from both Cora and Mrs. Molloy.[9]

Convinced by George's lie, Emma was disposed to countenance the match between him and her foster daughter, but she consulted her Springfield friends, including Judge Baker and Reverend Plumb, about the situation. In seeking their opinion, she revealed Graham's criminal background and detailed her past association with him. After a copy of George and Sarah Graham's divorce was obtained from Indiana, Mrs. Molloy's friends agreed that there was no legal reason why Cora should not wed Graham.[10]

No one thought to check for a second marriage.

Graham arrived in Springfield on June 1, the very day that Judge Baker was to take Mrs. Molloy out to the Cooper farm to show her the property, and he joined the outing.

Graham had come to Springfield hoping to find work on the railroad, but when the deal on the farm was finalized, it was agreed that he would stay on the farm as its manager. He and the Molloy family moved onto the property on June 15, 1885, and they named the place Highland Cottage. A month later, Reverend Plumb trekked to the Molloy farm to perform a marriage ceremony between George Graham and Cora Lee. Part of the reason for the hurried wedding was that Mrs. Molloy, given her frequent absences from home, was concerned about the impropriety of leaving George alone on the farm with Cora and two other young women.[11]

Everything went along smoothly at the farm for about a month after the marriage until sometime in August, when, according to Mrs. Molloy's later recollection, Graham began to fret about not having his children with him.[12]

But that wasn't the only thing he was fretting about.

5

The Disappearance
of Sarah Graham

NOT LONG after George and Cora were married, Mrs. Molloy forwarded
a newspaper notice of the wedding to Sarah Graham in Indiana. Mrs.
Molloy had never held Sarah in high regard as someone who could
"strengthen and control one of George's weak moral nature," and she
hoped that Cora's marriage to George would have an ameliorating influence on him. Upon receipt of the wedding notice, Sarah wrote to George
demanding to know what was going on, and he wrote back denying that
he had married Cora. Only after Sarah enclosed the newspaper clipping
in her next letter did he admit that he and Cora had gotten married.[1]

Now that the bigamous marriage George had hoped to hide from
his first wife was no longer a secret, he and Sarah entered into a ne-
gotiation of sorts. Sarah, according to Mrs. Molloy, had never shown a
strong motherly interest in her children and had expressed a willingness
to let them stay with their father. George proposed to give Sarah a sum
of money and take financial responsibility for the boys if she would turn
them over to him and stay out of his life. According to George, his offer
was in response to a threat from Sarah to expose his bigamy if he didn't
pay her off. In either case, whether George was trying to bribe Sarah
or she was trying to blackmail him, the two exchanged several letters
during the late summer of 1885 about his taking custody of Charlie and
Roy. Finally, Sarah agreed to meet George in St. Louis with the children.[2]

Instead of admitting that he was going to meet Sarah in St. Louis,
George told Cora and Mrs. Molloy that he was going to Fort Wayne to

pick up Roy, whom Sarah had agreed to turn over to him. He told Mrs. Molloy and Judge Baker that he had inherited some land in Fort Wayne after his father's death and that he planned to arrange its sale while he was in Indiana to help repay Baker's down payment on the Molloy farm. Some of the money he also planned to give to Sarah for her and Charlie's support in return for her allowing him to keep Roy. Convinced by another lie from the mouth of George Graham, Mrs. Molloy, with Judge Baker's help, came up with the money for him to make the trip. She then departed on September 10 for another series of revival meetings in Kansas.[3]

George left for St. Louis in late September and met Sarah and the boys there on September 28. Sometime after he reached St. Louis, he wrote a letter to Mrs. Molloy, then at Fostoria, Kansas, saying he had just arrived in Fort Wayne. He gave it a dateline of Fort Wayne, September 28, but it was postmarked in St. Louis on September 30, as though he had written it from Indiana and then dropped it in the mail during his return trip.[4]

In St. Louis, George tried to convince Sarah to return to Fort Wayne or to go to her uncle's house in St. Louis and leave the boys in his custody, but she balked at the proposition. According to her relatives in Indiana, George had told Sarah he was working for the railroad in Springfield, and she had left Fort Wayne with every intention of going all the way to Springfield. So, it's highly questionable whether she ever consented to turn over either of the children to George, as he later claimed. If she did, she must have had a change of heart once she reached St. Louis because she now insisted on accompanying the boys to Springfield, and all four Graham family members boarded a westbound train together on September 30.[5]

For Sarah Graham, it would be her last ride.

The Grahams arrived at the Frisco depot in North Springfield in the early evening of September 30. Having made prearrangements by telegraph from St. Louis, George took the boys to Fay's Restaurant and Boarding House on nearby Commercial Street for them to eat and spend the night. He told them that he and their mother were going on to Brookline but that it was too far from the train station to the farm for them to walk and he'd be back to get them the next day. After Graham dropped the boys off and left, Kate Fay, who knew Graham had recently married Cora Lee, asked Charlie how long his mother had been dead. He replied that she was not dead at all but was at the depot.[6]

Sarah Graham (Sketch from
*The Graham Tragedy and the
Molloy-Lee Examination*)

Graham went back to Sarah at the depot and, according to his later statement, asked her what she proposed to do now. Sarah replied that she planned to go wherever he went. Graham laughed and told her she was going to have a good time then because he was planning to walk five miles across country. Sarah said she guessed she could stand it if he could, and when he started off, she followed, even though it was a rainy, dreary night. The two took a streetcar to downtown Springfield, where they had dinner and Graham tried again to convince Sarah not to "ruin" him but instead to go back to St. Louis or go to Kansas City. He said he would send her money to live on, but Sarah "refused to listen" to George's entreaties.[7]

Leon Maurice, a downtown confectionary and restaurant owner, later remembered seeing a man and woman resembling George and Sarah Graham come into his business that night, and when the couple left about nine or ten o'clock, Maurice overheard the man tell the woman they had four or five miles to go. It was the last time anyone saw Sarah Graham alive.[8]

Except the person or persons who killed her.

And nobody saw George Graham again until the wee hours of the next morning when Peter Hawkins, a black man who worked on the Molloy farm and slept in a granary near the home, saw him approach and tap on a window. Cora Lee, Etta Molloy, and Emma Lee, who were all sleeping in the same bed, awoke, and Cora let him in. He told her he'd just gotten back from Fort Wayne and that he'd walked in from Dorchester, a train stop a couple of miles northwest of the Molloy farm. He then changed his wet, muddy clothes for dry ones and lay down to await breakfast.[9]

Later the same morning, Graham took a horse and wagon back to Springfield to pick up the boys. He retrieved Sarah's trunk, containing her clothes and other belongings, from the Frisco depot and took it to Fay's Boarding House. After removing a few things he could use, such as her Bible, a photo album, and some silverware, he left the trunk in storage at the boardinghouse. Mrs. Fay mentioned what Charlie had said the evening before about his mother, and George explained that the boys' mother had died so long ago that they did not know the difference between her and their aunt, who had come with them to Springfield for a visit to a nearby community.[10]

On the return trip to the Molloy farm, Graham told his boys that their mother was staying temporarily at Pierce City. He said he owned half of the Molloy farm, but that if he brought their mother there now, while Mrs. Molloy and Cora still had a stake in the farm and were living there, he and their mother would quarrel. He said that he hoped to get the other half of the farm and that when he did, he'd bring their mother there, but for now he didn't want Mrs. Molloy and Cora to know where Sarah was. He told Charlie and Roy to say she was in St. Louis if anybody asked them, and he repeated this instruction several times on the way to the farm.[11]

6

George Graham the Forger

AFTER GEORGE brought Charlie and Roy home with him to the Molloy farm, he explained that Sarah had decided she didn't want "to be bothered with them." He also said that he'd placed his Fort Wayne property in the hands of a real estate dealer for a quick sale and hoped that by November he'd be able to pay off some of the debts incurred on the farm since he and the Molloy family had moved in.[1]

In addition to the south gate at the front of the Molloy property, there was another gate on the east side, and the diagonal road or trail that ran by the house connected the two gates. Before the Molloy family moved onto the property, travelers along the Springfield to Brookline road had been in the habit of occasionally using the trail as a shortcut, but a few days after Graham returned to the farm with the boys, he put locks on the gates and posted "No Hunting" and "No Road Here" signs.[2]

About the same time, Graham chased Everett Cannefax, a young man from a neighboring farm, off the Molloy place when he started crossing the property near the well, even though Cannefax had ventured onto the property several times in the past without incident. Graham also showed Charlie and Roy the well and cautioned them not to go near it because they might fall in.[3]

Meanwhile, Mrs. Molloy was still busy with her revival campaign in Kansas. From Fostoria, she went to Abilene and from there to Council Grove, remaining several weeks at each place.[4]

Near the end of October, Graham happened to be at Fay's Restaurant when proprietor Benjamin Fay suggested that Graham needed to remove the trunk he had stored there for several weeks. Graham took Sarah's trunk to the Congregational Church and received Reverend Plumb's permission to store it in a vacant room above the pastor's study.[5]

Sarah Graham had written to her sister Abbie Breese from St. Louis on September 29, and Abbie expected Sarah to write again upon her arrival in Springfield. When she did not do so in a timely manner, Abbie and other family members began to worry. The family grew increasingly concerned when Abbie's letters to Sarah went unanswered. On October 16, George Graham finally wrote back to Abbie as though he were transcribing what Sarah had dictated to him. The letter explained that Sarah had a cancer on her hand and was unable to write herself. "Sarah" told her sister that she liked Springfield "real well," and the letter concluded, "George is awful fat, weighs 160 pounds." *Springfield Daily Herald* editor George M. Sawyer later cited Graham's playful impersonation of his first wife while concealing her disappearance from Abbie as a study in the total depravity of man.[6]

Abbie was not convinced by Graham's ruse. In late October, she wrote to Brookline postmaster John Potter inquiring about her sister. Not aware of Graham's marriage to Cora Lee, Potter wrote back saying he did not know anything about the whereabouts of Sarah Graham. Later, though, he asked Graham why he didn't write to his sister-in-law at Fort Wayne in reference to his wife's whereabouts, and Graham told Potter it was none of his business.[7]

But the conversation with Potter forced Graham to confront the reality that he had to deal with Abbie's inquiries. On November 13, he wrote a letter to Charlie's cousin as though it were coming from Charlie and directed his son to copy and sign it. In the letter, "Charlie" explained that his mother had the cancer cut off, but that her hand was still too sore for her to write. It also explained that Sarah was staying at Fay's Boarding House, while the rest of the family was at the farm. On December 22, Graham wrote another letter to Charlie's cousin assuring the Breese family that Sarah was all right, and he once again had Charlie copy and sign it.[8]

Abbie and her family, though, were still not persuaded by Graham's dissimulation, and they continued their inquiries. On Christmas Day,

Brookline constable William O'Neal received a letter from Marquis Gorham seeking information about his daughter Sarah.[9]

Mrs. Molloy came home for Christmas, and when Judge Baker saw her in Springfield on December 29, he reminded her that the farm transaction rested only on their verbal agreement and that, in case of his death, she stood to lose not only the farm but all the improvements she and Graham had made on the place. He said it was not very businesslike to leave matters in that condition, and he proposed to travel to Fort Wayne to inspect George Graham's Indiana land. If the property was as valuable as Graham represented and the title was good, Baker said he would attach a mortgage to the land to secure the $3,000 down payment he had made on the Molloy farm and then give Graham and Mrs. Molloy five years to pay it off. Pleased by the proposition, Mrs. Molloy said she would get Graham to agree to it when she returned to the Brookline farm.[10]

But George Graham's claim to have inherited property in Fort Wayne from his father turned out to be just another of his lies. Two days after Baker's conversation with Mrs. Molloy, Graham wrote Baker a letter admitting that he had no claim to the Indiana property. He assured the judge that he had the utmost respect for both him and Mrs. Molloy, and he rued his lack of moral courage in deceiving them and not telling the whole truth in the beginning. Not surprisingly, though, Graham was still not telling the whole truth because, in the letter, he referenced his trip to Fort Wayne the previous fall as though he had, in fact, made such a journey.[11]

A few days after receiving the letter from Marquis Gorham on Christmas Day, Constable O'Neal received another letter inquiring about Sarah Graham, this one from Fort Wayne attorney J. R. Bittinger, asking him to go out to the Molloy farm and see for himself whether Sarah Graham was there. On January 2, 1886, O'Neal trekked out to the farm to carry out the assignment, but he found only Etta Molloy, another girl (probably Emma Lee), and the Graham boys at home. Emma Molloy had gone back to Kansas for a revival at Dunlap, and George Graham was in Springfield. Unaware of the Cora Lee marriage, O'Neal asked where Graham's wife was, and Etta, thinking he meant Cora, told him that she, too, had gone to Springfield.[12]

Later the same day, O'Neal stopped at a neighbor's house and was discussing Mrs. Graham's whereabouts when the neighbor mentioned that Graham had been married only a few months. The neighbor said he thought he still had the newspaper notice of the marriage, but he looked for it and couldn't find it. O'Neal was a little surprised that Graham had only recently married, but it still did not dawn on him that he had two wives.[13]

A couple of days later, Graham came to Brookline, and O'Neal asked him where Mrs. Graham was. Graham replied that she was "out at home," meaning the Molloy farm. O'Neal then asked why she didn't write her folks to let them know where she was, and Graham, realizing he was talking about Sarah, fell back on the "sore hand" excuse. He added that he himself had not written because he didn't get along with her family.[14]

But Graham was beginning to feel the heat from all the inquiries concerning Sarah's whereabouts, and he decided to make a run for it. In order to finance his getaway, he forged three checks, written on an account of the D. C. Cook Publishing Company of Chicago, and he passed them on or about January 9 at three separate Springfield banks: one for a little over twenty dollars at the Exchange Bank, another for forty dollars at the Greene County National Bank, and the third for thirty-six dollars at the First National Bank.[15]

On January 10, Graham wrote to Mrs. Molloy at Dunlap informing her that Sarah was missing and that he was leaving Springfield: "I am in or about to be in the very greatest trouble of my life, and like all my trouble, it is the one cause, *Sarah*. I hardly know how to begin to tell you about it. The simple facts are, Sarah has not been heard from since I have had the children, and they do me the credit to suppose I have put her out of the world. They have been writing to all the officials they can find in reference to it, and tho' I knew this for two months, I paid no attention to it, not deeming it worthy of any." Graham concluded by asking Mrs. Molloy to write to him at Paola, Kansas.[16]

When Mrs. Molloy received the letter a couple of days later at Dunlap, she was with Rev. O. S. Munsell, a newspaper editor and Methodist minister at nearby Council Grove, where Emma had recently lectured. After reading Graham's letter, Mrs. Molloy handed it to Munsell to let him read it.[17]

The next mail brought Mrs. Molloy another letter from Graham at Paola saying that he would wait there for a return letter from her and that he was then going to Kansas City to look for work on the railroad.

In the same mail, Mrs. Molloy also received a letter from Cora saying that George had left.[18]

On January 14 from Paola, Graham wrote a letter to Abbie Breese upbraiding her for her persistent inquiries into Sarah's whereabouts:

> Dear Abbie:—Since writing you a few days since, I have concluded that I am about tired of your folks writing about the country about me, and we have decided to "take a walk" and go far enough this time that we will not be disturbed by your heathenish letter writing. As you didn't seem inclined to give me any information about our goods, I will send an officer after them when we want them. When you hear of us again, you will be civilized enough not to act so cranky. Now, go ahead and write to all the people of Brookline or Springfield, if you want to.
>
> Yours in disgust,
>
> Geo. E. Graham[19]

From Dunlap, Mrs. Molloy wrote to Graham at Paola advising him to return home at once. She assured him that she believed in his innocence, that he had nothing to fear from an investigation, and that running away would only arouse suspicion. She said that if he feared mob violence, he should go to Greene County's sheriff, Francis Marion Donnell, and seek protection. Trusting Graham's story that the harassment he had been experiencing from the Brookline officials was all a conspiracy on the part of Sarah's family to ruin him and that the Breeses and Gorhams knew all along where Sarah was, Mrs. Molloy told George he should not only welcome but should demand an investigation.[20]

Meanwhile, back in Missouri, Constable O'Neal trekked to Springfield on or about Wednesday, January 13, and went to the office of the county recorder, John Paine, to verify whether George Graham had recently married, as O'Neal's neighbor said. Armed with the knowledge that Graham had indeed acquired a new wife, apparently while still married to Marquis Gorham's daughter, O'Neal stopped at the office of Greene County's prosecuting attorney, John A. Patterson, to inform him of the situation and suggest that something be done about the bigamy. On his way back to Brookline, O'Neal stopped at the Molloy farm to inquire again about the whereabouts of the first Mrs. Graham. He found Cora Lee, Etta Molloy,

Cora Lee (Sketch from *The Graham Tragedy and the Molloy-Lee Examination*)

a girl he took to be Emma Lee, and a washerwoman he did not know on the premises. Cora told O'Neal that she didn't know where Sarah Graham was, and she asked O'Neal to come back in a few days, since George was not home. However, she made no effort at concealment and allowed the constable to go through several rooms in the house.[21]

Just as Mrs. Molloy was getting ready to leave Dunlap for Peoria, Illinois, for another revival, she received a wire from Cora saying she was in trouble and asking Mrs. Molloy to come home and bring George with her. Traveling with Emma Lee, Mrs. Molloy took a train to Kansas City, where she hoped to find Graham, since he'd said in his last letter that he was going there. (It's not clear whether Emma Lee joined Mrs. Molloy at Dunlap directly after O'Neal stopped at the farm on January 13 or O'Neal was simply mistaken about Emma Lee being there on that date.) When Mrs. Molloy and Emma stepped off the train in Kansas City on the evening of January 15, one of the first people they saw was George Graham. He reached for Mrs. Molloy's hand "as a drowning man clutches for life," she later recalled, and she was distressed to see that he had been drinking.[22]

They went to the nearby Union Depot Hotel, where Graham had registered as H. C. Edwards, and he booked a separate room for Mrs. Molloy and Emma Lee. At the hotel, Mrs. Molloy reiterated to Graham that he must go back to Springfield—that running away would only make him look guilty. He insisted that he couldn't go back, and he finally confessed to forging the checks. He explained that he had not gone to Fort Wayne to get his sons, as he'd previously said, but had instead met Sarah in St. Louis. He'd left her there, but because of her family's persistent inquiries, suspicion was beginning to build that he might have killed her. He was "nearly wild" under the accusation, and he'd forged the checks to get money so he could go looking for Sarah. He suggested that her family might have her hidden out in St. Louis and that they were only trying to make trouble for him. As usual, Graham's tall tale elicited the sympathy of Mrs. Molloy, who was convinced he had such a "sensitive organization" that he "could not hurt an animal, much less a human being." It was understandable, she thought, that he might do something impetuous under the strain of such unfounded allegations.[23]

Word reached Springfield on January 13 that the check Graham had passed at the Exchange Bank was no good. A brief story about the forgery in the *Springfield Daily Herald* the next day added that investigation in the immediate wake of the finding had revealed that Graham also passed forged checks at two other Springfield banks and that he had "shaken the dust of this vicinity from his feet and fled." Graham, the newspaper reminded its readers, was married to the foster daughter of temperance revivalist Emma Molloy and had been living on the old Cooper farm five miles southwest of Springfield.[24]

Being charged as a forger would soon be the least of George Graham's troubles.

7

George Graham the Bigamist

CHARLIE GRAHAM had watched his father abscond mysteriously, and now the elder Graham stood charged with forgery. Charlie began to question the lies his father had instructed him to tell, and, according to his later testimony, he broke down and confessed to Cora Lee that his mother had come to Springfield the previous fall rather than remaining in St. Louis. Cora got excited and exclaimed, "For God's sake, whatever you do, don't tell anybody that your mother came to Springfield."[1]

About January 15, Frank Molloy, Emma's fifteen-year-old son, traveled to Springfield and visited the First National Bank. After asking for and receiving information about the forgery on that bank, he informed cashier R. L. McElhaney that he thought his mother would come home and make the check good. McElhaney asked the young man a number of questions and surmised that Frank did not get along well with George Graham. In discussing the forgery, Frank said there was "something worse behind the whole matter," leading McElhaney to believe Graham had done something else he was hiding. The next day, though, Frank came back to the bank to clarify his statement. He said he'd simply meant that there was more money involved than the single check on the First National Bank.[2]

On January 16, John Potter wrote to Abbie Breese, enclosing an account from a Springfield newspaper of Graham's forgeries and subsequent flight. Potter told Abbie that he had not been able to learn anything about Sarah's whereabouts from the occupants of the Molloy farm, not even from Charlie and Roy, and he suggested that if Abbie could send a picture of her sister, it might help.[3]

While Mrs. Molloy was still in Kansas City, she received another dispatch from her oldest foster daughter. Cora was in "the sorest distress" over the forgery charges against her husband, and she beseeched Mrs. Molloy to come home at once. Assuring Graham that she would try to take care of his bad checks, Mrs. Molloy left Kansas City with Emma Lee on the morning of January 16 and returned home.[4]

On Monday, January 18, Mrs. Molloy went to Springfield to talk to Mr. McElhaney. He told her he was willing to let her make the check on the First National Bank good without involving the authorities, but he wasn't sure whether Charles Harwood, president of the Greene County National Bank, was willing to do the same. McElhaney accompanied Mrs. Molloy to the Greene County National Bank, where they prevailed upon Harwood to drop the matter if Mrs. Molloy paid the debt, and he agreed to do so. In the course of the conversation, Mrs. Molloy told the men about George Graham's background and explained how she'd become associated with him. Harwood suggested that she "had better give him up," but Mrs. Molloy said she could not do that. She told them that she believed there was something good in George and that he would yet be a good man.[5]

After making the check on the Greene County National Bank good, Mrs. Molloy returned with McElhaney to the First National Bank, where she then paid him the amount due his bank. Mrs. Molloy added that she'd like to talk with McElhaney about the matter in more detail, and he made an appointment to meet with her later that day.[6]

About 4:00 P.M., Mrs. Molloy returned, accompanied by Reverend Plumb, Rev. Samuel Alexander of the local Methodist Episcopal Church, and Judge Baker. McElhaney directed them into the boardroom, and when he entered a few minutes later, Emma Molloy and the three men were discussing the disappearance of Sarah Graham. Mrs. Molloy said George Graham had fled because he feared being arrested purely on the insinuations of Sarah's family and taken back to Indiana without due process. McElhaney asked her where she thought Sarah was. Mrs. Molloy said at first that she didn't know, but then she ventured that Sarah was in St. Louis. When the cashier asked where in St. Louis, Mrs. Molloy explained that Sarah came from "a common family" and that she believed the first Mrs. Graham had "gone to the bad." McElhaney asked what that meant, and Mrs. Molloy said that she thought if Sarah was not at her uncle's in St. Louis, she was probably in a house of ill fame there. McElhaney said that in either case, Sarah should be easy to find if Mrs. Molloy could provide a photograph and a detailed description. Mrs. Molloy had a photograph with her, but the cashier asked her to go home, write out a thorough description of Sarah Graham as well, and bring it back the next day.[7]

As soon as she had made the checks good, Mrs. Molloy sent word to Graham, who had gone to St. Joseph to get work on the Hannibal and St. Joe Railroad, and he almost immediately started back for Springfield. Mrs. Molloy recalled later that Graham came home of his own accord before receiving her letter and that he only learned of the checks having been made good after his arrival, but Graham himself said that he came home *after* being notified that the forgeries had been taken care of. Considering the constraints of time, he almost certainly learned by telegraph on the evening of January 18 that Mrs. Molloy had settled the matter with the banks.[8]

Reverend Plumb spent the next day, January 19, with Mrs. Molloy, helping her write out a description of Sarah Graham. Sometime during the day, Mrs. Molloy also wrote a letter to Constable O'Neal at Brookline. Later cited as evidence that she "wished to impress the world with the idea that she moved on an evangelical plane so pure, ethereal and exalted as to be far above the comprehension of ordinary mortals," the missive was written on a sheet of paper under an ornamental, printed letterhead that read as follows:

My Field—The World, Mark 16, 15.
My Name—Christian, Acts 11, 26.
My Creed—The Bible, Mat. 18, 15–17.
My Bro. and Sister—Mat. 12, 47–50.
My Hope—Life Eternal, John 6, 54.
My Work—Highways and Hedges, Luke 14, 22.
My Object—To Save Souls, Rom. 10, 1.
My Expectations—Rev. 7, 9–17.
OFFICE OF MRS EMMA MOLLOY
EVANGELIST & TEMPERANCE LECTURER
Home Address: Brookline, Mo.
Highland Cottage, Jan. 19th, 1886[9]

Detective Ed Davis, one of
the investigators in the Sarah
Graham murder case (Sketch
from *The Graham Tragedy and
the Molloy-Lee Examination*)

In the body of the letter, Mrs. Molloy informed O'Neal that she was home for a few days investigating the charges against Mr. Graham, and she asked him to come and see her at once and to bring all the letters he had received inquiring about Sarah Graham. She expressed her desire to "get at the *bottom facts*" of the case before she had to leave home again in two days. She said she would have come to see him already except that she had other matters that had to be taken care of.[10]

Later the same day, Mrs. Molloy, accompanied by Plumb, went back to Springfield with the description of Sarah Graham that McElhaney had requested. She gave it to him and asked him to let her know if he learned anything important. She then asked him whether he knew Ed Davis, a Springfield detective. McElhaney replied that he knew Davis well, and Mrs. Molloy asked him whether he could get Davis to tell Constable O'Neal to quit nosing around the farm. When McElhaney balked at the idea, Mrs. Molloy explained that she didn't want O'Neal coming around because he was scaring the young people.[11]

McElhaney turned over the picture and description of Sarah Graham to Detective Davis and Frank Erskine, a St. Louis detective who was working with Davis to track down the woman. The banker also told Davis of Mrs. Molloy's request that he quash Constable O'Neal's "nosing around," but Davis declined that assignment.[12]

On the evening of January 19, George Graham reached home, and the next morning, Mrs. Molloy summoned David Anderson, a neighbor and friend, to her house to seek his advice on how best to handle Graham's predicament. After Anderson arrived, he and Mrs. Molloy spoke in the front room, carrying on part of their conversation in the presence of a hired hand and other Molloy household members, but Graham, unknown to Anderson, was secreted in a bedroom.[13]

Mrs. Molloy told Anderson about Graham's forgeries and the fact that she had made the checks good. She said Graham regretted what he had done, and she showed Anderson a letter George had written to her from St. Joseph expressing his penitence and asking whether she and Cora could forgive him again after what he had done. Mrs. Molloy asked Anderson what other legal steps she might need to take. Anderson assured her that if forgery was all there was to the matter, Graham could probably live down the crime, but he cautioned her that he'd heard rumors that Graham was also guilty of bigamy. He asked whether it might be possible that Graham had deceived her and Cora.[14]

Mrs. Molloy replied that Sarah Graham had no legal claim on George because the couple had divorced a number of years ago. Anderson said he'd heard there had been a remarriage, but Mrs. Molloy and Cora did not believe that. Mrs. Molloy thought the bigamy charge was just something Sarah's family had stirred up. She thought it was George's misfortune that he'd ever been connected to Sarah and her family.[15]

Anderson warned Mrs. Molloy that not only was Graham suspected of bigamy, but he was also rumored to be involved in Sarah's disappearance. Anderson said John Potter had received several letters suggesting as much. Mrs. Molloy again blamed Sarah's family, saying they had "persecuted" George for a number of years. She repeated her belief that Sarah was probably in a "house" in St. Louis, and she thought Sarah would be found by the coming weekend. Mrs. Molloy said she wanted to see the letters Potter had received.[16]

After Anderson's visit, Charlie took him home in a buggy and continued on to Brookline. When Charlie returned home, he announced that while he was in Brookline, he had signed a letter that Constable O'Neal wrote to Abbie Breese. O'Neal had asked Charlie to write to his aunt, but Charlie begged off because his hands were stiff from the cold, damp weather. He allowed O'Neal to write the letter instead. Although Charlie dictated the general contents of the letter, he didn't know for sure what was in it because he didn't read it. The news threw Mrs. Molloy into a panic. "Maybe you have signed your father's life away!" she exclaimed. "Maybe you signed something that said you saw your father kill your mother."[17]

George Graham was at least as terrified as Mrs. Molloy, and he threatened to shoot some of the Brookline crowd for their meddlesome ways. No doubt he had John Potter and Constable O'Neal in mind as particular targets.[18]

Mrs. Molloy, Frank, Cora, and Charlie almost immediately set off in a wagon for Brookline. George Graham wanted to go, too, but Mrs. Molloy told him it would be better if he did not. The foursome traveled at a rapid clip, and during the short journey Mrs. Molloy expressed irritation that Constable O'Neal had not come to see her as she'd requested in her letter of the previous day.[19]

When they reached the village, Mrs. Molloy invited Constable O'Neal into the wagon for a conversation, and he agreed after some reluctance. They then drove off a short distance so they wouldn't have to talk in front of the whole town. Mrs. Molloy was "pretty hot," according to O'Neal, and wanted to know what he had forced Charlie to sign. Contradicting what Charlie had said, O'Neal claimed Charlie knew what he was signing because O'Neal had read the letter aloud after he'd written it.[20]

Unconvinced, Mrs. Molloy demanded to see the letter. Constable O'Neal said it had already been picked up, but Cora said that couldn't be true because no train had run. O'Neal then said the letter was in the post office and had already been sealed and stamped. After Cora offered to pay for a new envelope and stamp, O'Neal finally agreed to let them read the letter, assuming it was okay with postmaster John Potter. They went into the office, and Potter opened the letter and let them read it:

Brookline Station, Mo., Jan. 20, 1886

DEAR AUNT:—I seat myself to write you a few lines to let you know that me and Roy is well at present, and hope this may find you the same. Mother come to St. Louis, Missouri, with us, and pap left her there and brought us to Brookline, Mo. We have never heard of mother since. Pap married Cora Lee, July 18, 1885. Please write soon; direct in care of John Potter.

Charlie H. Graham[21]

After reading the letter, Mrs. Molloy handed it back to Potter and said it was all right—that she had no objections to its being mailed. During an ensuing conversation with O'Neal, as soon as she mentioned George Graham's name, the constable interjected, "See here, don't you talk about him. He is a forger; I have no use for such a man."[22]

Mrs. Molloy explained that she had taken care of the bad checks and that she intended to bring Graham back and have the matter investigated. She told O'Neal that George and Sarah Graham had been divorced several years, and she repeated her belief that Sarah would likely be found in a St. Louis bawdy house.[23]

The next day, January 21, Mrs. Molloy finally departed for Peoria to keep the revival engagement she'd previously scheduled.[24]

Now that Mrs. Molloy had covered Graham's bad checks and he had returned to the Molloy farm, the minor stink that the forgeries had caused in Springfield briefly died down. Although Constable O'Neal and others around Brookline still had their strong suspicions, most of Mrs. Molloy's friends and acquaintances were disposed to think well of her and her relations, and the Springfield press had not yet sniffed out what lay beneath the forgeries.[25]

But one of George Graham's hometown newspapers was already onto a nastier crime. Well aware of Graham's long, roguish history, the *Fort Wayne Daily News* published a report on January 21 headlined "George Graham: Some Ugly Stories Concerning the Disappearance of His Wife." The article began, "It would seem that the erratic George Graham will never cease, while life lasts, to furnish newspaper sensations." The newspaper reminded its readers that Graham had repeatedly been in trouble with the law and that he'd been sent to the northern Indiana prison three times, twice for horse stealing and once for forgery.[26]

The story described Graham's association with Mrs. Molloy in the publication of a temperance newspaper after he finished his last prison term. "Aside from a story implicating him and Mrs. Malloy [*sic*] in a liaison," the report continued, "not much has been heard from Graham since he came to this city to attend the funeral of his father, the late James Graham. The story of criminal relations between George and Mrs. Malloy was not credited here nor by the friends of that lady anywhere. The present sensation, however, has to do with the disappearance of Graham's wife, who was formerly known as Sarah Gorham, a daughter of Marquis Gorham, the well-known file-maker, of this city."[27]

The story then detailed Graham's marriage and remarriage to Sarah Gorham, the disturbing report of his bigamous marriage to Cora Lee, Sarah's departure from Fort Wayne in late September to join Graham, and the subsequent unsuccessful efforts of the Gorham family to locate Sarah. "Mr. Gorham, the father of the wronged wife, believes his daughter has been foully dealt with," the report concluded.[28]

The next day, the *Daily News* followed up with a story that reprinted several letters the Gorham family had received from the West relative to Sarah's disappearance. One was George's brutal reply from Paolo, Kansas, to one of Abbie Breese's inquiries, and another was the letter John Potter had written to Abbie on January 16 with an enclosed account of Graham's forgeries. The last letter was the one Charlie Graham had dictated and O'Neal had written at Brookline on January 20. Abbie had received it just hours before the *Daily News* went to print on January 22.[29]

These letters, the *Daily News* asserted, strengthened the probability that Sarah Graham had been foully dealt with, as the Gorham family feared, and the editor severely chastised Mrs. Molloy for her apparent involvement in the bigamous marriage, if nothing else:

> We come now to the inquisitorial part of this subject. How can Mrs. Emma Malloy [*sic*], who has posed before the country as a martyr to the cause of temperance, explain her connection with this affair? Mrs. Malloy knew that George Graham had a wife living at Fort Wayne, on the 18th of July, when he married her daughter. She knew, for she must have furnished him the money, that he was coming to St. Louis to meet his own wife two months after he had married another. How can Mrs. Malloy explain the lingering absence of the poor girl from Fort Wayne, who had been, with her children, an inmate of her home at Elgin and in Kansas? Does Mrs. Malloy expect the public forever to excuse the strange incidents that ever and anon mark her career? What strange infatuation is that which makes this lady write effusive love letters to an ex-convict and then permits him to marry her daughter with a wife still living?[30]

The *Daily News* called for an official investigation into Sarah's disappearance, including a requirement that George Graham and Mrs. Molloy be compelled to tell what they knew about the affair. Promptly taking up the challenge, Detective Davis wrote to the *Daily News*, asking the editors to send him copies of their January 21 and 22 stories about George Graham's misadventures.[31]

On January 24, Graham wrote to Mrs. Molloy in Illinois, once again expressing his contrition for the forgeries. In reference to Sarah's whereabouts, he added, "I hope the St. Louis search will be successful."[32]

Energized by the *Daily News* stories about Sarah Graham's disappearance and encouraged by Detective Davis's expressed interest in the case, Timothy and Abbie Breese left Fort Wayne for Springfield on January 27 to press bigamy charges against George Graham. Their purpose, of course, was not simply to prosecute Graham for his illicit marriage but also to keep him from taking flight while the search for Sarah continued. Armed with a power of attorney from Sarah's father, the Breeses also hoped to gain custody of Charlie and Roy. They reached Springfield on January 28, and the next day Timothy Breese went to Greene County authorities and pressed charges against Graham for bigamy. Later that day, Detective Davis and constable Rice Perrin of Springfield went out to the Molloy farm and arrested Graham on the bigamy charge, and he was lodged in the Greene County Jail in default of a $1,000 bond. The *Daily Herald* recounted the story the next day under the headline "Graham Again in Trouble."[33]

But neither the *Herald* nor its readers yet knew the full extent of George Graham's trouble.

8

The Search for Sarah Graham

INTERVIEWED BY reporters, Graham denied the bigamy charge, repeating the story he'd told Cora and Mrs. Molloy that he and Sarah had gotten divorced shortly after he went to prison the first time. Timothy Breese admitted the truth of that statement, but he said the couple had gotten remarried and that he was present at the wedding reception.[1]

On January 30, the day after Graham's arrest, Brookline deputy constable Joel Phillips went out to the Molloy farm to serve a summons on Charlie Graham, requiring him to testify at his father's upcoming preliminary hearing on the bigamy charge. The officer, according to a *Daily Herald* report, had the door "shut in his face" by the female occupants of the house and was not allowed to talk to Charlie. Phillips himself said only that he was denied entrance because the door was locked.[2]

On the same day, the *Fort Wayne Daily News*, following up its earlier stories about Sarah Graham's disappearance, reprinted an article from the *Wabash Courier*, which cited rumors that Graham, Mrs. Molloy, and Cora Lee had conspired to murder Sarah so that "she might not prove an embarrassing obstacle to the happiness of Graham and his wife No. 2." The *Courier* opined that while Mrs. Molloy was far from a model woman, she was not a murderer, and the *Daily News* echoed the sentiment: "Mrs. Molloy's guilt in the case consists in permitting her daughter to marry Graham without having first procured a divorce or evidence of his first wife's death."[3]

But many people around Springfield and Brookline were beginning to think she might be guilty of more than that.

On January 31, the *Springfield Daily Herald* reprinted the *Fort Wayne Daily News* stories about Sarah's Graham's mysterious disappearance, causing a sensation in Springfield. From his cell at the county jail, Graham wrote to the *Herald* the next day, answering the charge that he was involved in his wife's disappearance, and the letter was printed in the February 1 issue. He said the *News* account of his "career" was fairly accurate, although entirely one-sided. Pointing out that the case against him rested only on the assertions of Timothy Breese, he accused Breese of being a fugitive from justice and the Breese family of "having more than a passing acquaintance with the Indiana State prison." He admitted that the *Fort Wayne News* was well edited, but he claimed the editor, William D. Page, was a "malignant personal enemy" of his.[4]

"The slurs of the *News* against both Mrs. Molloy and Cora E. Graham (my lawful wife, Mr. Editor), are gratuitous, unmanly and uncalled for," Graham continued. "Both are estimable Christian ladies, and neither would for an instant aid, abet or encourage any illegal or underhand work." He said that if the prosecution should prove him guilty of any crime, he was prepared to face the consequences, but until more tangible evidence was produced, he asked that popular judgment be suspended and that he be granted the same impartiality and due process that anyone else should expect under the law. Graham, who was in regular contact with both his wife and his son Charlie, concluded by disputing the *Herald's* assertion that the officer who'd visited the Molloy farm two days earlier had the door slammed in his face. The "several females" who refused the officer admission were Mrs. Molloy's teenage daughters, Etta Molloy and Emma Lee, Graham explained, and they did not want to transact business with a stranger. Contradicting not only the *Herald* but the constable's official report of the matter, Graham said that the officer was eventually allowed into the house and that he only failed in his mission to talk to Charlie because he had not brought a warrant or other papers authorizing him to do so.[5]

Graham also wrote directly to the *Fort Wayne Daily News,* upbraiding editor Page for printing the sensational stories about him "at the expense of truth." Graham said he didn't claim to be "a model for the rising generation," but he did claim that he had tried hard since leaving Fort Wayne to redeem himself for his past transgressions and to secure for himself "a place among men." He added that much of his bad reputation in Fort Wayne could be attributed to the unfair coverage he'd received at the hands of the city's newspapers. "I have certainly been hardly used by the press of Fort Wayne," he asserted.[6]

Graham claimed Indiana governor James D. Williams had pardoned him in 1877 for his 1873 conviction for horse stealing because the governor concluded that Graham never should have been convicted in the first place. Graham also claimed that his Indiana conviction for forgery in 1879 resulted because the primary witness swore falsely against him.[7]

Graham continued in his letter to the Fort Wayne newspaper: "It is a fact that I *was* the husband of Sarah Graham and it is also the fact that I am *not* her husband now." He said he had engaged a detective to look for Sarah and that he was as anxious as anyone could be that she should be found. He repeated that the entire case against him rested solely on the assertions of Timothy Breese.[8]

Dismissing Marquis Gorham's reported concern over the welfare of his daughter, Graham said he had a letter in his possession in which Gorham had ordered Sarah to leave his home and never come back. After Gorham's ultimatum to his daughter, Graham yielded to Sarah's entreaties and took her away from Fort Wayne to Elgin, Illinois, even though he was under no legal obligation to do so and did not plan to have anything else to do with his first wife after rescuing her from her dire circumstance. Graham said Sarah knew all about these matters and would not like to have them aired in public should the bigamy charge against him come to trial.[9]

As for the charges against Mrs. Molloy made by the *Daily News*, Graham said they were "all mud" that would "rub off when dry." Calling Mrs. Molloy "an earnest, true, christian lady," Graham said he was thoroughly indebted to her for any advancement he'd made during the past several years and that any attempt on his part to defend her would be like "a poodle attempting to defend a lion."[10]

Editor Page responded the very next day to what he called "Graham's Gush." He said, "Mr. Graham must permit us to look at the case from a different standpoint than one which only contemplates his peace of mind.

What the public is interested to know is, what has become of Sarah Graham?" Page accused Graham of being a selfish ingrate who only sought "to draw attention to himself as the unfortunate party" and who seemed incapable of sticking to the issue at hand—namely the whereabouts of his first wife. The editor labeled Graham's claim that Sarah had agreed to willingly turn her kids over to him as preposterous. He also cited Graham's letters to the Breese family assuring them that Sarah was all right but was unable to write herself because of a sore hand. If she had since unaccountably disappeared and Graham wanted to take his "place among men," as he now claimed, why had he not informed the Breeses of Sarah's disappearance rather than trying to hide it from them? "We have tried hard to pity George Graham," Page concluded, but "we can only see the character of Graham in a hideous aspect."[11]

A few days later, Mrs. Molloy also wrote to Page, explaining that "some kind of friend" had sent her a copy of the *Daily News* containing the conjectures about Sarah Graham's disappearance and "the innuendoes upon myself for my course in the past six years, regarding Mr. Graham." Mrs. Molloy said she wasn't surprised that any time appearances might be against Graham, his past misdeeds would be held up to "public excoriation," but she was surprised "that after eleven years of the best of my life has been given to the work of restoring to society the wrecks it has made, renovated by the grace of God, that those who have been familiar with my life and work should be so ready to believe the worst of me."[12]

Everyone knew, Mrs. Molloy continued, that it was almost impossible for a man who had ever been convicted of a crime to be forgiven by society or to find work. "If it is a crime to aid such a one, then I am guilty of numberless such crimes." She did not deny that she had taken an interest in Graham ever since he'd appeared at her door, "forsaken by friends, out of employment, and sick at heart with the world's scorn." No one in distress ever appealed to her, she said, that she did not try to help.[13]

Sarah Graham's disappearance was not proof of her death, Mrs. Molloy said, reminding the editor that Sarah's children had sworn they left her in St. Louis. Mrs. Molloy said the charge that she'd claimed Sarah was in a house of ill repute was cruel. Instead, she thought Sarah might be with her brother in Washington Territory, since that was where she'd told George she was going. At any rate, Mrs. Molloy was convinced that

Sarah's friends *"know exactly where she is."* If they did not know, they were entitled to sympathy, and no one was more eager to solve the mystery of Sarah's whereabouts than Mrs. Molloy and Cora Lee.[14]

Mrs. Molloy concluded,

> If George Graham has been guilty of a crime, we cannot shield him, but until he is proven guilty I must believe him innocent. No one is more cognizant of his weaknesses than myself, but no one knows his good qualities so well, either. The last words his father ever spoke to me were: "You have been a mother to my unfortunate boy. Don't let go of him while there is any hope." When I meet that father at the judgment, he will know that I tried to fulfill his request.
>
> Emma Molloy[15]

After reading Mrs. Molloy's letter in the *Daily News,* the editor of the *Wabash Courier* felt called upon to respond. His reaction was typical of the mounting censure Mrs. Molloy faced because of her close association with Graham. Mrs. Molloy, whose life was as "full of scandals as a dog is of flees [sic]," was now involved in her biggest scandal ever, said the *Courier* newsman, and she had already lost many friends in Wabash because of it. Despite conceding that Mrs. Molloy had presented a plausible defense of herself and had made a reasonable request that her friends withhold judgment until all the facts were known, the editor concluded, "Either Mrs. Molloy is the most indiscreet woman in the world, or she is a very bad one."[16]

George Graham's arrest for bigamy was little noted except in Springfield, where the arrest occurred, and in Indiana, where both Graham and Mrs. Molloy were from. One person from outside those areas who did take notice was editor James Hagaman of the *Concordia Blade,* who said he wasn't surprised by the news of Graham's arrest. Hagaman had "judged him to be a villain" because of a threatening letter Graham wrote to the *Blade* when he lived in Kansas a year ago and because of other concerns Hagaman had about him. "It seems quite strange that Mrs. Molloy should have been wholly ignorant of the kind of man he was."[17]

Graham's preliminary examination on the bigamy charge began on February 4 before justice of the peace Daniel B. Savage. In consideration of the intense interest in the case, the hearing was held in the circuit

Charlie Graham (Sketch from *The Graham Tragedy and the Molloy-Lee Examination*)

courtroom, and about two thousand curious spectators jammed into the room. Graham was represented by attorneys George S. Rathbun and O. H. Travers, while prosecuting attorney John A. Patterson, assisted by local judge Walter D. Hubbard, argued the state's case. The prosecutors introduced legal documents showing Graham's marriage to Cora Lee in 1885 and his 1871 marriage to Sarah Gorham. The defense countered with a document showing Graham's divorce from Sarah in 1873, but the state then produced a record of the 1878 remarriage to Sarah Graham.[18]

Timothy Breese took the stand to corroborate Graham's two marriages to his sister-in-law. Breese also denied having been connected with a highway robbery in Kansas or ever having been charged with counterfeiting, as Graham had alleged.[19]

Charlie Graham was called as a witness to tell what he knew of the whereabouts of his mother. With George Graham present and monitoring his son's every word, Charlie dutifully recited the story he'd been coached to tell. Young Graham said that he, Roy, and their mother came from Fort Wayne to St. Louis, where they met their father, and that he and Roy continued to Springfield with their father, while their mother remained in St. Louis. The last time he saw her, Charlie said, was on the platform at the train depot in St. Louis.[20]

The next morning, February 5, Justice Savage formally charged Graham with bigamy and ordered him held for his appearance at the May term of the Greene County Court. "Bond was fixed at $1,000," the *Daily Herald* reported, "and in default thereof the reckless George went to jail."[21]

Later the same morning, Cora, who had been at Graham's side throughout the preliminary examination, wrote to Mrs. Molloy relaying the outcome of the proceeding. "I am altogether too heart-broken and torn to pieces to write you a long letter this morning, but I will try to write you a longer one after I get out home." She said that no one in Springfield would put up the $1,000 bond because the public was "so prejudiced by the newspaper articles and the transaction about the notes. Everything looks as if there had been a remarriage in 1878, although the lawyers say it is possibly a forgery. George still declares to me that he never was remarried to Sarah."[22]

On the morning of February 6, Timothy and Abbie Breese, accompanied by Constable Perrin, Greene County deputy sheriff Joseph Dodson, and A. O. Mack, visited the Molloy farm to talk to Charlie and Roy Graham. Cora met the party at the door and let them into the house. Timothy Breese asked Cora whether she had any objection to his talking to the boys in the presence of the deputy, and Cora replied that she would rather he did not—that, in such a case, she would want a witness from her side present. However, she did not mind Breese talking to the boys in her presence alone.[23]

Breese then asked Cora what she thought about the disappearance of Sarah Graham. Cora said she didn't know anything about it, and she turned the question back on Breese, asking him what he thought about it. Breese replied that some people thought Sarah was concealed on the Molloy property. Cora stoutly denied the allegation, adding that if that was what people thought, she wanted the proper authorities to come and make an official search at once. She told Breese that since he'd asked, she would give him her honest opinion—that he probably knew himself where Sarah was.[24]

"No, indeed," Breese exclaimed, "if we did, I would not be here."

Cora broke into tears and said she did not want to talk about it anymore. After a brief lull, she excused herself and went into another part of the house. Presently she returned with Charlie and Roy, and she was carrying several Bibles or Testaments. She distributed them among those gathered in the room and asked them to join her in Bible reading and worship, explaining that it was a family tradition. The group took turns reading from the fourth chapter of John, and Cora led them in prayer to close the impromptu service.[25]

Afterward, Abbie Breese started talking to Roy, who was sitting on her husband's lap, and when Dodson tried to engage Cora in conversation, he couldn't gain her attention because, according to the deputy, she "seemed to be listening intently to what Roy was saying to Mrs. Breese." The group exchanged pleasant conversation for another hour, and Timothy Breese told Cora that although he'd previously shared the opinion of those who thought Sarah was concealed on the farm, he no longer believed that to be the case. Cora gave Deputy Dodson a picture of Sarah and asked him to give it to Detective Davis, and the Breese party then left without the Graham boys and without having gained any new clues as to Sarah's whereabouts.[26]

But the visit sorely distressed Cora Lee. She sat down to write the letter to Mrs. Molloy that she had promised her the previous day. She told Mrs. Molloy that Mr. Breese had been there almost all morning, and she described the conversation she'd had with him about Sarah's whereabouts.[27]

Later in the day, Cora sent for David Anderson, the neighbor in whom Mrs. Molloy had confided a couple of weeks earlier. When Anderson and his wife arrived, Cora escorted them into the kitchen, where it was warmer, and asked them to sit down, but the visit had scarcely commenced when Cora noticed Constable O'Neal, O'Neal's deputy, and Timothy Breese passing the Molloy place in a wagon. Cora grew very agitated and excused herself. She took George Graham's pistol out of Charlie's pocket and left the house, taking hired hand John Brumley along with her. With the pistol under her apron, Cora started with Brumley toward the east gate of the Molloy farm, where she thought the men would try to enter. They passed on toward Springfield, though, without making any attempt to enter the property, and Cora returned to the house after about ten minutes. She set the pistol down near Anderson and Charlie Graham. Charlie, who, as a thirteen-year-old Missouri farm boy, was used to handling firearms, picked it up and put it back in his pocket.[28]

Cora explained to Anderson and his wife that she was afraid that Breese had come back to "kidnap" Charlie and Roy and that she thought the men in the wagon were "full of Brookline whiskey." She then turned her attention to the reason she'd summoned Anderson, asking him whether he might be willing to sign as one of George's bondsmen to get him released from jail. Anderson replied that she needn't bother her friends about the bond because Graham was under suspicion for an even greater crime than bigamy. Sentiment was, therefore, too strong against him. As he had during his previous visit, Anderson again asked whether Cora thought Graham might have deceived her and Mrs. Molloy, but Cora was adamant in her devotion to Graham. She said a minister had joined them together until death parted them and that she would stand by George even if he'd committed "ten thousand crimes." Anderson realized it was no use trying to reason with Cora, and he and his wife excused themselves and left. A couple of days later, Cora wrote Anderson that she'd gotten George's bond reduced to $500, and she renewed her request that he sign as a bondsman. Anderson declined to answer the letter or to pay Cora another visit.[29]

On February 6, the same day the Breeses visited Cora, Graham wrote to Mrs. Molloy from his jail cell, beseeching her to bail him out. He said he had previously been inclined to believe that the Breese and Gorham families were as much in the dark about Sarah's disappearance as he and the Molloy family were, but that he was now convinced the whole thing had been premeditated and the Breeses and Gorhams were fully aware of Sarah's whereabouts. "If I could be in Fort Wayne a week," he continued, "I could unravel the whole thing. I believe Breese could produce Sarah in forty-eight hours if he wanted to, and it maddens me to think that I must be kept cooped up here while they have full liberty to perfect their plans and crush me."[30]

A day or two after his visit to the Molloy farm, Breese started for home and Detective Davis accompanied him as far as St. Louis, where they met Detective Erskine. Acting on Charlie Graham's assurance that his mother had been left in St. Louis, the three men vainly scoured the city, including the "institutions of depravity." They learned that Sarah, her husband, and their two boys had spent two nights at the Grand Central Hotel, but they turned up no other sign of Sarah Graham.[31]

Breese returned to Indiana, where he reported that he'd learned very little about Sarah's possible whereabouts, but that he'd found Charlie and Roy were "kindly cared for." Meanwhile, Davis carried the investigation back to Springfield and learned that George Graham and his two sons had reached that place on the evening of September 30. Mrs. Fay told him that Charlie had said his mother was also with them but had been left on the train. Charlie thought his mother and his father were going to a train station near the Molloy farm and then would walk together to the farm from there. The detective concluded that Charlie had later been instructed to say his mother was left in St. Louis, and the focus of the search for Sarah Graham now turned to the Springfield-Brookline area.[32]

In answer to Graham's letter of February 6 asking to be bailed out, Mrs. Molloy replied on or about February 8, saying that she would "raise heaven and earth to find that woman," but she currently had no funds of her own to pay George's bond and nobody whom she felt at liberty to appeal to for bail money. She urged George to be patient, assuring him that Sarah would turn up sooner or later and that if there was no second marriage, everything would be all right.[33]

From his jail cell on February 8, Graham wrote a letter to the *Springfield Daily Leader*, responding to the rampant rumors about Sarah's disappearance. "I admit, mysterious disappearance," Graham said, "if she has disappeared." He added that he and others (presumably meaning Mrs. Molloy) had detectives engaged in a search for Sarah, and he claimed that he had personally written the description of her that had been furnished to Detective Erskine and published in the *St. Louis Missouri Republican*.[34]

"To the allegation that I am connected with or responsible for the alleged disappearance," Graham concluded, "I can enter a vigorous denial. There could be no possible motive for such action on my part. The testimony of both of my children is unequivocal on the point that they bade their mother good-by at the Union depot in St. Louis."[35]

Following up on her letter to George on February 8 that urged him to be patient, Mrs. Molloy wrote to him again the next day, assuring him that she was convinced of his innocence and that she would not let him be convicted on false evidence. "Anything I can will be gladly done."[36]

On February 10, Mrs. Molloy again wrote to Graham, inquiring as to what steps his lawyers had thus far taken. "Have they tried to get a transcript of the court record for 1878? It seems to me if no such license is recorded, that would entitle you to a new hearing, and would immediately release you." She beseeched him not to hide anything from her but to tell her the worst. "This agony of mind is killing me. I cannot think you would do so insane a thing as to marry Cora, when you knew there had been a second marriage." She admitted, however, that she was puzzled as to why such a marriage had not already been disproven by the absence of any record of it.[37]

Mrs. Molloy didn't wait to learn what steps Graham's lawyers had taken. That very day, she wrote from Peoria to the Allen County probate judge, under the name of Mrs. M. M. Emerson, asking him to please furnish her with a transcript of the marriage of George Graham and Sarah Graham or Sarah Gorham in December 1878 "and relieve the anxiety of a mother's heart."[38]

Mrs. Molloy's advice to Graham to be patient and her assurances that she believed in his innocence were not what he'd hoped to receive from her. Responding to her letter of February 8, he wrote back on February 10: "No, you will not raise heaven and earth to find that woman. When they really want her, they will produce her." He went on to suggest that the Gorham and Breese families had hatched a plan, out of mere spite, to hide Sarah out in Indiana, where she couldn't be found, and then accuse him of disposing of her.[39]

9

Mrs. Molloy as "An Object of Suspicion"

ALTHOUGH MOST of Mrs. Molloy's friends and acquaintances in Springfield stood by her when Graham's forgeries were revealed, sentiment began turning against her after the inflammatory *Fort Wayne Daily News* stories appeared and Graham was subsequently arrested for bigamy. In early to mid-February, Reverend Plumb wrote to Mrs. Molloy at Peoria, apprising her of the mounting censure she faced in Springfield. Rumor had begun "to connect her name in an ugly manner with the mystery of Sarah Graham's disappearance," and he advised her to consult an attorney. He recommended H. E. Howell, a prominent Springfield lawyer and judge.[1]

In mid-February, Mrs. Molloy traveled from Peoria to her hometown of South Bend, Indiana, to be at the bedside of her sick father. From South Bend on February 19, she mailed a lengthy letter to Howell. By way of introduction, she mentioned Reverend Plumb, "who knows better than any one else all the pitiful circumstances of this case of Mr. Graham's, which has plunged me into the saddest disaster of all my life."[2] She wrote:

I entered into this work of prison and temperance reform about eleven years ago; entered into it as a fireman rushes into a burning building with no thought for himself, but with one inspiration to save the perishing. I have received many heart wounds, have come forth scarred and burned, but I have the consolation of knowing that many hearts have been comforted and many homes made brighter by my labors, and I trust many souls saved to God.

Never in all my life have I failed to put out my hand helpfully to the outcast, and the unfortunate, or to speak a word of hope to the erring. It has been a part of my religion to remember that Christ came to "seek and to save that which was lost"; and it has never once entered my mind, that if I should make any mistake, or err in judgment, that all "good and professed Christian" people would turn against me, and that, as David says: "False witnesses would rise up against me and lay to my charge things which I knew not." So I find myself stunned and bewildered by the information that Mr. Plumb gives me, that *"almost the entire population of Springfield believe me to be a bad woman."* It seems strange that any should think that if I wanted to descend to anything low and vile that I would need to bring into my home those who were helpless to take care of themselves, and spend my entire time in constant drudgery to support them. You can readily see that I am not so devoid of any personal attraction that if I wanted to live a criminal life, I could not find some one who would *support me* instead of having some one on my hands to support.[3]

Mrs. Molloy then chronicled the history of her association with George Graham, starting with her making his acquaintance while he was in prison. After he got out, he gradually became, she said, "like one of my own children." She admitted that if she had been more "worldly wise," she might have forbidden the hasty, questionable marriage between Cora and George, but Cora, who'd worked closely with George in the newspaper office, seemed to be madly in love with him. Cora was not a child, she knew George's history, and she was willing to take the risk. Mrs. Molloy said that neither she nor Cora doubted George's story that he and Sarah had been divorced and that nobody thought to inquire about a second marriage. Although Mrs. Molloy knew firsthand about the relationship between George and Sarah until the newspaper failed and the family moved to Springfield, she admitted that for much of what had happened since that time, she had trusted in what George had said. He had told her that he left Sarah in St. Louis and that she was going from there to Vancouver in Washington Territory, where she had a brother in the army, and that she was going to cook for the soldiers. Charlie and Roy had told the same story about leaving their mother in St. Louis. Mrs. Molloy said she therefore believed, when she heard about Sarah's disappearance, that George could not possibly be involved.[4]

Mrs. Molloy concluded her account of her association with Graham by telling Howell about her making the bad checks good and then leaving for Peoria. "George's arrest and imprisonment and subsequent events you are all familiar with," she said. "Mr. Plumb, when he reads this, as well as Judge Baker, will tell you that this history is in substance what I told them last spring, before George and Cora were married. Can you see that I have done anything wrong—anything that is unchristian—in this whole transaction, or anything that should entitle me to the bitter censure of the people of Springfield?"[5]

She continued:

If it transpires that George has deceived us, and as Mr. Plumb states there is a record of a second marriage, then George must suffer for so cruelly and wickedly deceiving us, who have spared no labor or pains to save him to a life of usefulness and happiness. If he *has* done this he must reap what he has sown, bitter and hard as it is to those of us who have striven so hard to save him. We can do no more than to see that he has a fair trial. The law must take its course. No one could possibly suffer under all this more than Cora and I, but *if he is proven guilty,* then I shall believe in the *insanity of crime,* for surely no sane man of his mental ability *would come back,* knowing that he was guilty, and after he was arrested, and knowing that he could not escape the records, still stoutly deny his guilt.

I am writing at the bedside of my father, who for a week past has been hovering between life and death. All this strain has been so fearful upon me that I have not been able to sleep for a week past, nor have I been able to retain any food to speak of since Mr. Plumb's letter came. He is a good man and I believe advises me wisely. His information regarding George's probable guilt has been almost a death blow to me. He says the people of Springfield say, "I dare not come back *for fear of arrest.*" What have I done to be arrested for? I certainly have no fears of that kind, but the necessary expenditures for getting ready to work the farm have plunged me into debt nearly $400. I must earn the money before I can come home to pay these debts.

It seems the most cruel blow of all to have Mr. Plumb write me that I "must either come home at once and make my record clear from the time I first knew George and Sarah to the present time, or he does not believe I can do temperance work any more *at all anywhere.*" I am not on trial. I have done nothing to injure anyone, public or private, unless it be, as the world will say, foolishly clinging to the frailest hope, and periling everything in attempting to rescue one "whom it seems is next to impossible to save." The future world will show whether the effort has been *wholly in vain.* Do you think God will let my usefulness be destroyed because I have made this seeming "failure?" Is it possible that the church with which I am connected, which preaches a "salvation to the uttermost," will help to crush me for carrying out the lesson taught in Matt. 25: "I was an hungered and ye gave me meat; I was thirsty and ye gave me drink; I was a stranger and ye took me in; I was naked and ye clothed me; I was sick and ye visited me; I was in prison and ye came unto me." "Inasmuch as ye have done it unto the *least of these,* ye have done it unto me."

I can only leave all this in God's hands, for I believe he is just, and will, in the end, vindicate me. If George should prove guilty, his bitterest enemy could wish him no more terrible fate than to be torn from a home where we all loved him, and desired nothing so much as that he would be good and happy, and the ultimate salvation of his soul, and be sent to so terrible a place as Jefferson City prison is represented to be. I cannot endure to think of it. I am afraid it will kill Cora.

Now, Judge, I have done as Mr. Plumb directed—I have told you the whole story as concisely as possible. Will you tell me what I ought to do? If I stop my work the family at home must suffer, and I can't pay my debts. God had opened the way for me to have work for several weeks yet, and I cannot but think if I were so wicked that *He had rejected me* the door would be closed. The minister who has made my engagements knows the whole history, and has seen the Springfield papers. Some one very kindly provided him with full copies. I have done by George just as I promised his dead father I would the last time I ever saw him—clung to him through evil and good report. All this has been with the consciousness that I must answer to God for all my influences over him. He will tell you that ever since I have known him, he has never had aught but the best and kindliest Christian influences, and no one he has ever known has ever striven harder to lead him to Christ. If this is a crime in the eyes of the world, then I must suffer for it. Christ says "the servant is not greater than his lord. If the world hate you, ye know that it hated me before it hated you." If I have been led astray in all this, it has been through God's word. If you will read Isaiah 56:6 to 11th, you will find my Divine directions. I have no desire to parade my work, done silently and patiently for the Master, before the world; but there are many others who could testify that George is not the only one who has been the object of my care and solicitude.

If it should transpire that all my friends should fall away and I should become "for the work's sake," an object of suspicion, and my life work torn from me by those who will not do this work themselves, I can only say, "Thy will be done." God must have some place in the world for me, and He will show me what he wants of me. I am waiting His directions.[6]

Mrs. Molloy concluded by saying that she was enclosing a small fee as a retainer, in case she needed Howell's counsel, although she felt it would hardly compensate him for reading her very long letter. She said she had written it with many interruptions and "a constant prayer that God will bring the right to the light."[7]

While Mrs. Molloy was penning her lengthy communication to Judge Howell, both Cora Lee and George Graham were busy inscribing letters to Mrs. Molloy.

On February 18, Cora wrote that she had visited George and that he clung to her, "cried like a child," and begged her not to desert him. Graham offered to go before circuit judge W. F. Geiger or the prosecuting attorney and plead guilty to the bigamy charge if it meant Cora would stay with him. After Cora came home, she wrote to George that yes, she would stand by him if he was guilty and confessed but that he need not confess if he was not guilty. However, if he claimed not to be guilty and was later proved guilty, she would cut him loose forever. Cora admitted that even George's own attorney thought he was probably guilty and had suggested that George confess so that he might get a reduced sentence. "It is just killing me by inches," she told Mrs. Molloy.[8]

Despite the opinion of George's attorney, Cora still held out a glimmer of hope that the record of the second marriage might be fraudulent, and she closed the letter by asking Mrs. Molloy whether she could go to Fort Wayne and examine the county marriage records without letting the recorder know who she was.[9]

Mrs. Molloy had, of course, already made a clandestine inquiry about the marriage record, but whether Allen County officials ever responded to her letter to the probate judge is not known. And, as it turned out, it didn't matter because Cora had already learned the answer to her question. Following up her letter of February 18, she wrote to Mrs. Molloy again on February 19:

My dearest mother:—Bereft of everything save God, I will try to write you a word to-day. My strength has failed me and I have been sick all day. George told me *all* yesterday and the Fort Wayne record is *all right,* and I have been sorely deceived. I have no word of reproach for him, and pitied him so when he clung to me and prayed for me not to *hate* him. Of course I feel just as I always have felt. I cannot write you all about it, but I *must* see you. Don't write anyone a word about this but me. Won't you come home and do try to get things arranged so that I won't go entirely insane! I hope George will go before the Prosecuting Attorney and Judge Geiger and tell them, and thus get a lighter sentence. Oh! I pray you in the name of God *don't* say anything harsh or unkind of him. Do let me hear from you at once. He said he would have told me at the very first, but he thought it would be a mercy to me if I could go through the rest of my life and not know it. He said when he saw me, and saw how completely crushed I was, and how fast this was wearing me out, that he could not stand it without confessing everything to me. Oh! he has suffered if he has done wrong. I have everybody else to fight now; for God's sake in this awful despair *don't desert me.* I cannot write more. Come home as soon as you can. If I could only find some one who feels as I do to talk with about it. Yours as ever, only covered with clouds of despair.

C.[10]

On February 19, George wrote to Mrs. Molloy, responding to rumors of sexual impropriety between the two of them that had reached her at South Bend through her friends in Springfield. "As there never was any criminal intimacy between you and I, there can be no evidence from Indiana or *any place else* proving such a fact." In closing, he assured Mrs. Molloy, contrary to what he'd already confessed to Cora, that no matter what evidence might be produced against him for the crime of bigamy, he was *"before God innocent."*[11]

The next day, he wrote Mrs. Molloy again, elaborating on his previous day's statement. "The rumors of crim. con. from Indiana were *Breese's assertions* and were made in reference to Cora as well as yourself, and of course have no basis in fact." Graham advised Mrs. Molloy to sue the newspapers that had printed such insinuations and told her he was writing a full history of his life in which "the earnest, true, pure noble humanity and generosity you have always displayed toward me shall be treated in full."[12]

But events were on the horizon that would strain to the breaking point the goodwill between George Graham and Emma Molloy.

10

A Ghastly Discovery

STILL NURSING their suspicion that Sarah Graham might ultimately be found on the Molloy place, John Potter, Isaac Hise, and several other men from the Brookline area trekked out to the farm on Thursday morning, February 25. Using a windlass, the men lowered Hise into the old shaft located about three hundred yards northeast of the house, and Hise discovered the nude, decomposing body of a woman. Convinced it was Sarah Graham, Potter hurried to Springfield to alert Greene County authorities while Hise and the other workers went about retrieving the body from the well. Henry Fellows and Joseph Studley joined Hise at the floor of the well, and the men wrapped the body in sheets and blankets. Realizing the material was not strong enough to hold the body, they sent someone to the Molloy house to fetch two more blankets. They wrapped the additional blankets around the body and then hoisted it to the surface. The men also found various articles of women's apparel at the bottom of the well and brought them out.[1]

Meanwhile, Potter reached Springfield shortly after noon. Detective Davis promptly wired Abbie Breese to inform her of the discovery, and Abbie replied that she would start for Springfield as soon as possible. Since an inquest would be necessary to officially determine the identity of the deceased and the cause of death, coroner Z. Van Hoose hastily gathered a coroner's jury of six men.[2]

It was between 3:00 and 4:00 P.M. by the time Potter, Sheriff Donnell, Van Hoose, the impromptu coroner's jury, and a ragtag assortment of

Above: Shallow ravine where the well, in which Sarah Graham's body was found, was located, as the land appears today (Photo by the author)

Left: Headline about the discovery of Sarah Graham's body (From *Springfield Express*, March 5, 1886)

A HORRIBLE STORY!

The Mystery of the Disappearance
of Mrs. Sarah Graham
Cleared by

The Discovery of Her Dead and Murdered Body on the Molloy
Farm.

Found in the Bottom of a Well
Sixty Feet Deep
With a

Bullet Hole in the Breast—Greene
County the Scene of
the Most

Wanton Murder Ever Recorded
in the Annals of
Crime.

Circumstances Point to George E.
Graham as the Slayer of
His Wife.

newspaper reporters and other curiosity seekers got back to the Molloy farm. When they arrived, the body, sewn into the sheets and blankets, lay on the ground near the well, and the articles of clothing were scattered nearby. Hundreds of people from the surrounding countryside had also arrived and were milling around.[3]

Van Hoose qualified the jury and ordered the body exposed. The covering was opened up, and the ravaged female corpse was exposed to the huddled crowd. "The flesh has sloughed from the face and upper part of the body so that identification from the features was rendered impossible," said the *Springfield Daily Herald*, "but the lower limbs retained their form in a remarkable degree."[4]

Found among the women's clothing brought up from the well were a chemise and a corset with corresponding apertures in the right side that were thought to have been made by a bullet. A close examination of the body revealed a hole in direct line with the openings found in the garments. The coroner's jury and others on the scene tentatively concluded that the woman had been shot to death.[5]

After the hasty preliminary examination, the body was placed in a coffin and the clothes were gathered up for removal to Springfield, where the inquest was scheduled to resume in a more formal setting at the courthouse the next morning.[6]

Before leaving the scene, a *Herald* reporter called at the house to get Cora Lee's reaction to the horrific discovery. Cora was lying down and complained of feeling sick. She said she knew nothing about the body, and she asked that people not prematurely judge her and Mrs. Molloy. She offered a fainthearted suggestion that perhaps Timothy Breese had dumped the body in the well during his visit a few weeks earlier, but she did not insist on the idea once the reporter pointed out that the extreme decomposition of the body rendered such a theory implausible.[7]

Back in Springfield, Sheriff Donnell informed Graham of the discovery of a woman's body on the Molloy farm, and the prisoner, fearing mob action, exclaimed that he was not safe in the part of the jail where he was being held. The sheriff agreed, moving him to a steel cell and placing extra guards nearby. That evening, a reporter interviewed Graham in his cell. Clinging to the story that he'd left Sarah in St. Louis, Graham rejected the idea that the woman found in the well was his first wife. He claimed to have sent money to Sarah since he'd left her in St.

Louis. As the reporter started to leave, Graham added that regardless of what he might be guilty of or blamed for, he wanted the newspaperman to state that Mrs. Molloy was entirely innocent.[8]

Informed later the same evening that Graham still maintained he'd left his first wife in St. Louis, Mrs. Fay repeated that the boys had told her their mother came with them to Springfield.[9]

The next morning, February 26, "excitement was at fever heat" in Springfield over what was evidently a heinous murder, and the efforts of law officers to fix the guilt on George Graham met with "the cordial approval of public sentiment," according to a *Herald* reporter. A large crowd gathered at an early hour and surrounded the courthouse on the public square in anticipation of the coroner's inquest, but the taking of testimony was postponed until the afternoon because one of the jurors was absent and had to be replaced.[10]

In the meantime, the jury, law officers, and members of the press adjourned to Eli Paxson's undertaking business to view the remains, with the public being denied admission. The body lay in a coffin wrapped in blankets, and when it was exposed, "The sight was sickening." One of the jurors, pharmacist Charles Neiswanger, cut open the body to try to determine the course of the alleged bullet. From appearances, it had entered the right breast, broken a rib, and passed through the right lung. Although no bullet was found, the evidence, including powder burns on the clothing corresponding to where the bullet would have entered the body, convinced the jury that the victim had been shot. A deep cut in the abdomen suggested that the woman had also been stabbed.[11]

When the inquest resumed at 2:00 P.M. at the courthouse, the courtroom was jammed with an estimated fifteen hundred spectators. Another one thousand people were turned away for lack of room. With prosecuting attorney John Patterson conducting the hearing, Charlie Graham was the first witness called to the stand. He admitted that he'd lied at his father's preliminary hearing on the bigamy charge and that his mother had, in fact, come to Springfield with him and Roy. He'd lied, he said, because his father told him to. When the articles of clothing taken from the well were shown to him one by one, Charlie, with remarkable calmness, identified them as his mother's. He said that Mrs. Molloy and his mother sometimes quarreled when they lived together in Elgin and Washington. In conclusion, he stated that no one had instructed him on what to say during the present examination except Cora Lee, who'd told him to tell the truth.[12]

Kate Fay took the stand and repeated the story she first told Detective Davis and had affirmed to the *Herald* reporter the previous evening—that when the boys first came to her restaurant, they said their mother was on a train at the Springfield depot. Mrs. Fay also mentioned the trunk that Graham had left temporarily at her place the previous fall. John Potter, Isaac Hise, and Henry Fellows were among those testifying about the discovery of the body, and both Potter and Constable O'Neal related the story of Mrs. Molloy coming to Brookline upset over the letter Charlie had signed. The inquest was then adjourned until the next day, when Abbie Breese was expected to have arrived from Indiana to testify.[13]

The *Springfield Daily Leader* had withheld publication of the letter George Graham wrote on February 8, shortly after his incarceration for bigamy, in which he vigorously denied any involvement in his first wife's disappearance and cited his sons' statements that they'd left their mother in St. Louis to back up his claim. Now that Charlie's testimony to the coroner's jury on the morning of February 26 had exposed the lie in his father's letter, the *Leader* printed it later the same day. Interviewed about the contents of the letter, Detective Davis vehemently refuted Graham's additional claim that he had personally been involved in writing to Detective Erskine in St. Louis and instigating the search for Sarah Graham. Davis said he knew from his own certain knowledge that Graham had "never had any intercourse whatever, either in person or by letter, with Erskine," and he concluded, "Graham is a villain of more than ordinary shrewdness."[14]

On Friday evening, February 26, a *Springfield Express* newsman called at George Graham's cell to interview him concerning the discovery of the woman's body on the Molloy farm and subsequent developments. As usual, when one of his stories was proved to be a lie, Graham had another one ready to fall back on. Offering what the reporter called "a remarkable statement," Graham now admitted Sarah had come to Springfield with him, as Charlie had testified at the inquest, but he denied that the woman found in the well on the Molloy property was his first wife. He said if the woman's body was so decomposed that parts of the skin and other tissue fell off when the rescue workers retrieved it from the well, as had been reported, it could not possibly be Sarah's body because he had seen Sarah as recently as January 16, when he'd met her in Kansas City and paid her $100 "to keep her mouth shut in regard to the case of bigamy with which I am charged." Graham ventured that Sarah was probably back in Indiana with her kinfolk and that the body taken from the well had been placed there by or through the direction of the Breese family as a frame-up.[15]

In late February, Emma Molloy had been holding a revival at Elmwood, Illinois, about thirty miles west of Peoria. When Sarah Graham's body was found, she was staying at the home of a Methodist minister in Elmwood, where she was prostrated by nervous exhaustion from overwork. Requests to interview her on the evening of February 26 were denied by her physicians, who stressed that her illness had nothing to do with the horrific discovery on her farm because she had not yet been told about it. She must have been informed very soon afterward, though, because she quickly shook off her illness and departed for Springfield the next morning.[16]

When the coroner's inquest resumed on Saturday morning, February 27, a crowd even larger than the day before made such a rush on the courthouse that the courtroom was filled to overflowing ten minutes after the doors opened. The crowd was disappointed to learn that Abbie Breese had missed her connection in St. Louis and would not reach Springfield in time to testify that day.[17]

Instead, Peter Hawkins, who'd worked on the Molloy farm from late July to early October 1885, took the stand. He said that Graham and Frank Molloy got into a big dispute shortly after he came to work on the farm, and Mrs. Molloy threatened to have Graham arrested for threatening her son. Frank went away to school shortly after this.[18]

Despite the tension between Graham and Frank Molloy, Graham spent a lot of time with Mrs. Molloy, Hawkins continued, even more than he spent with Cora. Hawkins once saw Graham and Mrs. Molloy walking with locked arms. He also saw Cora and Graham walking together on the farm several times, including three times near the well not long after Graham brought the boys to live with him. When Hawkins complained of a smell coming from the well, Graham told him a hog had fallen in the well, and once, during a wet spell, Graham forbade Hawkins and a neighbor from drawing water from the well, explaining that it was too nasty.[19]

Hawkins said that Cora went to Brookline early on the evening of September 30 and that she was gone longer than usual, but she arrived home about 9:00 P.M., shortly after Hawkins heard the train whistle as it passed

Roy Graham (Sketch from *The Graham Tragedy and the Molloy-Lee Examination*)

Nichols Junction, Dorchester, and Brookline. Most damning, Hawkins said he heard two shots about two and a half hours later coming from the general direction of the well. An hour or so after that, Graham came home. Graham called to Hawkins, who slept in a granary a short distance east of the house, but the hired man didn't answer. Hawkins then heard Graham talking with Cora at the east side of the house and overheard him say, "We got off at Nichols."[20]

Roy Graham, the next witness, repeated much the same testimony as his older brother concerning his trip from Fort Wayne to Springfield by way of St. Louis the previous fall. He said it was his understanding, when he and Charlie were left at Mrs. Fay's, that his mother and father were going out to the Molloy farm together and that the boys would join them the next day. Like Charlie, Roy identified some of his mother's clothing, and he also mentioned her trunk.[21]

During the noon hour, a *Daily Herald* reporter called at the Greene County Jail to interview Graham. He at first refused to answer questions, but he finally agreed to give a statement revealing everything he knew about his first wife's disappearance.

"I might as well admit the charge of bigamy," he began, adding that he had denied the charge as long as he could but was now willing to acknowledge it. As in his statement to the *Express* reporter the night before, Graham admitted that his sons had told the truth at the inquest about their mother coming with them to Springfield, but he still maintained that the woman whose body was found at the bottom of the well on the Molloy farm was not his first wife. He said that on the train from St. Louis to Springfield, Sarah agreed to leave the boys with him at the Molloy farm while she continued to Washington Territory to visit her brother, and Graham gave her seventy-five dollars to help with the expense.

After leaving the boys with Mrs. Fay, George and Sarah rode a streetcar to downtown Springfield and then went to the Gulf depot, where Sarah bought a ticket for Kansas City and George bought one for Nichols Junction (aka Junction City). Graham concluded his story as follows:

> We went on the midnight train, and I left her at the Junction. I walked from there to the farm about 3½ miles. It was very muddy, and I got home about 3 o'clock in the morning.
>
> Some time after that I got a letter from her, dated at Independence, Mo. She said she had been sick and must have money. I sent her $10, and told her it was all I had. I told her there must be a limit to these demands. On the first of January she wrote me again from Kansas City and demanded more money, threatening to expose me unless I sent her $100. I got the money from three banks here; you remember how I got it—by forging three checks. Well, I met her in Kansas City. I traveled under an *alias,* and registered as H. C. Edwards. I stayed with her one night in Kansas City. She occupied my room. I gave her $100, and have never seen nor heard from her since. I went up to St. Joe and got a job on the Hannibal & St. Joe railroad. I received word from home that the bank matter had been settled, and telling me to come back. The next development was my arrest for bigamy, and here I am.

"This story," noted the reporter, "was told with circumstantial minuteness as to dates, etc., that evidenced careful preparation."[22]

It wouldn't be the last carefully prepared, minutely detailed story told by George Graham.

After Graham completed his statement, the reporter asked him about the missing trunk that Roy had mentioned in testimony that morning, and Graham explained that Sarah had taken it with her to Kansas City. The missing trunk had first been mentioned in testimony by Mrs. Fay the previous day, and Reverend Plumb's wife had told her husband about it when he returned home that evening from an out-of-town trip. Plumb remembered the trunk George Graham had left at the Congregational Church, and he retrieved it and turned it over to authorities. When testimony resumed after the noon recess, the trunk was produced in court, and both Roy and Charlie, who were called back to the stand, identified it as their mother's trunk. Charlie also said that his father had taken a number of his mother's items out of the trunk before storing it.[23]

Reverend Plumb then took the stand and told about George Graham storing the trunk at his church. He also described meeting Mrs. Molloy the previous spring and becoming friends with her and her family. He said he thought Mrs. Molloy considered Graham "a weak man—not a wicked man."[24]

John Brumley, who'd worked on the Molloy farm the previous winter, also testified at the inquest on Saturday. He told of the trip Mrs. Molloy and others took to Brookline when Charlie signed the letter to Abbie Breese. He said that although George was home at this time, he had instructions from Cora to tell anyone who might inquire that George was not there. Brumley said Mrs. Molloy and Graham were on "pleasing" terms. He saw them hugging and kissing on two occasions. He thought Cora was in the same room at the time.[25]

The last witness of the day was Etta Molloy. She said that the Molloy family and the Graham family had all lived together peaceably at Washington, Kansas, and that she never knew of any difficulty between Sarah Graham and either Mrs. Molloy or Cora Lee. She knew of no special kinship between Mrs. Molloy and George Graham. She said she heard nothing about the whereabouts of Sarah Graham except the boys saying their mother was in St. Louis. Etta admitted that George Graham sometimes carried a pistol, but she said she did not hear any gunshots on the night Graham came home from St. Louis. She said she did not think Cora or anyone else had gone to the post office that evening, and, to the best of her recollection, Peter Hawkins was not even on the Molloy place that evening because he had gone to visit a neighbor. Etta said she, Cora, and Emma Lee slept together in the same bed that night and that Cora had been home the whole night.[26]

Now that Sarah Graham's trunk had turned up, a *Herald* representative went back to Graham's cell at the close of the day's testimony and asked him how he explained the lie he'd told earlier in the day about Sarah taking her trunk to Kansas City. Graham at first denied having made such a statement, but he finally admitted he'd taken the trunk to Plumb's church but didn't want it known because there were circumstances connected to the trunk that those who were out to get him could use against him. The *Herald* man concluded that Graham was "weaving a net around himself that is growing stronger and more intricate every hour."[27]

Timothy and Abbie Breese reached Springfield on the evening of February 27, and approximately one thousand people were at the Frisco depot to greet them when they arrived. Detective Davis conducted the couple to the Southern Hotel just off the public square on South Street, and later that night Abbie summoned Justice Savage to the hotel. Acting on the law in Missouri (and many other states) that allowed individual citizens to file criminal complaints, Abbie swore out warrants for the arrest of George Graham, Cora Lee, and Emma Molloy for the murder of Sarah Graham, and Savage, upon a finding of probable cause, issued the arrest orders.[28]

11

Mrs. Molloy under Arrest

THE WARRANT for the arrest of Cora Lee was placed in the hands of deputy sheriff Tom Cox, and he and an assistant promptly trekked out to the Molloy farm to serve it at 1:00 A.M., February 28. Taken into custody, Cora Lee was brought back to Springfield and guarded at Cox's residence, while Charlie and Roy Graham were also escorted to Springfield and turned over to Abbie Breese.[1]

It was still early Sunday morning when Mrs. Molloy arrived in Springfield, and she, too, was promptly arrested. As she stepped from the train at the Frisco depot in North Springfield, she was met by Judge Baker, and they started together toward a waiting carriage until they were halted by a call of "Hold on, Judge!" Sheriff Donnell approached with a warrant in hand, read it to Mrs. Molloy, and took her into custody.[2]

Donnell escorted Mrs. Molloy to the Metropolitan Hotel on College Street, where she was closeted in a room and left in the custody of deputy Clay Roberts. She had sobbed bitterly during the ride to the hotel, and after her arrival, she was sick and vomiting. When a detective (probably Detective Davis) called on Mrs. Molloy at the hotel, she told him, "As God is my judge, I am innocent of any guilt in this matter. I never knew that Mrs. Graham was near my farm or that her remains were in the old well. I only hope that success will attend the officers in their search for the murderer. From what I have learned in the last few days I am inclined to believe that George Graham killed his wife. If it is so, all I can say, God pity him."[3]

Mrs. Molloy was reluctant to speak to the press without her attorneys present, but she did venture that Graham should confess and save the innocent. She said it was "hard for her to be dragged down by him" after she had stood by him for so long. After her attorneys arrived, she consulted with them until mid-afternoon, when deputy Frank Williams took her to his house and placed her under guard there.[4]

Shortly after she was brought to Springfield, Cora wrote a lengthy letter to George, which began, "In the deepest grief I have ever known, I write you this morning to beseech you if you bore me any love or if you ever bore any love to your two children, that if you are guilty of this awful crime, to confess it." Cora said she was under arrest for something she was "as innocent of as a newborn child" and was guarded by deputies to protect her from possible mob action. She again urged George to make a full confession if he was guilty because, although his life might be choked out, there was yet a chance for a "full and free pardon from God."[5]

Cora told George that "Mamma," as she called Mrs. Molloy, was also under arrest, and she implored him not to let the two of them suffer for something they were innocent of after they had faithfully stood by him. Cora added that she was also accused of marrying him when she knew he was not legally separated from Sarah. She said he knew this was not true, and she never would have married him if he had not assured her that everything was all right.[6]

Cora concluded with yet another appeal for George to confess and save her for the sake of his children, whom she loved as though they were her own. "I pray you to plead guilty and I pray you let your soul be saved. . . . I am constantly praying God to make you see and do the right. Bereft of everything but God, I am what is left of Cora."[7]

Later in the day, reporters called at the Cox residence to interview Cora. On the advice of her attorney, she, like Mrs. Molloy, had little to say, but one newsman did pry a tearful admission out of her. Although she loved George and never would have thought he was capable of such a horrible crime, she now believed he was guilty of killing Sarah. She stoutly protested her own innocence and expressed confidence that she would be cleared.[8]

In response to rumors of mob violence, Timothy Breese and prosecutor Patterson went out on Sunday to the Brookline area, where the most persistent rumors were circulating, to urge that the law be allowed to take its course. Breese, who also visited the Molloy farm to examine the well where his sister-in-law's body was found, said he wanted Graham to have a trial so that all the facts in the murder of Sarah Graham could be brought to light.[9]

On Sunday afternoon, Deputy Roberts, who'd had charge of Mrs. Molloy earlier in the day, visited Graham at the county jail and told the prisoner that Mrs. Molloy had expressed a belief that he killed his wife and that, in justice to her and Cora, he should confess. Reacting in anger, Graham asked for pen and paper and scribbled a hasty note to Mrs. Molloy: "I have been getting all day a history of your movements, including the Judge Baker talk this morning. I am prepared to do you *full* justice, also to Cora, but you must not make an exhibition of your feline qualities against me. You can not with impunity take part in any attack on me. Yours as I am treated, Geo. E. Graham." Handing the note to Roberts, he said, "Give that to Mrs. Molloy. I think it will shut her mouth."[10]

The note was promptly delivered to Mrs. Molloy, and after reading it, she said to tell George that she was powerless to help him because all her property was tied up in debt to Judge Baker. Speaking of George, she added, "I stood by him and thought him innocent until the dead body was found in the cave. Now I don't know what to think."[11]

12

George Graham the Murderer

PROMPTED, at least in part, by Cora's entreaties, Graham was busy throughout Sunday evening preparing a confession. The statement was addressed to judge W. F. Geiger and prosecutor John Patterson, and Graham summoned Geiger to the jail at midnight on Monday, March 1, 1886, to hand the statement to him. It appeared later that morning in a *Daily Herald* extra. Graham said he was making the statement to save innocent people and to spare the expense of a drawn-out legal proceeding. He declared "decidedly and emphatically" that Mrs. Emma Molloy and Mrs. Cora E. Graham were "completely innocent, both morally and legally, of any knowledge *of* or complicity *in* the death of Sarah Graham. Neither of them had the most remote idea that any crime had been committed. Both of them have always acted with the utmost honesty and good faith." Graham added that he was making this declaration out of a sense of justice to Mrs. Molloy and Cora, even though he'd been informed that both women had turned against him.[1]

Graham then launched into a history of his involvement with Mrs. Molloy and Cora Lee and of his strained marital relations with Sarah. He said he'd lied to Mrs. Molloy and Cora when he told them he had never married Sarah a second time and that they'd believed him implicitly. "In their minds, therefore, no impediment existed to my marriage with Miss Lee."[2]

He next described his exchange of letters with Sarah during the late summer of 1885 and the couple's supposed negotiations concerning his gaining custody of the boys. When they met in St. Louis, though, Sarah balked at turning the children over, and when they reached Springfield, she said she was going out to Brookline with him.[3]

He tried to talk her out of it, but she insisted and accompanied him to the downtown restaurant. After leaving there, Graham said, he and his estranged wife walked to the depot of the Kansas City, Springfield and Memphis Railroad (usually called the Gulf Railroad) at Main and Mill Streets, where George again tried in vain to talk Sarah into boarding a train for Kansas City. Finally, believing that Sarah would surely not attempt to walk five miles across country on a dark, rainy night, George set off on foot for the Molloy farm, but Sarah came right along after him.[4]

It was about 1:30 A.M. on October 1 as George and Sarah neared the east side of the Molloy farm. They stopped in the road just outside the gate that led onto the property, where they engaged in conversation. George picked up a stick and started whittling with a small knife that had a blade about an inch and a half long, and Sarah had a small limb in her hand. George made one final attempt to get Sarah to turn back and not "tear up everything," but she refused to be assuaged, vowing that she was going to go up to the house and "clear Cora out." George spitefully reminded her of a "liaison" that she had supposedly had during the family's stay in Elgin, Illinois. In anger, Sarah struck at him with the stick, and when he threw up his hand to ward off the blow, the knife cut her on the left side of the throat.[5]

Sarah cried out that George had killed her, and he shoved her roughly away, causing her to fall violently to the ground. When George leaned over her and saw the blood flowing profusely from the wound in her neck, he realized "it was all up" with him, and he rashly decided that the only thing to do now was to finish her off and try to cover up the crime. He pushed the knife into the wound to its full length, and Sarah died almost instantly.[6]

Graham stood for some time already regretting his crime and contemplating how to dispose of Sarah's body. He finally undressed the body to make it harder to identify in case of discovery or else to minimize the transfer of blood to his own clothes. He then lugged the corpse to the abandoned well that sat in a ravine on the Molloy property, about twenty yards northwest of the gate, and dropped it in. Returning to the road, he dismissed his initial plan to burn or otherwise dispose of the clothing and instead took the clothes to the well and dropped them in also.[7]

Graham sat beside the well contemplating his foul deed and considering his next move. As the first streaks of daylight began to appear, he returned to the road, walked up the hill on the east side of the Molloy property, and then turned west and walked past the house. About a hundred feet beyond it, he turned back and approached the house from the west. He went to the west bedroom, where Cora and Etta were asleep, and tapped on the window until they awoke and Cora let him in. Graham stressed that Cora was totally in the dark about the crime and did not know until early January that Sarah came even as far as St. Louis because he'd told her that he traveled to Fort Wayne to get the boys.[8]

Evidence that had thus far been adduced during the ongoing coroner's inquest, of course, suggested a decidedly different theory of the crime than the scenario Graham outlined in his confession. A crucial point of discrepancy involved the murder weapon. The coroner and his expert witnesses were convinced that Sarah Graham had died of a gunshot wound, not from stabbing, even though the alleged fatal bullet was not found. Many people thought Graham was lying to protect Cora Lee. They believed she had been in on Sarah's murder from the beginning, and some, in fact, thought she was likely the one who had pulled the trigger. The skeptics also rejected George's story that he and Sarah had walked from Springfield on the fateful night, arguing instead that Cora had met them in a buggy or wagon, either in Springfield or at a train stop near the Molloy farm. The three had started off together and George and Cora had killed Sarah somewhere along the way before they reached the Molloy farm. They had disposed of the body, not by throwing it in the well but by lowering it with some sort of hammock or harness.[9]

Graham maintained, however, that the supposed bullet wound on Sarah's body must have gotten there by some other cause, since the only wound he inflicted was a stab wound to her neck. He suggested that experts needed to reexamine the clothing that had supposedly been pierced by the bullet and burned by gunpowder. He said he owned only one firearm, a .38-caliber American bulldog pistol, and that he had not even taken it with him to St. Louis.[10]

Graham claimed Peter Hawkins's testimony at the inquest was a falsehood "from beginning to end." He said he did not say to Cora that "we" came in from Nichols Junction, as Hawkins had testified, but instead he told her he walked home from Dorchester. Even if he had made the alleged statement, Hawkins would not have been able to hear it since Graham knocked for entrance on the west side of the house and Hawkins slept in the granary on the east side.[11]

He said he had decided to confess the whole truth primarily for Cora's sake. She was "the *one* thoroughly good, pure woman" who had come into his life, and he thought continuing to fight the charge against him might jeopardize her well-being. As for Mrs. Molloy, he said that she had long been "a very near and dear friend" and that he had "abused and mistreated her confidence shamefully."[12]

Graham wanted it known that fear of mob violence had nothing to do with his confession because, he said, "I don't scare." A Springfield correspondent to a Fort Wayne newspaper agreed, remarking that the prisoner's "imperturbable demeanor under the circumstances" was extraordinary. "Altogether he is a most remarkable phenomenon in the criminal line." The correspondent added that Graham was well read in law, theology, politics, and literature, as well as being a fluent public speaker and a "vigorous writer."[13]

13

Mrs. Molloy behind Bars

GRAHAM'S CONFESSION created a great sensation on the streets of Springfield, and a large crowd gathered on the public square Monday morning. When the coroner's inquest resumed, a standing-room-only crowd packed the courtroom. Prosecutor John Patterson announced that Abbie Breese was in such delicate condition that she was unable to appear in court, and the jury repaired to the Southern Hotel to take her testimony. She was hysterical throughout the interview and broke down completely as she identified her dead sister's garments and other belongings.[1]

When the jury returned to the courtroom, Julia Stokes, who had been employed at the Molloy home to do some sewing in August of the previous year, was called to the stand. She said that she'd once seen Mrs. Molloy and George Graham holding hands as they returned from a walk and that she thought they were "too intimate not to be kin-folks."[2]

Fifteen-year-old Emma Lee was the next witness. She said that she'd never heard of any difficulty between Sarah Graham and either Mrs. Molloy or Cora Lee during the time the Graham and Molloy families had lived together or near each other, and that both Mrs. Molloy and Cora thought well of Sarah. Emma had never noticed any special intimacy between Graham and her foster mother. She said she slept in the same bed with Cora on the night Graham came home from St. Louis and that Cora never got up until Graham reached the house.[3]

Charlie Graham was then recalled, taking the stand for the third time. Contradicting Emma Lee's testimony, he said that his mother occasionally had trouble with Mrs. Molloy and Cora Lee because his father sometimes treated them better than he did her. He said he'd seen his father and Mrs. Molloy sleep in the same bed together and that his father and Cora Lee had occupied the same bed before they were married.[4]

The inquiry concluded at noon Monday, with the verdict to be announced later that day. Sometime the same day, Mrs. Molloy wrote a note to Cora Lee, whom she addressed as "My Darling Child":

> God is our refuge and strength, a very present help in time of trouble. We are having our darkest time. Rest in the Lord and wait patiently for him. Our friends have not all deserted us. I am so sure God will not let us be destroyed, for he knows we are innocent. Be brave. Be careful what you say and who approaches you, for all the adversaries are gathered against us. But God will give you wisdom. I'm praying for you.
>
> Mamma[5]

On Monday afternoon, the coroner's jury met in Patterson's office and reached a verdict that Sarah Graham had come to her death at the hands of George Graham by means of a pistol shot to the right breast and "other unknown means." The jury also concluded that Emma Molloy and Cora Lee were accessories to the crime. The verdict came as a blow to the two women, who had expected to be exonerated by Graham's confession. Instead, they would now face a preliminary hearing to determine whether there was probable cause to hold them until their cases could be heard by a grand jury.[6]

Although George Graham claimed his confession was not prompted by fear of mob violence because he didn't scare, his professed calm wasn't for lack of a reason to be concerned. Hundreds of men milled around in the vicinity of the courthouse on Monday night, and the "entire community was on a tip-toe of expectancy." In southwest Missouri in 1886, the possibility of a lynching was a very real threat. Springfield itself had been the scene of two lynchings of black men, one in 1859 and one in 1871, but extralegal killings overall in Missouri were neither as common nor as racially motivated as in some of the Deep South states like Georgia and Mississippi. Lynching in Missouri, where the Old West and the Old South met, was used to mete out rough justice to white offenders almost as often as it was used as an instrument of racial oppression. In 1866, a group of vigilantes calling themselves the Regulators had lynched two white men in northwest Greene County and then rode into Springfield and took over the town before lynching a third man just south of Springfield. And just eleven months ago, in April 1885, the infamous Bald Knobbers had lynched two white men south of Springfield in neighboring Taney County. But the feared mob action against George Graham never materialized on this night, and the knots of curiosity seekers and would-be vigilantes gradually broke up late in the evening.[7]

Shortly after midnight on Tuesday, March 2, Graham notified the press that he was preparing another statement in which he "would fully show the origin and operation of many things that seem mysterious." He said it would take several days to complete and that it would be backed up with direct evidence. If the assertions contained in his statement should strike anyone, he said, it would simply be because they were in the range of his fire. He said he had tried to do full justice in his statement from twenty-four hours earlier and that had he "been treated in a different manner by a party whose name has been used in connection with this case," he would have gone to his grave without revealing any of "these sensational features." However, he said, "The attempt of Mrs. Molloy by her agents to have a mob close my mouth determined me to speak." He said that he'd already told the whole truth as far as the murder of Sarah Graham was concerned but that "in other circumstances" he was inclined to "Grant's whisky ring motto . . . , 'Let no guilty person escape.'" This was a reference to a scandal during the Grant administration in which whiskey distillers in St. Louis and other cities bribed government officials to avoid paying proper liquor taxes. Grant instructed his treasury secretary, who was investigating the case, to "let no guilty man escape."[8]

At Graham's request, an officer was dispatched to the Molloy farm to retrieve a box of letters that contained, according to Graham, correspondence between him and the two recently arrested women, which he planned to use to back up the "sensational features" of his forthcoming statement. However, the letters were nowhere to be found, and Charlie Graham later said Cora Lee had burned them on the day his mother's body was found, after all the officers had left the Molloy farm.[9]

Early Tuesday morning, March 2, Detective Davis returned from Kansas City, where he'd gone to investigate Graham's claim to have met his first wife at the Union Depot Hotel under the name of H. C. Edwards. Davis found that Graham had indeed registered as Edwards at the hotel on the date Graham had specified; however, he had not met Sarah Graham but rather Emma Molloy and her foster daughter Emma Lee, who were registered in a different room. This was, of course, the occasion when Mrs. Molloy had met Graham to try to convince him to return to Springfield.[10]

Also, on Tuesday morning, March 2, Emma Molloy and Cora Lee appeared with their attorneys before Justice Savage, who committed them to jail to await their preliminary hearing on March 12. Since the Greene County Jail contained no suitable place to house women, the defendants were placed under guard in Springfield.[11]

The same day, March 2, a group of citizens of Brookline Township got together and drafted a series of resolutions in the form of a letter to Judge Geiger and prosecuting attorney Patterson, demanding that a special grand jury be impaneled to dispose of the case against the accused murderers of Sarah Graham in a timely fashion. "We listened to and coincided with the wish expressed by T. L. Breese and seconded by yourselves with the understanding that a speedy trial would be forthcoming," the letter concluded ominously, "but outraged justice will not be passive if there be continued delay." M. B. Loyd and T. F. Spragins signed the letter on behalf of the citizens of Brookline.[12]

Tuesday evening Emma Molloy wrote a long letter to Graham, responding to the rumors he had heard that she had turned against him and was trying to get him lynched. Headed "My Poor Boy," it read as follows:

> This is, perhaps, the very last letter I shall ever be permitted to pen you. I am committed, with Cora, as an accessory to the terrible murder of which you know I am as innocent as a child unborn. In all the flood of misrepresentations and malice that has been so unjustly heaped upon me, I have not yet opened my mouth in my own defense, because the excitement over Sarah's murder is so intense that I have feared mob violence, not only for you, but for Cora and myself. Reason and judgment will yet prevail. We are not to be tried by the newspapers, but by the courts, and I expect to be tried by the higher tribunal—the judgment bar of God. All that you can say will not alter God's verdict when we are all put in His scales, and stand before Him in the judgment. I do not write this to deter you from saying anything that, before God, you think you ought to say for the good of the world, or the cause of Christ, but be care-

ful that in your hot haste to avenge a supposed wrong you do as grave and
terrible a wrong to me as you did to poor Sarah, and then wish through
all eternity you had done full justice by one who has never shown you
a solitary injustice or done you a wrong. You have never had anything
but kindness from me from the first hour that you came to me, a poor,
sorrowful outcast, and in the tenderness of the religion (in which no one
knows better than you that I am sincere and have lived out in all my associations with you), I cared for you as my own, you know how unselfishly.
Now all the newspapers are trying by sensational reports to confirm the
charge that I helped to plan the murder, and am equally guilty with you.
People who seem to care more for a sensation than for an innocent human life are imposing upon you by falsehoods about my utterances, and
about Judge Baker and I "trying to close your mouth by mob violence."
I think this chapter of horrors would be complete were you to be hung
in the same town where I am. I have for this reason refused to speak a
word in my own defense thus far, and Judge Baker only wants to see justice done and the right vindicated, and is emphatically opposed to mob
violence. No one on our side has any desire to persecute you, terribly as
we have suffered in the attempt to be kind to you. You, in your hot haste,
did a wrong to poor Sarah that you can never undo, and have put yourself
in a position where you may tear down those who are innocent, but can
never again build them up. Without the least cause may perhaps impair
the whole work of my life by unguarded and hasty utterances, that can
never be recalled. Is this a just reward for the unselfish devotion of years?
"By our words we shall be justified; by our words we shall be condemned."
Remember in these days you are speaking for eternity. I am simply holding still in God's hands. He will do right by me, and I have commended
you to Him. With every prayer for God's help for myself, I have still to cry,
"God have mercy upon George," and I pray that He will give you true re-
pentance. If in the fury of this gale I go down, I have commended myself
and the dear helpless children under my care to God. I have only tried to
do what God and I could in the last few years, and if God deems my life-
work done, and it can be possible that I shall stand charged with the grave
crime of helping to murder the mother of your innocent babies, and the
law cannot protect me, I shall say, "God's will be done." Don't say anything
that you will not be willing to meet at the bar of God, for this life is but a
small portion of the life eternal. No one pities you more than the one who

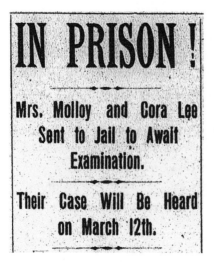

IN PRISON !

Mrs. Molloy and Cora Lee Sent to Jail to Await Examination.

Their Case Will Be Heard on March 12th.

IN MEMORIAM

A Grand Tribute to the Memory of the Lamented Sarah Graham.

Immense Throngs of the Best People of Springfield Attend Her Funeral.

Headline announcing the arrest and incarceration of Emma Molloy and Cora Lee as accomplices to the murder of Sarah Graham (From *Fort Wayne Daily News*, March 2, 1886)

Headline describing the funeral of Sarah Graham (From *Fort Wayne Daily News*, March 3, 1886)

has stood by you all these years, and who has prayed as earnestly for you as any one on earth, and now can only commend you to God's mercy. We shall meet at God's bar. He will do us all full justice.

Yours in the fear of God,

Emma Molloy[13]

On Wednesday morning, March 3, Mrs. Molloy and Cora Lee were moved to the Polk County Jail at Bolivar, thirty miles north of Springfield, to be kept there until the preliminary hearing.[14]

Sarah Graham's funeral service was held on Wednesday afternoon in Springfield at the Christ Episcopal Church on East Walnut Street. The building was filled to overflowing with mourners, mostly women, although Abbie Breese, her husband, and the deceased woman's two sons were the only family members present. The service was "solemn and impressive" and caused "many in the audience to shed tears of sympathy." After the service, the remains were interred in Maple Park Cemetery, one mile south of the public square.[15]

14

Taking Sides:
A Whirlpool of Excitement

SYMPATHY FOR the dead woman and her family elicited during the funeral service naturally intensified sentiment against the accused murderers. Ironically, the most vitriolic feelings were reserved for Emma Molloy, who, of the three defendants, was the one charged only as an accessory after the fact. Charlie's testimony on the final day of the inquest that he had seen his father and Mrs. Molloy sleep in the same bed especially turned many people against Mrs. Molloy, although his similar statement alleging that his father and Cora slept together before they were married seemed not to inflame the public's attitude toward Cora in the same manner. In fact, at least one observer reported a growing sentiment in Cora Lee's favor after her arrest.[1]

The Sarah Graham murder case made headlines across the country, and the widespread publicity revived gossip about George Graham's criminal deeds and Emma Molloy's supposed immorality in many of the places where they had previously lived or Mrs. Molloy had lectured. The *Wabash Courier* resurrected the 1882 Wohlgamuth scandal, and a dispatch from La Porte claimed Graham had been arrested for horse stealing but had escaped prosecution during the brief time he'd sojourned there. A report from Elgin reminded readers that George Graham and Emma Molloy's names had been "scandalously connected" in that place. A Peoria correspondent said that although Mrs. Molloy initially had a great number of supporters in that city, many were now turning against her, and the writer even accused Mrs. Molloy of stealing from the family with whom she stayed while in Peoria. Editor Charles Barrett of the *Washington Post* once again brought up the supposed tryst between Emma and George in a Kansas City hotel and published a satirical edition of the *Morning and Day of Reform,* labeling Mrs. Molloy a "hypocrite and she-devil" whose creed was "Mormonism and free love." The *Atchison Champion* accused Mrs. Molloy of helping to plan Sarah Graham's murder. The *Leavenworth Times* said that if Charlie Graham's testimony was to be believed, "the revivalist and the wife murderer often laid down to pleasant dreams together." Yet Mrs. Molloy would then "arise from her bed of crime . . . and go forth to do battle with the devil," rejoicing that she was "not as other people are, filled with the sins and iniquities of the world." The *Times* opined that the veil of Mrs. Molloy's "hypocrisy and deceit," which only harmed the Christian religion, should be torn asunder.[2]

But the "whirlpool of excitement," as one newspaper called the sensation surrounding the murder case, was greatest in the Springfield area. During the coroner's inquest, so many people had turned up to witness the proceedings that the courthouse could not accommodate them all, even on a standing-room-only basis, and the case remained an all-consuming topic of conversation on the streets of Springfield in the days that followed. Local newspapers, containing stories about the latest developments in the case, could not print enough copies to keep up with demand, and readers swamped the papers with letters to the editor expressing their opinions about the case.[3]

Many of the letters took aim at Mrs. Molloy. A Springfield woman named Mary suggested that Graham was, by Mrs. Molloy's own assertion, completely dependent upon and under the influence of the mesmerizing temperance revivalist, whom Mary compared to Cleopatra and other women throughout history who had tempted men into wrongdoing. Another woman, signing herself "Citizeness," echoed the same idea and suggested that Graham had shown more character since his incarceration than either of the women. A letter writer from Elgin, Illinois, said he, his wife, and others who had known Sarah Graham were particularly outraged by Mrs. Molloy's "attempts to blacken the reputation" of Mrs. Graham, whom the writer described as "a lady in the fullest and truest sense."[4]

A resident of Washington, Kansas, recounted the supposedly scandalous history of Emma Molloy and Cora Lee when they lived with Graham in Washington, and he accused Mrs. Molloy of being "one of the basest and most brazen hypocrites that ever stole the livery of heaven to serve the devil in." Whether she actually participated in planning the murder, the letter writer allowed, was a matter of divided opinion, although he thought she likely had some knowledge of it and, if not, was at least morally responsible. The identity of the letter writer, who signed himself "Veritas," was a matter of conjecture back in Washington. Mrs. Molloy herself thought Veritas was lawyer J. W. Rector, whom she'd opposed when he ran for state legislator while she was in Washington, and many observers in Washington agreed.[5]

Graham resented the suggestion that he was dependent on Mrs. Molloy, and he fired off a letter to the *Springfield Daily Herald* chronicling his life since he'd been released from the Indiana prison in such a light as to show his self-sufficiency. He did, however, admit that he was greatly indebted to Mrs. Molloy for the help she had accorded him.[6]

Against the outpouring of criticism toward Mrs. Molloy, she still had a thin army of supporters in Springfield, and they rose to her defense with letters of their own.

Writing to the *Daily Herald*, an anonymous "Citizen" decried the "slanders of hearsay" that had recently been published in local newspapers. He noted that many people seemed to "devour all sensational stories" connected to Mrs. Molloy "with mouths open for more," and that they were "making more to-do over her seeming downfall" than they were over Graham's heinous crime. Continuing in a vein that would prove prophetic, the writer predicted that the contagion of gossip would likely reach Graham's "cage of steel and cause him to vomit forth a mess fit for an epicure in scandal. How greedily would such a dish be swallowed—just so it was anything connected with this woman—even though it came from a confessed liar, thief, forger and wife-slayer."[7]

Someone who identified himself only as an "Acquaintance" also wrote the *Herald*, refuting what he considered the three main points of attack against Mrs. Molloy: her hurried trip to Brookline to see the letter Charlie signed, her suggestion that Sarah could be found in a St. Louis brothel, and her sanctioning of the bigamous marriage between Graham and Cora Lee. The writer said that Graham had fostered in Mrs. Molloy's mind the idea that he was a victim of a conspiracy and that, therefore, when Charlie came home and announced that O'Neal had gotten him to sign a letter without his reading it, it was only natural for Mrs. Molloy to be concerned, as any parent or guardian would have been under similar circumstances. "Acquaintance" said that Mrs. Molloy's remark about Sarah being in the St. Louis brothel was made in confidential conversation with R. L. McElhaney and several other men at McElhaney's bank as they were discussing Sarah's possible whereabouts, and that when Mrs. Molloy suggested that the St. Louis "houses" should be searched, she was only echoing what George Graham had intimated to her about his wife's possible whereabouts. Finally, the letter writer said that Graham was "no slouch of a criminal" and that he had deceived both Emma and Cora into believing there was no impediment to his marriage with Cora. The writer admitted that Mrs. Molloy had made a terrible mistake, but he said it was one of judgment, not of the heart.[8]

Although Mrs. Molloy's backers were a distinct minority in Springfield, opinion was less united against her in most of the places where she had previously lived and worked, and her friends from across the country wrote her many letters of support, some of which found their way into publication. Emma Dixon, who'd worked with Mrs. Molloy in Indiana temperance campaigns, wrote to her "sister in Christ," assuring her that thousands of people in her home state still supported her. Couching her letter in biblical language, Mrs. Dixon said she was sure that Mrs. Molloy would soon be vindicated and would "stand before the world innocent as thou dost before God and all thy friends." The letter first appeared in the *Daily Herald* and was subsequently picked up by other newspapers.[9]

In response to the negative press about Mrs. Molloy, her attorneys also wrote to the *Herald,* enclosing several letters of recommendation that men who'd been associated with George Graham in business or temperance work had written on his behalf. The lawyers asked that the letters be reprinted to show those who questioned how Mrs. Molloy could possibly have been ignorant of Graham's crimes that she was far from the only one who had been duped by his smooth manner.[10]

Rev. O. S. Munsell of Council Grove was one of those who contacted Mrs. Molloy in the immediate wake of her arrest, wiring a telegram to express support and sympathy for her on behalf of her many friends in Council Grove. On March 5, Mrs. Molloy, from her cell at the Polk County Jail, wrote two letters in reply, one addressed to the "dear people of Council Grove"—and meant for publication in Munsell's newspaper—and the other a private communication addressed to her "Council Grove Friends." In the first letter, Emma said she was passing through "the very blackest shadow" of her "sorrowful life," but that she felt sure God would not let her "errors of judgment" destroy all the work she'd done. In the other letter, which Munsell chose to publish as well, Emma expressed her gratitude for the support of her friends in Council Grove. She said that on the advice of her lawyers, she could not say much about the murder case, but that she felt sentiment was starting to change in her favor. She thought that no one in Springfield really believed she was guilty of being an accessory to murder, but many were still intent on blackening her character so as to destroy her "future usefulness" in the cause of temperance. Declaring her complete innocence of the crime, she said her main mistake was in "having a heart too pitiful for the erring and weak" and "incapable of understanding a nature that *could* so betray" someone who had been a constant benefactor and trusting friend. Noting that many people were asking why she and Cora did not more strongly condemn Graham, Mrs. Molloy said that George's having to answer to God for the black crime on his soul was sufficient and it was not for her and Cora to join "in the general clamor." But this should not be interpreted, she said, "as any palliation in our minds of his terrible sin. He might as well have murdered *our whole family.*"[11]

In a column following the letters, Munsell editorialized in strong support of Mrs. Molloy, whom he characterized as "a wronged, betrayed, and injured woman." Munsell attacked "the editors and journalists who in this terrible affair have deliberately and persistently sought to blacken the character and ruin the life of this woman, but have not one word of condemnation for . . . the bigamist, the adulterer and murderer who has so basely deceived and wronged her." Munsell said the real reason for the attacks on Mrs. Molloy was that she was "an active and successful temperance lecturer on the one hand and an earnest, untiring, devoted evangelist on the other." Thus, "these 'manly' Gentlemen of the press malign, abuse and slander her as they would not dare to slander a man, knowing full well that merited chastisement both personal and legal would be their sure reward. Shame on a set of cowards who vent their malice against temperance on the one hand and Christ and His church on the other by safely and magnanimously slandering two helpless women."[12]

On March 6, a *Springfield Daily Herald* newsman traveled to Bolivar to visit Emma Molloy and Cora Lee. Although the sheriff had been beset with a constant stream of callers, some mere curiosity seekers, requesting to see the celebrated female inmates, the reporter was granted admittance. He found Emma and Cora in an eight-by-eight-foot steel cage inside a larger cell on the second floor. Five other women occupied the main cell, but Emma and Cora had the interior cage to themselves. Mrs. Molloy showed the newsman some of the many letters of support she had received, including the one from Emma Dixon. Reading from it, she became overcome with tears before composing herself and reading portions of other letters. Throughout the interview, Mrs. Molloy "frequently gave way to her feelings," while Cora Lee "maintained a stolid indifference throughout and seemed to feel far less keenly the humiliation of the surroundings."[13]

In his report of his visit to Bolivar, the *Herald* newspaperman, who considered himself among the distinct minority of Springfield citizens who was disposed to await dispassionately the outcome of the legal proceedings in the Sarah Graham murder case before passing judgment on Emma Molloy, marveled at the furor surrounding the noted revivalist's arrest. Although Springfield residents were following the case intently, the *Herald* man felt they probably did not appreciate the fervent interest that Mrs. Molloy's implication in the crime had created in other parts of the country. The widespread sensation was extraordinary, said the newsman, but then Mrs. Molloy was "no ordinary woman," as those who had been "entranced by her eloquence and been brought within range of her personal magnetism" could readily attest.[14]

15

The Preliminary Hearing, Part One

EMMA MOLLOY and Cora Lee were brought back from Bolivar on March 10, 1886, and guarded at a Springfield hotel. On Friday morning, March 12, people flocked into Springfield from the surrounding countryside, some coming from as far away as fifty miles, in anticipation of the women's preliminary examination. Long before the hearing was scheduled to begin, the courtroom was jammed with spectators, many of them women, "eager to catch a glimpse of the prisoners."[1]

The preliminary hearing was the prosecution's opportunity to present evidence establishing probable cause. Defense attorneys could cross-examine witnesses to try to impeach the state's evidence but could not call their own witnesses. The hearing got under way at 9:00 A.M. before two justices, Daniel Savage and Z. M. Rountree. The defendants were represented by judge H. E. Howell and attorneys B. R. Brewer, James M. Camp, George S. Rathbun, and O. H. Travers. The latter two had previously represented George Graham at his preliminary examination on the bigamy charge. Prosecutor John Patterson and judge Walter Hubbard, who'd represented the state in the earlier proceeding, also argued the case against Cora Lee and Emma Molloy.[2]

The morning session was consumed by the arraigning of the defendants and the swearing in of witnesses. When the examination resumed after the noon recess, Thomas J. Delaney appeared as counsel for George Graham and demanded that his client's preliminary hearing be held in conjunction with that of the two women, but the judges ruled

Photo of the old Greene County courthouse, where most of the proceedings in the Sarah Graham murder case took place (Courtesy of the Springfield-Greene County Library)

that it should be held separately. Mrs. Molloy and Cora Lee came into the court escorted by judge James Baker, his wife, and several other ladies. Mrs. Molloy looked as if she'd been crying, while Cora Lee maintained "her dare-devil expression." Both defendants listened attentively as testimony got under way.[3]

The first few witnesses, including Isaac Hise and Henry Fellows, testified concerning the discovery of Sarah Graham's body. Deputy Joseph Dodson took the stand and told of his visit to the Molloy farm with the Breeses in early February. He'd also been back to the Molloy farm yesterday looking for more evidence. Dodson and his team had found additional articles of feminine clothing and sundry other items, including a pair of scissors, in the well. The search party also found scattered in the nearby pasture what appeared to be numerous scraps of knit underwear that had been cut into pieces with scissors.[4]

Court adjourned for the day with Dodson still on the stand. When the hearing resumed on March 13, the courtroom was once again full, although fewer would-be spectators inundated the public square. Among those who took the stand after Dodson completed his testimony was John Potter, who told of his communications with the Breese family in trying to locate Sarah Graham and of the discovery of her body. David Anderson described the two separate occasions on which he was summoned to the Molloy farm by Emma Molloy and Cora Lee. Coroner Z. Van Hoose testified that the coroner's inquest had found what, in his opinion, was a gunshot wound to Sarah Graham's body and that there was no evidence of a severe knife wound about her head or neck. In keeping with the prosecution's theory that Sarah's body had not been thrown into the well by Graham but rather lowered down by him and Cora Lee, Van Hoose testified that the body was generally free of bruises and abrasions. The court then recessed for the weekend.[5]

A couple of days earlier, about the time the preliminary hearing began, George Graham had been transferred to a different cell, and during the hurried move, some of his papers and other personal effects were left behind at his old cell. Among the items was a small pocket Bible that had belonged to Cora Lee, and throughout the book Graham had marked certain passages of scripture that appeared to apply to his current situation. The *Daily Herald* obtained a memorandum of the marked passages and published it on Sunday, March 14, as a "Scriptural Compilation." Graham had marked several verses from the "time to every purpose" section of Ecclesiastes, and several passages he'd marked in Psalms seemed to suggest that he considered himself "a dead man out of mind" and "a broken vessel" who had been slandered and plotted against. But the most provocative passages, which many observers took as references to Emma Molloy, were verses Graham had marked in Proverbs describing the ruin of a man at the hands of an "adulteress" and a "whorish woman."[6]

Dr. Van Hoose completed his testimony when the hearing resumed on Monday, March 15. Although he and the pharmacist, Charles Neiswanger, did not find a bullet in Sarah's body, Van Hoose claimed the search had not been exhaustive. Even though there was no exit wound, he was convinced that the victim had been shot. Neiswanger and Dr. E. A. Roberts followed the coroner to the stand to back up his testimony.[7]

The testimony of Abbie Breese consumed the rest of the day. When Sarah's garments were shown to her, Abbie again broke down as she had during the coroner's inquest, and Mrs. Molloy and Cora Lee wept as well. Abbie also identified several of the items that Graham had taken from Sarah's trunk, including her Bible, and that were subsequently found at the Molloy residence. Over a defense objection, Abbie's testimony that Sarah strongly disliked Emma Molloy and Cora Lee was allowed.[8]

Also found among the papers Graham left behind in his previous cell was a piece of writing that seemed to be a private soliloquy. It was not addressed to anyone in particular and may not have been meant for publication. However, on March 15, editor George Sawyer wired its contents to the *Chicago Inter Ocean*, for whom he acted as a stringer, and it was published the following day in that newspaper. Sawyer might have been concerned about unduly influencing the outcome of Cora Lee and Emma Molloy's preliminary hearing if he published the piece locally, but, if so, he had a quick change of heart because he reprinted it a few days later in his own *Springfield Daily Herald* under the heading "Graham's Meditation." Graham began by comparing his disgrace to the fall of Caesar, and then, mixing his allegory, he likened the actors in his personal tragedy to Dickens characters. Emma Molloy would be his Lady Dedlock from *Bleak House*, Graham said, and Cora was a mixture of Hortense from the same book and Agnes Wickfield from *David Copperfield*. "Poor Sarah" was Dora from *David Copperfield*, and Graham likened himself to Pip in *Great Expectations* because he was "brought up by hand" and it was "a mighty hard hand."[9]

Graham next set forth a bitter denunciation of Emma Molloy and Cora Lee, accusing them of plotting to have him killed. He said their avowed love for him was phony and motivated only by "a desire to gratify their unholy passions." He said that he would have given his life for them, but to know they were seeking it was "carrying self-preservation too far."[10]

Graham concluded,

> Emma, in her letter, points me to "the bar of God." I can have no confidence in a religion which will allow her and Cora to implore me to tell the truth, and then endeavor to have me mobbed for fear I will tell the whole truth. . . . What a difference even now in our conditions. Emma and Cora are simply "under guard," are allowed full and free communications with

everyone, have complete use of the mails, and have a fair chance to make a defense. I am completely isolated, can see or talk with no one, and what defense is made for me is made in spite of every obstacle the prosecution and my co-defendants can throw in the way. I feel sometimes like writing a full, true and complete history of the past four years. Wouldn't it be sensational?[11]

When the hearing resumed on March 16, Charlie Graham took the stand. He said that when the Graham and Molloy families lived in Elgin, his father went to Mrs. Molloy's house almost every night and often stayed late. When prosecutor Patterson asked why he went there, the defense objected, and the two sides got into an exchange over the admissibility of testimony pertaining to Emma Molloy's and Cora Lee's reputations for morality that lasted the rest of the morning. Defense attorney Travers said such testimony had no bearing on whether the defendants had abetted the murder of Sarah Graham, and Howell added that the testimony of one questionable witness should not be allowed to destroy the reputation of an eminent and well-respected woman like Emma Molloy. Patterson and Hubbard countered that they only wanted to establish motive. They intended to show that George Graham had lived in an adulterous relationship with both Emma Molloy and Cora Lee for several years and that the two women therefore had strong reason for wanting Sarah dead. They hoped to prove that Cora Lee was the one who actually fired the fatal shot and that Emma Molloy not only helped conceal the body but was an accessory before the fact to the murder.[12]

After a noon recess, Justice Savage ruled that the disputed testimony would be allowed. Prompted by the prosecution, Charlie Graham set about attacking Mrs. Molloy's moral character. He said he often saw his father and Mrs. Molloy holding hands and that he'd seen her sitting on his father's lap "a good many times." When the two families lived at Elgin, Mrs. Molloy sometimes wrote notes to his father summoning him to her house. When the Grahams lived with the Molloys in Washington, Charlie heard his mother arguing with Cora Lee and Mrs. Molloy over his father. Charlie said he also saw his father in bed with Cora Lee and Mrs. Molloy in Washington. He saw the same behavior after he came to live on the Molloy farm, and his father and Mrs. Molloy would hug and exchange "familiarities" whenever one of them was going away.[13]

Both the prosecution and the defense wanted Frank Molloy to come from La Porte, Indiana, where he was now going to school, to testify at the hearing, and sometime on March 16 Judge Baker and Mrs. Molloy sent for him. Frank, however, declined to make the trip, claiming he knew almost nothing about the occurrences at the Molloy farm because he'd been in Marionville attending school most of the time. The only pertinent knowledge he had, he said, was that Graham had shooed him and a schoolmate away from the well one time when they'd gotten too close to it.[14]

Word of Charlie's statements incriminating Emma Molloy and Cora Lee was almost immediately relayed to George Graham. In response to the rumored plans of defense attorneys to impeach the testimony, Graham dashed off a letter to Cora Lee that same afternoon. As soon as court recessed, Sawyer took possession of the letter, and he published it in the *Daily Herald* the next day:

My Dear Cora:—For however bitter you have become against me, I can never regard you as other than the dearest one in the world to me. I want to caution you in reference to the course I understand your attorneys intend to pursue in the matter of Charlie's testimony to-day. Now, dear, you claim to be a Christian woman; you say you desire nothing so much as to see me converted. Can you expect me to believe in the sincerity or truth of your religion or believe you are in earnest if you countenance the attempt to degrade the boy and make it appear that he testified falsely? Cora, you know Emma Molloy knows and I know that little Charlie swore to the exact truth to-day. A Christian should not lie. The whole history of the past three years is bound to come out. Why not boldly grapple with it and admit what is true? You and I can at least have the excuse that we were all the world to each other. And, mark what I tell you, the tendency now is that you will be bound over and Emma go free. In that case, just as sure as there is a God in heaven, she will desert you just as unscrupulously as she has me. The sneers with which Emma and yourself are said to have received Charlie's evidence to-day were sadly out of place.[15]

Graham continued in the same vein, urging Cora to "brush away the sophistries" and let the whole truth come out. He ended by advising Cora not to believe the "(mis) *Leader* attacks." The *Springfield Leader,* a conservative Democratic daily edited by D. C. Kennedy, was, of the several Springfield newspapers at the time, the most severe in its criticism of George Graham, and it apparently had reported that Graham was denouncing both Cora Lee and Emma Molloy, although issues of the *Leader* from the period in question do not survive.[16]

Although Graham had initially said he would withhold his tell-all statement until after the preliminary hearing, he allowed Sawyer to read it on the evening of March 16. Sawyer wired a description of the statement to out-of-state newspapers, including the *Fort Wayne Daily Gazette*. Without giving specifics, Sawyer said the statement would give dates and places of assignations between Graham and the female defendants and that it would not be "a Sunday school tract." He promised to send the full statement as soon as he was at liberty to do so.[17]

Not long afterward, Graham placed the entire statement into the hands of an unnamed Springfield citizen, giving Sawyer full access to it. As soon as Judge Baker learned that Graham had turned over the document, Baker approached Sawyer and asked him not to publish it, at least not until after the preliminary hearing. Sawyer compromised, agreeing to release only excerpts of the statement as long as the hearing was going on.[18]

When the preliminary examination resumed on March 17, the prosecution continued its questioning of Charlie Graham. Among other evidence, the state elicited a statement from Charlie that he had not seen a pistol in his father's possession at St. Louis or during the trip to Springfield the previous fall.[19]

Upon cross-examination, defense lawyers did indeed attack Charlie's testimony, as rumor had suggested they would. For six hours, Travers grilled the witness about life in the Molloy and Graham households in Elgin and Washington, but "the boy was cool and collected," according to the *Herald,* and Travers was unable to bring out any significant inconsistencies in the story Charlie had told the previous day. In reference to the notes Mrs. Molloy had written to George Graham at Elgin, Charlie said his mother grew very upset upon finding several of them in his father's coat. Charlie said he didn't read the notes himself, but he remembered that one of them was signed, "Yours truly, Mrs. Emma Molloy." Charlie also said that he often went along when his father visited Mrs. Molloy's house in Elgin and that he was sometimes in the same room when Mrs. Molloy sat on his father's lap. Even his mother was present at least a couple of times. Charlie stated that all the members of both families, including his mother, seemed to be on friendly terms when they weren't arguing.[20]

On the afternoon of March 17, Charles F. Barrett, editor of the *Washington Post,* who was in Springfield to attend the trial, went out to the Molloy farm, accompanied by another newsman who called himself "Baxter" in dispatches to out-of-state newspapers. Although Baxter's identity is not certain, he was perhaps editor D. C. Kennedy of the *Leader* or J. G. Newbill of the *Express.* Baxter and Barrett reached the farm about 2:00 P.M. and found curiosity seekers still thronging around the well that had yielded Sarah Graham's body almost three weeks earlier. At the house, they found a new occupant moving in, and he allowed them to search through the belongings that had been left behind. Among the items they discovered was a batch of letters from William Wohlgamuth to Emma Molloy that she had held on to. They also found a diary and expense account that Graham had kept, which showed the movements and whereabouts of the various members of the Molloy household with specific dates and times. The two men turned the letters and diary over to Patterson when they got back to Springfield.[21]

When the hearing resumed on March 18, Charlie's cross-examination continued throughout much of the day, and again the defense attorneys were unable to break his testimony. They did, however, elicit admissions showing that on the occasions when he saw his father in bed with Mrs. Molloy and Cora Lee, all the parties were dressed in at least nightclothes and that the doors to the room were open. He and the other young people in the household came and went into the room freely, although he was sometimes told to stay out. Hoping to establish that the prosecution had determined even before the inquest to try to implicate Mrs. Molloy in the murder, the defense tried to get Charlie to say when he'd first told Patterson and Hubbard about seeing his father in bed with her, but Charlie claimed not to remember.[22]

During the first few days of the preliminary hearing, Graham's attorney, Thomas J. Delaney, had sat with Mrs. Molloy and Cora Lee's lawyers, consulting with them from time to time, and he was accused of selling out his own client. Some observers thought he was actually in the employ of "the two hundred thousand dollar friend of Mrs. Molloy" (that is, Judge Baker). Perhaps sensitive to such charges, Delaney, for the first time, did not appear at the preliminary hearing on March 18.[23]

John Brumley, who'd taken the stand near the end of the day on March 18, continued his testimony the next morning, mainly recounting events surrounding Graham's forgery, including Mrs. Molloy's frantic trip to Brookline to see the letter Charlie had signed. Brumley also testified that Cora Lee had instructed him to cut wood on the side of the road away from the well. In the afternoon, Charlie was recalled briefly, and then Mrs. Fay took the stand and chronicled her dealings with George Graham and his boys the previous fall.[24]

Graham wrote a letter on March 19 to Judge Geiger, complaining that prosecuting attorney Patterson was denying him his constitutional rights, and it was published in the *Herald* the following day. Graham said that he had been held for almost three weeks without a preliminary hearing, that Patterson was not allowing him to correspond with the outside world, and that his efforts to mount any kind of defense were being hampered. He admitted the crime for which he was charged was heinous, but he said there were other men in the Greene County Jail who were also charged with first-degree murder but were not denied basic constitutional rights. Graham asked Judge Geiger to issue an order requiring that he be granted the few rights to which he was legally entitled.[25]

When the hearing resumed on Saturday, March 20, the testimony of Peter Hawkins, who'd briefly taken the stand late Friday afternoon, consumed most of the day. Hawkins mainly echoed what he had said at the inquest, although the defense, on cross-examination, tried hard to find inconsistencies in his testimony and to paint him as a weak-minded, unreliable witness. The final witness of the day was Fannie Scott, who testified that she had visited the Molloy farm the previous August. When she asked how long Graham had been widowed before he married Cora Lee, Mrs. Molloy said three or four years.[26]

On the evening of March 20, Sawyer wired portions of Graham's statement, with its "startling revelations," to the *Chicago Inter Ocean* and a few other newspapers across the country, and the excerpts were scheduled for publication the next day. Written with "the skill of a novelist," the narrative included minute details that, according to Sawyer, left "no room for doubt." An extraordinary case was about to get even more sensational.[27]

16

Graham's Great Story

ALTHOUGH SAWYER released parts of Graham's long-awaited statement to the *Inter Ocean* and other out-of-town newspapers, he continued to delay local publication. So, when the preliminary hearing resumed on Monday morning, March 22, some of the hysteria surrounding the case had briefly died down, and the rush on the courthouse was not as hectic as it had been during previous sessions.[1]

Julia Stokes was the first to take the stand after the weekend break. She repeated her testimony from the inquest that she'd seen Graham and Mrs. Molloy walking hand in hand last summer when she was at the farm. She admitted that they did not attempt to conceal the behavior, but she said they did seem to want to conceal parts of their conversation. The defense suggested there was nothing out of the ordinary in having a private conversation.[2]

Constable William O'Neal reiterated the story he'd told previously about Mrs. Molloy demanding to see the letter that O'Neal had written to Abbie Breese and Charlie had signed. Although he allowed Mrs. Molloy to see the letter, he admitted that when she also asked to see the letters the Breese family had sent him, he showed her part of one letter but didn't show them all because he thought she was concealing Graham.[3]

Isaac Hise was recalled to confirm part of O'Neal's story, and then R. P. Norman, who lived beyond the Molloy farm toward Brookline, testified that the gate leading through the Molloy farm had been locked about October 5 or shortly before. Everett Cannefax testified that he was crossing the Molloy property a day or two before the gate was locked and that when he saw Graham and Cora Lee walking arm in arm near the well, Graham ordered him out of the pasture. When Charles Neiswanger, the pharmacist, was recalled, the defense tried to undercut his credibility as an expert witness, suggesting that bruises and abrasions on Sarah Graham's body from being tossed into the well might not have been discernible after five months.[4]

Although editor Sawyer had balked at printing Graham's statement in the *Herald* while the preliminary hearing continued, he must have known that word of the story he'd sent to Chicago and other cities would quickly leak to Springfield sources, and the *Springfield Republican* forced his hand when it printed what Sawyer called a "garbled recital" of Graham's statement in its Sunday edition. Sawyer decided to publish a more thorough synopsis, the same one he'd wired to the *Inter Ocean*, and it appeared as a *Herald* extra on Tuesday morning, March 23.[5]

The statement, or "Graham's Great Story," as the *Inter Ocean* had dubbed it, was dated March 4, 1886, and it began as follows:

> To the Public: In putting forth the following statement I make no pretensions of being actuated by that high and holy impulse—a desire to improve society or raise the tone of public morals. Having been adjured by Mrs. Emma Molloy and Mrs. Cora E. Graham to "tell the truth and nothing but the truth" in this matter, and these ladies having ventilated their opinions of the writer with a freedom that is charming (?) to contemplate and shown a familiarity with adjectives that would have delighted Lindley Murray, I have concluded, as an addenda to their adjuration, to tell the whole truth.[6]

Graham chastised Cora for having deserted him during his darkest hour in order to save herself. He said, "However guilty I may be, Cora Graham and Emma Molloy are in no position to join in the general chorus against me." He claimed that "if there had been no Emma Molloy or Cora Lee there would be no George Graham in the steel cage of Greene County to-night."[7]

He then detailed the history of his association with Mrs. Molloy and Cora Lee, giving precise circumstances as to dates and places. He said that he and Mrs. Molloy grew very friendly while they lived at Elgin, but that nothing improper occurred between them beyond her sometimes sitting on his lap or giving him a harmless kiss—until November 17, 1882, when he "unbosomed" himself and professed his smoldering love for her. She protested mildly at first, but on December 17 at Mrs. Molloy's home, they engaged in their first act of "criminal intimacy."[8]

Graham said he and Mrs. Molloy continued to have sexual relations at her house on a frequent basis after that. On Christmas afternoon, Graham continued, Mrs. Molloy confided to Cora Lee that she was intimate with Graham, and she also admitted that she'd had a similar affair with Jerome Talbott in 1876, that Ed Molloy knew about it, and that she and her husband had stayed together only for the sake of the children.[9]

On January 1, 1883, Mrs. Molloy left for Richmond, Indiana, for a revival. Graham said Mrs. Molloy had never really confessed her love for him until one day, shortly after she left, he received a letter from her that "fairly electrified" him. Mrs. Molloy had copied "the most passionate poems" from Ella Wheeler's *Poems of Passion* and enclosed them in her letter.[10]

Graham said he had intended to back up his claims with letters Mrs. Molloy had written to him, but many of the letters were among those that Cora Lee had burned. He still had a few letters that he'd brought with him to his cell or that someone had delivered to him there, and he could substantiate some of his claims with those letters.[11]

On January 4, while Mrs. Molloy was in Richmond, Graham first had sex with Cora Lee at the Molloy residence in Elgin. After that, Graham's "lordly attendance," as Sawyer phrased it, "was about equally divided between the two women."[12]

On March 3, Cora learned she was pregnant, and on May 21 she had an abortion, the operation being performed by a doctor in Elgin whom Graham identified only as Dr. D. E. B. Twice more this "perplexing state of affairs" occurred in the Molloy household, and abortions were procured both times. In each instance, Graham identified the location where the abortion was performed and gave the initials of the attending physician.[13]

Graham next gave an extensive listing of dates and places of assignations between himself and the two women in Chicago, Kansas City, and other cities. Among these was a rendezvous on October 8, 1883, in Crestline, Ohio, at the Olive House, where he and Mrs. Molloy registered as B. F. Mallory and wife. At the Union Depot Hotel in Kansas City, Graham, Mrs. Molloy, and Cora Lee stayed in the same room on April 22 or 23, 1884, registering as George Graham, wife, and mother. Again on June 6, 1884, Graham and Mrs. Molloy spent the night together at the Union Depot Hotel in room 6 or 10. At the Breevort House in Chicago, Graham and Cora Lee stayed in room 13 on the night of July 16, 1884. On May 1, 1885, Graham and Mrs. Molloy occupied room 7 together at the Union Depot Hotel in Kansas City. (This, of course, was the alleged tryst that had caused such a stir just prior to Mrs. Molloy's temperance campaign in Springfield.) Graham said he also had a rendezvous with Cora Lee at the Morgan House in Kansas City on May 17, 1885.[14]

"And so it went," Sawyer explained. "The foregoing is an imperfect skeleton of the sensational disclosure."[15]

Graham allowed that some people might find his tale improbable, but he doubted whether either Cora Lee or Emma Molloy would deny its truth on oath. He mentioned several people, including Lina T. Peake of La Porte and Martha Wessner of Washington, who could confirm parts of his story. He concluded,

> It may be true, as Solomon says, that the "words of woman are as sweet as honey and smooth as oil, but her end is bitter as wormwood and sharp as a two-edged sword." I have the consolation, small though it be, of knowing that though my bark goes down amid the turbid waters of illicit love, the shores of time are covered with just such wrecks.
>
> George E. Graham[16]

When the *Herald* containing Graham's statement hit the streets early Tuesday morning, it created a "profound sensation" throughout Springfield, and when it came time for court to convene later that morning, defense attorneys announced that Mrs. Molloy was prostrated and would not be able to appear. The hearing was thus adjourned for the day. Later it was learned that she was vomiting, and a rumor circulated that she had taken poison in a suicide attempt, although her doctor said her only ailment was nervous prostration.[17]

Interviewed in his cell the same day, Graham expressed chagrin that his statement had been released prematurely because he was afraid it might hurt the women's case. He said if they had treated him fairly, he never would have written it. Informed that both Mrs. Molloy and Cora Lee denied the truth of his statement, he said their denials were all it took to convince him that their professed religion was a sham. He expressed renewed anger that they had turned against him when Sarah's body was found instead of holding fast to a belief that he was not guilty, and he reiterated his belief that they had tried to incite a mob against him. Told that Mrs. Molloy thought he was just trying "to break her down," he said if that had really been his motive for issuing his statement, he could just as easily have implicated her in the murder. He also scoffed at the notion that Mrs. Molloy had attempted suicide, saying he knew that she had similar attacks every few weeks.[18]

Although Patterson was hanging on to Graham's diary, which had recently been found at the Molloy farm, he turned the Wohlgamuth letters back over to "Baxter" with the stipulation that they not be published in Springfield or nearby newspapers. Baxter promptly sent the letters to the *Fort Wayne Daily News,* and one of the missives, showing Wohlgamuth's "strange infatuation for the revivalist," was published in that paper on March 23. It was written when Mrs. Molloy was living in Washington and after Wohlgamuth had gotten over his initial anger at being rejected by her a couple of years earlier. He asked Mrs. Molloy's pardon for the harsh things he'd said to her in the aftermath of his infatuation with her. Wohlgamuth told Mrs. Molloy that his wife, Edna, had forgiven him and was also ready to be friends again with her if she would just write to her. Both he and Edna would welcome Mrs. Molloy into their home if she wanted to come for a visit, and he asked her at least to come to their town to speak. "I want to hear you once more," he said. "I am truly, Will."[19]

Editor William Page explained to his readers that there were several letters in the batch he'd received but that some of them were "unfit for publication." One of them in particular referred to "an act on the part of Mrs. Molloy that led her husband to get a divorce." All of them showed that Mrs. Molloy had "entire possession of Wohlgamuth's affections." Page allowed that the letters had no bearing on the Sarah Graham murder case except to show "the kind of influence she wielded over a certain class of ill-balanced minds." It was easy to imagine the sort of power she might have had over "an unprincipled fellow like Graham."[20]

Mrs. Molloy's health was reported to be improving on March 24, but the preliminary examination was again postponed due to her continued illness. A rumor that was perhaps fueled by friends of Mrs. Molloy circulated on this day that Graham had been paid for his extraordinary statement, but Sawyer, citing a letter Graham had previously written to a St. Louis newspaper correspondent refusing an offer of money in exchange for exclusive rights to the statement, denied that Graham had received remuneration.[21]

Graham's spicy statement was reprinted in newspapers across the heartland, especially in those areas where Mrs. Molloy had lived or lectured, and most editors joined in the chorus of condemnation of what was seen as her blatant hypocrisy and moral depravity. A few of Mrs. Molloy's friends in the press remained loyal, charging that she was being attacked only because of her status as a prominent female temperance orator, but even some of the newspapers that had generally supported Mrs. Molloy prior to her becoming embroiled in the Sarah Graham murder case turned against her or else remained silent. For instance, the *Sabetha Herald,* which previously thought Mrs. Molloy had made "an excellent impression" in Sabetha and throughout Kansas, decided that, at the least, she must be insane to have become so deeply involved with a villain like Graham.[22]

A number of editors refused to publish Graham's sensational statement, but even they were not necessarily motivated by goodwill toward Mrs. Molloy. For instance, the editor of the *Goshen Weekly News* made it clear he was no friend of Emma Molloy, and he thought she should suffer for her transgressions. Yet he declined to publish Graham's "indecent" statement, despite requests to do so, because he thought Graham was merely "trying to divert attention from his own worthless carcass and gain sympathy by attempting to show Mrs. Molloy in the worst possible light, and with this end in view, makes matters appear worse than they really are."[23]

17

The Preliminary Hearing,
Part Two

ON THURSDAY, March 25, Mrs. Molloy was still sick, but the preliminary hearing resumed that afternoon when she waived her appearance. Pharmacist Charles Neiswanger and John Potter, who'd recently stepped down from his job as Brookline postmaster, were briefly recalled, but neither brought forth any significant new testimony. A. J. McMurray, another man who'd been present at the Molloy place on the day Sarah's body was found, testified that Cora Lee had been anxious to shield Charlie and Roy from the well during the recovery operation.[1]

Mrs. Molloy finally made her reappearance at the hearing on Friday morning, March 26, but she remained only an hour or so. A. J. Clements, assistant cashier of the First National Bank, was the first witness to take the stand. He recounted Mrs. Molloy's making George Graham's forged checks good, her opinion that Sarah Graham might be found in a St. Louis brothel, and Frank Molloy's coming to the bank and saying there was "something worse behind the whole matter." According to Clements, Mrs. Molloy told him that she first knew George Graham when he was just a baby in Pittsburgh, Pennsylvania.[2]

Abbie Breese was briefly recalled but offered no substantial new evidence. Cashier R. L. McElhaney took the stand and essentially confirmed Clements's earlier testimony.[3]

Maurice, the Springfield confectioner, testified that on or about the night of last September 30, a man and two women, one of them veiled, came to his store about 8:00 or 9:00 P.M. The man seated one of the women, while the veiled woman went back outside. The man promptly went outside, too, and then returned and sat down with the first woman. Pretty soon, a veiled woman whom Maurice took to be same woman who'd come in earlier entered the store, looked around a bit, and then turned and left. The prosecution wanted to prove that the veiled woman was Cora Lee and that she'd come to Springfield in the spring wagon on the night in question instead of going to Brookline as Peter Hawkins had thought. However, Maurice couldn't be positive the first veiled woman was the same person as the second. He also couldn't identify the woman seated with the man, although he vaguely remembered that the clothes she wore were similar to those found on Sarah Graham's body. He also couldn't tell whether the first woman and the veiled woman even knew each other, but he was pretty sure the man was George Graham. When the couple got ready to leave, the man said to the woman that they had four or five miles to go.[4]

Although Mrs. Molloy wasn't well enough to attend the whole session on March 26, she did write a letter that day to a friend in Indiana. Later published in the *Indianapolis Journal* and reprinted in other newspapers, it represented her first written statement since Graham had leveled his charges of immorality against her. Without specifically refuting the charges, she opened with a reference to the "flood of slander and misrepresentation" to which she had been subjected, and she expressed her appreciation for the continued support of her many friends in Indiana. She assured her friend that she knew nothing about Sarah Graham's murder until she read about it in the papers when she was on the way back to Springfield from Peoria and that she was arrested simply for having befriended someone whom she'd considered "the football of fortune."[5]

Addressing the charges of immorality more directly, Mrs. Molloy said Graham had now repaid her kindness by "striving to excuse his crime by the most terrible and baseless slanders, even despoiling the grave to drag forth the dead to heap his abuse upon them." (This was a reference to Jerome Talbott.)[6]

Mrs. Molloy concluded that she had been tried "by a judicial mob" who was more anxious to blacken her character than to find Sarah's killer, but that much of the "filth and slum" that had been presented at the preliminary hearing would not be permitted in a circuit court. Therefore, she still hoped to clear her name and "not die under a cloud."[7]

Emma Molloy as she appeared
at the time of her and Cora's
legal troubles (Sketch from
*The Graham Tragedy and the
Molloy-Lee Examination*)

At the hearing on Saturday, March 27, editor J. G. Newbill of the
Springfield Express related conversations he'd had with Mrs. Molloy and
George Graham since Mrs. Molloy's arrest, but he offered no new revelations. The prosecution next placed into evidence Mrs. Molloy's "My
Poor Boy" letter to George Graham, her long letter from South Bend to
H. E. Howell, and several letters Charlie Graham had written or copied for his father and sent to his folks in Indiana. The state then rested
its case. Defense attorney O. H. Travers immediately filed a motion to
dismiss the charges against his clients, but after some legal sparring, he
withdrew the motion and was granted a request for adjournment until
Monday so the defense could prepare its case.[8]

A large crowd jammed the courtroom when the examination resumed
on Monday morning, March 29. When the court called on the defense
to present its case, Travers announced that he and his team had decided
not to introduce any evidence because his clients had nothing to defend.

He then resurrected his motion to dismiss the charges, but it was quickly overruled. Travers said, "Very well"; the defense was ready to argue.[9]

Judge Hubbard, after a few minutes' recess to prepare his books and notes, began the prosecution's closing argument. Calling the Sarah Graham murder case "the most remarkable known to the present generation," he said there was sufficient evidence to charge Cora Lee as an actual participant in the crime, and he asked that she be held for first-degree murder. He admitted that the state lacked evidence to charge Mrs. Molloy as an accessory before the fact, but he said she had helped conceal the crime and should be held under a steep bond as an accessory after the fact.[10]

Hubbard attacked several points in Graham's confession, claiming he was only trying to shield Cora. Hubbard thought the idea of a woman walking five miles across country on a rainy, dreary night was absurd, and he cited the fact that Sarah's shoes had only a little mud on them when they were found in the well as proof. Graham's claim that Sarah had been killed with a knife was also meant to shield Cora, Hubbard argued. He also discounted other points in the confession, such as Graham's claim that he'd stabbed Sarah about the neck, because the neckline and upper part of Sarah's clothes showed no signs of blood. Her head wound and the blood on her hood, Hubbard said, were more consistent with having been struck with a heavy club. The state also did not believe Graham's story that the body had been thrown into the well, and Hubbard cited Cannefax's testimony of having seen Cora with Graham near the well just a few days after the murder as evidence that she was aware of the crime. Why else would Graham have let her anywhere near the well?[11]

Hubbard also cited several other circumstances against Cora. Charlie had told Cora in January that his mother came to Springfield, and yet Cora concealed this knowledge rather than turn it over to authorities. Cora knowingly entered into a bigamous marriage with Graham, and thus she had a strong motive to have Sarah out of the way. The presence of Sarah's Bible and other items in the Molloy home were proof of Cora's guilty knowledge.[12]

Turning his attention to Mrs. Molloy, Hubbard gave her credit for her renowned Christian work, but the state, he said, was no respecter of position or rank. Among other evidence, Hubbard cited Mrs. Molloy's improper relations with Graham, her settlement of his forgeries, her concealing him in her home, her false stories about Sarah's where-abouts, and her intense excitement on the day she came to Brookline to see Charlie's letter as circumstances against her in the present case.[13]

Attorney James Camp answered for the defense. He said his clients were innocent not only of the criminal charges against them but also of improper relations with Graham. Both women were unfortunate victims of misplaced confidence. He cautioned the state and the community at large against overstepping the bounds of justice in their "hot haste" to avenge a wrong and thereby convicting innocent parties. Camp said Cora had burned the letters on the day Sarah's body was found because Constable O'Neal had ransacked the house earlier in the day in his determination to find anything he might use against the family. Prosecutor Patterson's strong denial of this allegation brought a burst of applause from the courtroom audience.[14]

On Tuesday, March 30, the defense brought out its "big guns," Howell and Travers. Howell began the morning session, arguing that all he was asking for his clients was the same presumption of innocence to which anyone else would be entitled. But that was not happening in this case, he said. Citing Mrs. Molloy's "My Poor Boy" letter to Graham, Howell said that if a woman less well known than Mrs. Molloy had been engaged in prison work and had routinely referred to the ex-cons whom she took under her wing as her "boys," no one would have thought anything about such a letter, yet Mrs. Molloy's letter had been repeatedly cited in this case as proof of a sinister or immoral association with George Graham.[15]

Howell implied that Mrs. Molloy was being targeted precisely because she was well known. No woman could go through the temperance crusades, the political campaigns, and the work of prison reform that Mrs. Molloy had been through and "come out unscathed and free from slander." And, unfortunately, Howell added, an attack upon a man's virtue in this country "does not break him down," but a similar attack upon a woman "blasts her forever."[16]

"Mrs. Molloy is as incapable of hatred," Howell continued, "as she was of murdering poor Sarah Graham. . . . If Emma Molloy is present when George Graham yields up the ghost, she will be by his side offering up prayers for the salvation of his soul. You can call that hypocrisy if you want to."[17]

Howell's theory of the crime was similar to what Graham had confessed to, except he allowed that Graham had probably shot Sarah as well
as stabbed her. The murderer then stripped to his underclothes to avoid
getting blood on his outer garments, carried Sarah's body to the well, and
dumped it in headfirst, which accounted for the flesh later falling away
from the face. He took Sarah's scissors from her satchel and then tossed
the satchel and Sarah's other belongings into the well. Using the scissors,
he cut up his underwear and scattered the pieces in the pasture before
tossing the scissors in, which accounted for why they were not found in
the satchel. Graham then put his outer clothes back on and went to the
house.[18]

Howell attacked Charlie Graham's credibility, pointing out that he
had admitted to lying at his father's preliminary hearing for bigamy. Why
would he not lie at this preliminary hearing as well? But even if part of
what Charlie described was true, Mrs. Molloy's conduct was "open and
above board," not evidence of a clandestine love affair. And even if everything Charlie said was true, it made no difference because Mrs. Molloy
was not on trial for immorality. The courtroom audience, though, was
little swayed by Howell's arguments. During the midst of his criticism of
Charlie Graham, Patterson rose to the boy's defense, eliciting applause
from the spectators.[19]

As proof of Mrs. Molloy's innocence of concealing Sarah's murder,
Howell pointed to the fact that Mrs. Molloy had undertaken to bring
Graham back to Springfield after he'd forged the checks and fled. Except for Mrs. Molloy's efforts, George Graham would now be long gone
instead of locked in the Greene County Jail.[20]

Taking over in the afternoon, Travers used most of his speech also
attacking Charlie Graham. He implied that Charlie was a liar, just like
his father. "As he swore to a lie at the instance of his father," Travers said,
"so would he swear to a lie at the instance of those who are whooping
up this prosecution." And Travers wanted to know why Charlie had not
also been arrested as an accessory to his mother's murder, since Charlie
had concealed more evidence than anyone.[21]

But even if Charlie told the truth, his testimony was not nearly as damaging as it had been interpreted. There was no way, Travers said, that Mrs.
Molloy, Cora Lee, and George Graham would have been in bed together

for sexual purposes when the doors were left open and people were freely coming and going throughout the house. Not even in "the vilest haunts of abandoned humanity" would one witness such conduct.[22]

As for Cora Lee, Travers said, she was guilty only of loving Graham "too well." When Charlie told her his mother came to Springfield and Cora exclaimed, "For God's sake, don't tell it," hers was a natural reaction of a loving wife who feared her husband might be implicated in a serious crime. Afterward, though, she had instructed Charlie to tell the truth at the inquest.[23]

Travers challenged the prosecution to put Etta Molloy and Emma Lee on the stand, but he knew Patterson and Hubbard would not do so because Etta and Emma would testify that Cora Lee was home all night until Graham arrived in the wee hours of October 1. Travers concluded, "Graham, villain as he is, murderer as he will be convicted—he told the truth when he said these women were innocent of all knowledge or participation in this crime. But the state has magnified every little spring branch in this case into an unfordable stream—every insignificant molehill is elevated to the grandeur of a mountain."[24]

In his closing speech later the same evening, prosecuting attorney Patterson assailed the defense for its unmanly attack on Charlie Graham. Patterson admitted he did not know just how George and Sarah Graham reached the Molloy farm on the fateful night, but he would assert that they did not walk the whole distance as Graham said in his confession. Patterson believed George Graham had tarried in St. Louis for two days instead of just one because he had made arrangements to meet someone, probably Cora, in Springfield on the evening of September 30. The prosecutor also didn't know exactly where the murder was committed, but he was prepared to suggest that "Cora Lee, the coolest member of this trio, had the nerve to fire the fatal shot." He thought the murder had probably been committed at the back part of the pasture, not at the gate or the well, and later the body was carried to the well and "lowered or thrown in." If George Graham was going to kill his wife by himself, he would have done it elsewhere instead of killing her at the farm and concealing her in the well, where there was a good chance it would be discovered and he would be tied to the crime. In answer to the defense's charge that Cora Lee and Emma Molloy had been slandered by the press, Patterson thought the newspapers had done them "no injustice," and he asked that Cora be bound over without bond on a charge of first-degree murder and that Emma be held under heavy bond to await the action of a grand jury.[25]

The next morning, March 31, Mrs. Molloy and Cora Lee were brought into the courtroom, "looking haggard, careworn and anxious." When the court came to order, Justices Savage and Rountree announced their decision. They found probable cause to believe that Cora Lee was an accessory before the fact and should be held without bail and that Emma Molloy was an accessory after the fact and should be held under a $5,000 bond. Many of the spectators burst into applause, but the justices immediately called for order. The defendants received the verdict with "assumed indifference" and were led out of the courtroom and back to the home of deputy Frank Williams, where they had been staying under guard. Later the same day, the defense attorneys applied to Judge Geiger for a writ of habeas corpus, but the judge took no immediate action on the petition.[26]

George Graham expressed disappointment when the news of the preliminary examination's outcome was relayed to him on the afternoon of March 31. He said he'd hoped the women would be cleared, as he thought it would be better for his own case when he went to trial not to have "the impediment of accessories." However, he was outraged by the course Mrs. Molloy's attorneys pursued in painting him as a fiend during their closing speeches.[27]

The same day, Graham got Sheriff Donnell to serve a restraining order on Abbie and Timothy Breese, preventing them from taking Charlie and Roy back to Indiana. However, he later withdrew the order.[28]

The citizens of Springfield and observers elsewhere across the land greeted the news that Mrs. Molloy would be held in connection to Sarah Graham's murder with "general satisfaction," although some felt she should have been charged, like Cora, as an accessory before the fact. Opponents of prohibition, in particular, received the news of Mrs. Molloy's trouble almost with jubilation and tried to use it to score political points. The Democratic Party of Leavenworth, for instance, adopted a resolution that Emma Molloy was a "typical and symbolic" representative of the "prohibitory-Republican standpoint."[29]

As soon as the preliminary hearing was completed, renewed rumors of mob action toward George Graham began to circulate. According to editor George Sawyer, it was common knowledge that an organized band of men in the general area of the Molloy farm had been having weekly meetings "since the inauguration of this sensation" to discuss taking the law into their own hands, but they had been postponing any action at least until the hearing was finished. The question now uppermost in everyone's mind was, "What next?"[30]

18

Mrs. Molloy's Champion
Rises to Her Defense

ON APRIL 3, several prominent citizens of Springfield, including Judge
Baker and Judge Howell, put up Mrs. Molloy's $5,000 bail money, and she
was released, pending her appearance at the May term of Greene County
Circuit Court. Cora Lee, meanwhile, was transported back to the Polk
County Jail at Bolivar. Her petition before Judge Geiger for a writ of ha-
beas corpus had still not been heard, since the judge was out of town.[1]

Within days after the preliminary hearing for Cora Lee and Emma
Molloy came to a close, the Ozarks Publishing Company issued a 125-
page pamphlet about the Sarah Graham murder case up to that point.
Titled *The Graham Tragedy and the Molloy-Lee Examination*, it was
distributed throughout the Ozarks and beyond for twenty-five cents
per copy. It was mainly a reprinting of articles about the case that had
previously appeared in the *Herald.* The publishers chose not to print
George Graham's sensational "statement," explaining that although they
had the original complete manuscript in their possession, they thought
it was too prurient and too prejudicial against the female defendants for
publication while their case was still being adjudicated. If the allegations
of immorality against Cora Lee and Emma Molloy should subsequently
prove true, they would publish the entire statement then. (Evidently the
full statement was never published and has been lost to time.)[2]

On April 10, Judge Baker wrote a lengthy letter in defense of Cora
Lee and Mrs. Molloy. It was published in the *Springfield Herald* the next
day and subsequently reprinted by other newspapers. Baker reminded

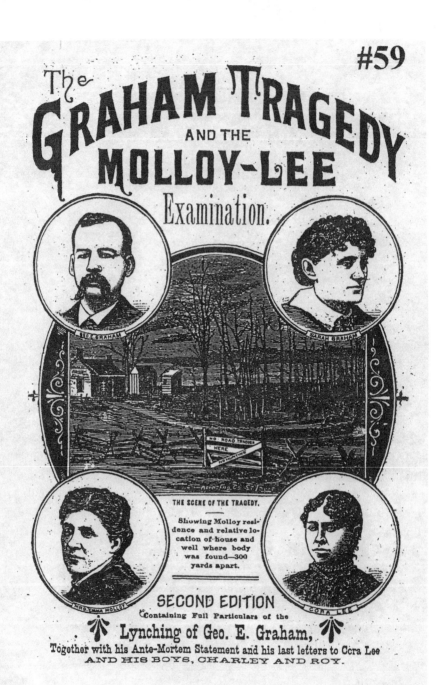

Cover of *The Graham Tragedy and the Molloy-Lee Examination,* a sensationalist tract originally published in early April 1886

readers that Mrs. Molloy had first learned about the discovery of Sarah Graham's body while she was away from Springfield and that she had arrived back in town when "public excitement was at its highest." For his act of humanity in meeting Mrs. Molloy at the train station and for his continued friendship with her during the preliminary hearing, Baker had been censured by many but commended by others. He said it was owed to both his critics and his supporters to state why he believed Cora and Emma were innocent not only of involvement in Sarah's murder but also of the charges of immorality leveled against them.[3]

Baker explained that Graham was "adroit in the art of deception" and that both Miss Lee and Mrs. Molloy believed his story that he and Sarah had divorced and never remarried. The two women were not aware of a second marriage and, therefore, were not willing parties to the bigamy. The only logical theory of the murder, the judge said, was that it was committed to conceal the bigamy from Cora Lee and Mrs. Molloy.[4]

To substantiate his point, Baker cited several letters exchanged in confidence among Graham, Mrs. Molloy, and Cora Lee during the weeks leading up to the discovery of Sarah's body. These were among letters Mrs. Molloy had turned over to Judge Howell upon her arrival in Springfield from Peoria. In one letter, written on February 10, 1886, just a couple of weeks before Sarah's body was found, Graham was still proclaiming to Mrs. Molloy his innocence of bigamy. Baker also cited Cora's letters to Mrs. Molloy in early to mid-February showing Cora's growing concern that George might have deceived her and that there might indeed have been a second marriage. "These letters written in all the freedom and confidence of affectionate members of the same family," Baker said, "conclusively prove that these ladies were ignorant of both the second marriage with Sarah and of the murder."[5]

Baker said that Graham had not only concealed from Cora Lee and Mrs. Molloy the fact of his remarriage to Sarah, but he had even lied to them about his trip to St. Louis, telling them instead that he had gone all the way to Fort Wayne. Mrs. Molloy did not learn otherwise, Baker said, until January 1886, over three months after the murder, and he cited correspondence between himself and Graham and between Mrs. Molloy and Graham to back up his statement.[6]

Baker then turned his attention to the preliminary hearing, first attacking the credibility of Peter Hawkins. Hawkins had testified to unloading a trunk, supposed to have belonged to Sarah Graham, at the Molloy farm on the day that Graham went to Springfield and brought the boys back from Fay's Boarding House. All the other testimony in the case showed conclusively that Sarah's only trunk was the one Graham left at the boardinghouse and later took to Plumb's church. Baker said Hawkins's testimony that Cora Lee had gone to Brookline on the night of the murder was equally unworthy of credit, since Etta Molloy and Emma Lee had both said at the inquest that Cora stayed home all evening. But even if Cora did leave that evening, Hawkins himself had testified that she was back home well before he heard the fatal shots.[7]

Etta and Emma could also have refuted the supposedly damaging testimony about Cora Lee and Mrs. Molloy's guilty knowledge of the presence of Sarah's Bible and other items in the Molloy home. George Graham had brought them home, explaining that when he and Sarah parted, she had told him to take them because she didn't want anything that he had previously given to her as a gift.[8]

Cora Lee having been seen near the well with Graham in the days following the murder was purely coincidence, Baker suggested. All the members of the household strolled across the property on a regular basis, occasionally coming near the well.[9]

Mrs. Molloy's actions surrounding the letter Constable O'Neal had written for Charlie were used to suggest her complicity in covering up the murder, but they actually showed just the opposite, Judge Baker argued. In the O'Neal letter, Charlie told his aunt that his mother had been left in St. Louis, while previous letters that Charlie had written at his father's direction because Sarah had a "sore hand" informed Abbie that her sister was staying in Springfield. If Mrs. Molloy had been aware of these previous letters, she would not have said "all right" and handed the O'Neal letter back to be mailed, knowing that it contradicted what Abbie had previously been told.[10]

Baker said that Charlie's testimony impeaching the character of Mrs. Molloy and Cora Lee should never have been allowed, and he accused Justice Savage and Justice Rountree of letting themselves be influenced by the "public excitement and prejudice" surrounding the case. At any rate, much of Charlie's testimony was absurd, according to the judge, such as his claim to have seen his father and the two women in bed together at Washington one morning after his mother and Etta Molloy had gone downstairs to prepare breakfast. Not only was Etta or Sarah liable to come back upstairs at any moment, but the doors were left open and any other household member could have walked in. Indeed, Charlie had even testified that the room where the threesome was lying in bed together was the same room where everyone in the household normally dressed. "The basest and most degraded of women would not be guilty of such conduct in the presence of each other," Baker asserted, "much less in the presence of these children, and with the wife of the man and another young woman at any moment liable to enter."[11]

"As to the charges made by Graham of criminal intimacy with these women," Baker said, "I have only to say I do not believe them." He reiterated that Graham had served several terms in the penitentiary and had since committed bigamy, murder, and three forgeries. He'd even suborned his own son to commit perjury.[12]

Baker said that he still valued the character and friendship of Mrs. Molloy and that many of those who were bitterly denouncing her were "actuated by their hatred of her Christian and temperance work." Her alleged want of virtue was merely a pretext.[13]

The judge concluded by quoting from letters between Mrs. Molloy and George Graham during the weeks leading up to the discovery of Sarah's body. The language evinced no special intimacy, and Graham emphatically repudiated the rumors that had begun to circulate connecting the two of them in an illicit relationship.[14]

Not everyone was convinced by Baker's defense of Mrs. Molloy, of course. For example, editor James Hagaman of the *Concordia Blade* was not unexpectedly one of the skeptics. Although allowing that Baker had made a few good points, Hagaman thought that the judge's argument overall was "lame and impotent." However, Baker's letter did seem temporarily to curb the tide of slanderous gossip about Mrs. Molloy, at least in Springfield.[15]

Near the time Baker's letter appeared, Mrs. Molloy also wrote a letter in her own defense to an unknown party in her hometown of South Bend. More reproachful in tone toward George Graham than any previous statement she'd given, it was published in the *South Bend Tribune* and was reprinted in the April 21 *Springfield Leader.* Mrs. Molloy said she would "not condemn an Indiana dog" on the word of those who were attempting to swear her life away.[16]

She said she'd been told that Graham had received "a large bonus" for his sensational statement and that she had nothing but "contemptuous pity" for him. She continued,

> The man who in cold blood could murder his first wife, of course would have no conscience in stabbing to death the two women who, in their faithfulness to him have nursed a viper unconsciously. . . . Those who wish to receive the testimony of a man who boldly proclaims that he has no desire to better the world, against a woman who has given her whole life as an oblation on the altar to save others possesses a credulity that it would be useless to try by any testimony to overthrow.[17]

She, like Baker, pointed out that the prosecution had deliberately chosen not to put her daughter, Etta, and her foster daughter Emma on the stand, knowing their testimony would have been detrimental to the state's case. She asked her friends in South Bend not to lose faith in her but to await further developments, assuring them that she was preparing a statement that would give a true history of "this remarkable chapter" in her "somewhat eventful life."[18]

Mrs. Molloy concluded,

> Those who think it is remarkable that I should be so deceived in Graham should remember that he has been leading the entire press of this country in a will o wisp chase for weeks past, and they know less about this case than when they begun. The attention of the whole country has been skillfully diverted from his crime to attend to my wholesale butchery, and all because I was so unfortunate as to have been in the past engaged in Christian and temperance work, making me the target for the shaft of soulless reporters and the jibes of newspaper men, who rejoice more over the downfall and destruction of one Christian worker than over the punishment of ninety and nine self confessed criminals like Graham.
>
> Emma Molloy[19]

Graham, of course, was loath to let any perceived attack go unanswered. He replied to Mrs. Molloy's letter as soon as it appeared in the afternoon *Leader,* and unwilling to postpone publication of his response even until the next edition of that paper came out, he sent his missive to the *Herald,* which published it the next morning. Graham said Mrs. Molloy's letter contained a "glowing (I might say *red hot*) eulogy" of her many real or imagined virtues, but he cited its self-sacrificing tone as an example of her hypocrisy. Her supposed magnanimous deeds, he said, were done only for her own glory. He added that if she had ever "evidenced a desire to be on friendly terms with Graham," as she claimed, such fact had not come to his knowledge. He signed his letter, "Yours disgustedly, Geo. E. Graham."[20]

About the time Graham's letter was published in the *Herald,* the *Leader* received the same or a similar communication from him, but the *Leader,* now edited by S. K. Strother, declined to publish it "for the good reason that it objects to giving countenance to such a cowardly murderer. Nothing that George E. Graham or anyone implicated in his case may write will be published by the *Leader,* unless it may be classed as news." Alluding to the *Herald,* Strother added, "We hope our esteemed morning contemporary will take notice of this."[21]

Perhaps there was a taste of sour grapes in Strother's determination to abstain from muckraking because the *Herald* had generally been scooping the *Leader* in its coverage of the Graham murder case. In fact, Mrs. Molloy and her friends threatened to sue the *Herald* and a few out-of-town newspapers for their scandalous stories about her, but the *Herald* was cowed neither by the *Leader*'s challenge to print only hard news nor by the prospect of a lawsuit. Issuing a warning of its own, the *Herald* suggested that there was a lot that was known about Mrs. Molloy and the other "dramatis personae in this tolerably celebrated case" that had not yet been published.[22]

With Judge Geiger's health failing, Cora Lee's attorneys applied to circuit judge W. I. Wallace of Lebanon, Missouri, for a writ of habeas corpus. The hearing began at Bolivar on April 22. Judge Baker and Judge Howell for the defense argued that Cora was being held not based on the evidence but because of public opinion. Their client was ill with typhoid fever, and they revealed that she was also pregnant. Common decency therefore dictated that she be allowed bail. The prosecution countered by reiterating some of the evidence, including the fact that Cora and George were seen together near the well shortly after the body was dumped there. No "sane man," according to Patterson, would take a person where he had disposed of a body unless that person was in on the crime. Branching into Mrs. Molloy's case, the prosecutor cited her continued concern for Graham after Sarah's body was discovered, including her "My Poor Boy" letter, as evidence of her complicity in the crime. On April 23, Judge Wallace ruled that Cora Lee should be admitted to bail on $5,000 bond, although she remained in jail at Bolivar until her friends could come up with the money.[23]

The April 23 issue of the *Springfield Daily Herald* published a letter signed "Pro Bono Publico," calling on Mrs. Molloy to put forth a written denial of the salacious charges Graham had leveled against her. Graham himself later claimed authorship of the letter, but if, indeed, it was an example of his volunteer work, he wasn't the only one urging Mrs. Molloy to issue a formal rebuttal. Her friends were advising her to make a public statement without further delay, and she was, in fact, preparing a detailed denial. However, she was taking time to assemble affidavits and other evidence to support her statement. For many of her critics, the denial would come too late.[24]

19

Lynched by "The Three Hundred"

SHORTLY AFTER 1:00 A.M. on Tuesday, April 27, 1886, a large body of horsemen rode into downtown Springfield from the west along College Street and surrounded the courthouse at the corner of College and the public square. Almost all the men were armed, and nearly all had handkerchiefs tied across their faces to disguise their identities. Numbering about 150, they were grouped into separate "divisions" and appeared to be well organized. Eight or ten of them dismounted at the jail, located on College Street at the rear of the courthouse, and they rapped on the door.[1]

When night watchman R. W. Douglas opened the door, the small mob presented their weapons and marched Douglas into the sheriff's quarters, where two of them grabbed Sheriff Donnell by the arms just as he was rousing from bed and putting on his pants. Donnell offered no resistance because, according to his later statement, he'd never seen so many shotguns and revolvers in his life and "they handled them in a way that was too careless for comfort."[2]

One of the men went to a drawer where Donnell usually kept the keys to the jail, as though he knew right where they should be, but the drawer was locked. When Donnell declined to hand over the key to the drawer, the men started rummaging through his pockets and saying they didn't want to hurt him but planned to have Graham one way or another. Fearing for her husband's safety, Mrs. Donnell let the vigilantes have the key to the drawer, from which they quickly retrieved the jail keys.[3]

Two men guarded Donnell while the rest, taking Douglas with them, unlocked the door leading to the cells. Douglas refused to say which cell was

Today, Weaver Elementary School marks the approximate spot where George Graham was lynched. (Photo by the author)

Graham's, but one of the men looked into Graham's cell and recognized him. Within five minutes, the men had the door to Graham's cell open.[4]

The prisoner thought the men were bluffing at first, but realizing they weren't as they entered his cell, he became defiant, calling them "God damn Brookline murderers." One of the men put a shotgun to Graham's head and ordered him to shut up and put on his clothes. Graham sobbed briefly as he dressed, but he quickly regained his composure and told the gang they could hang him, but they couldn't scare him. Graham coolly asked for a chew of tobacco, and when the request was granted, he took a plug from beneath his bedding and bit off a chaw.[5]

The vigilantes tied Graham's hands, put a rope around his neck, and herded him outside. They put their prisoner into a spring wagon they'd brought along for that purpose, and they made Douglas get in the wagon as well. The cavalcade then started east on College Street, crossed the public square, and turned north on Boonville. The commotion at the jail had aroused a gaggle of curious onlookers, and many of them trooped along behind "the march of death." Periodically the rear guard of the night riders stopped to warn the spectators back, but some still straggled along at a safe distance.[6]

The march continued north to within a couple of blocks of the dividing line between Springfield and North Springfield (that is, Division Street), then wound its way west and slightly north, finally halting at a blackjack oak tree about three hundred yards north-northwest of the woolen mill on or near the site of present-day Weaver Elementary School.[7]

The "regulators," as one newspaper called the vigilantes, drove the spring wagon beneath the oak tree, and the rope around Graham's neck

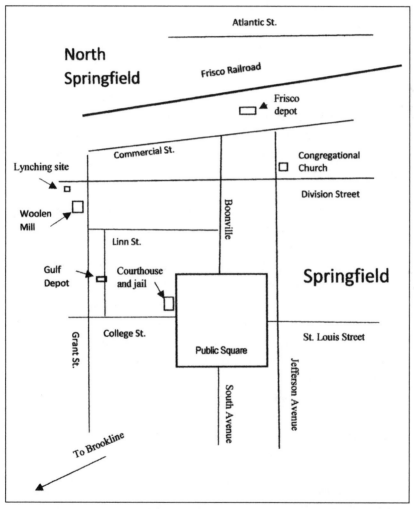

Map of Springfield, circa 1885, showing the streets and sites pertinent to the Sarah Graham murder case, including the location of the lynching (By the author)

was tied to a limb about nine feet off the ground. Given an opportunity to say any last words, Graham said, as reported several minutes later by one of the masked lynchers, that he alone was not responsible for Sarah's death, that he did not, however, care to implicate anyone else, and that neither Cora Lee nor Emma Molloy was guilty of complicity in the crime.[8]

The vigilante horde drove the wagon out from under Graham, but the rope was too long, allowing his feet to hit the ground. Two of the gang lifted him up while others adjusted the rope around the limb. The ones holding Graham up then let go, and he swung with his feet barely touching the ground. He hung in that position for over twenty minutes before finally choking to death.[9]

It was after 3:00 A.M. when most of the gang rode away to the south and then went west out of town. About thirty men remained at the tree warning away onlookers, but they, too, rode away to the west a half hour later, leaving the curiosity seekers free to approach the body.[10]

They found Graham dead with blood oozing from his mouth and nose. Pinned to his coat was the following message under the heading "Arbitrary Notice":

When the Coroner is in possession of this paper, Geo. E. Graham will be dead, and as little punishment will have been inflicted as if he had been hanged by legal authority.

It is a matter of right to the community and justice to humanity that we, "The Three Hundred," ignore the law in this instance.

We recognize that our criminal statues are not equal to all occasions, therefore we have resolved to remove from our midst the worst criminal who has ever infested our country before he gets the "benefit of clergy," that we may hereafter and forever live and be without his presence and vicious influence.

We heartily welcome all strangers to citizenship who are pure of purpose and act in good faith, but we give this, too, as a warning to ex-convicts and murderers who may hereafter invade our country to impose upon our credulity.

We also give warning that any persons of any rank or station who DARE to discover the actors in this tragedy will be surely and speedily DISPATCHED TO HELL, where all things are revealed to the curious.

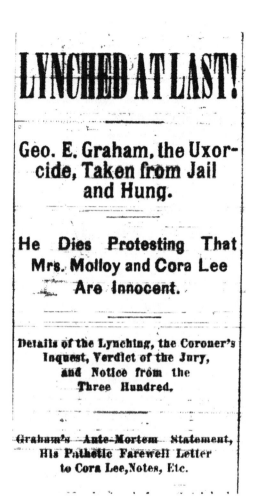

Headline announcing the lynching of George Graham (From *Springfield Express*, April 30, 1886)

In Justice to the memory of Sarah Graham, a loving wife and dear mother, whose life was sacrificed at the altar of Hecate, We Subscribe Ourselves

CITIZENS OF GREENE Co. Mo.

To Sheriff Donnell: Keep your mouth shut if you recognized any of us or you will die the death of a dog.[11]

Released after the lynching, night watchman Douglas returned to town to get the sheriff, and the two of them went back to the tree at 5:00 A.M. to cut down Graham's body. It was conveyed to Eli Paxson's undertaking establishment just off the square on South Street, where a coroner's inquest was held early that morning. After listening to the testimony of Sheriff Donnell, Mrs. Donnell, Douglas, and one other man, the jury reached the predictable verdict that George Graham "came to his death by being hung by the neck until dead by parties to this jury unknown."[12]

Informed of the mob action against Graham even as he was being taken out of jail and transported to the hanging tree, Mrs. Molloy reportedly accepted the news with no display of emotion. However, Judge Howell, who saw Mrs. Molloy early Tuesday morning, said later that she had "expressed regret at the suddenness and awfulness of Graham's death." Howell added, "She bore herself in a manner that greatly increased my regard for her and convinced me more than ever of her innocence."[13]

Rumors of mob violence toward the two female defendants arose in the immediate wake of Graham's hanging, and a report circulated that Mrs. Molloy had left for Bolivar on Tuesday morning "to escape the outriders." She was, in fact, still in Springfield, and a representative of the *Springfield Leader*, which accused the rival *Herald* of instigating the false story, interviewed her later that day. "I shall not run from any mob," she declared. "I am innocent of any crime. I am prepared to die at any moment, and when the mob comes to hang me, I shall meet them at the gate lest in their haste to hang somebody they make a mistake and murder some one they do not wish to."[14]

Mrs. Molloy also told an Associated Press correspondent that she had "not a word of sympathy for Graham's crime," but she deplored mob violence. She said certain citizens of Greene County had been threatened simply for believing her innocent. Requesting that her friends be patient, she said she would soon make certain things clear, but that she had been thus far withholding a thorough statement "to avoid precipitating the tragedy which came Monday night anyway."[15]

Word of Graham's lynching was wired to Bolivar on Tuesday morning, and unlike Mrs. Molloy, Cora Lee was overcome when the news was conveyed to her. "O, my God, my God!" she exclaimed, as she fainted away. After she revived, she started rocking back and forth and moaning in anguish, "O, George, George." She denounced the method of Graham's death but otherwise refused to talk about it.[16]

Graham's body remained on display at the undertaker's firm throughout the day on Tuesday, and an estimated five thousand curious spectators filed by to get a look at the murdered murderer. The burial, post-poned to allow all the gawkers ample time to view the corpse, took place without fanfare on Wednesday morning at Hazelwood Cemetery on the southeastern outskirts of Springfield.[17]

A number of communications to and from Graham came to light shortly after his death.

A letter from Cora that was found on his body contained "a number of mystic signs" and "many insinuations that could only be understood by the parties interested." This letter was apparently never published.[18]

A few days before the lynching, Graham had written an "ante-mortem statement," and he put a copy in a sealed envelope and placed it in the hands of editor J. G. Newbill of the *Springfield Express* with instructions that it should not be opened without Graham's permission. It was opened almost immediately after his death and subsequently published in various newspapers, including the *Express.* Addressed "To all Whom it May Concern," it began, "When this statement shall have been brought to public notice I will be beyond the jurisdiction of any earthly tribunal; and, standing face to face with the judgement bar of a court before whom all earthly courts pale into insignificance, I fully recognize the importance of my speaking the truth and nothing but the truth." Graham went on to say that knowing he was facing imminent death, he wanted to reiterate once and for all that he was solely responsible for the murder of Sarah Graham and that neither Cora Lee nor Emma Molloy had any knowledge whatsoever of the murder until the body was discovered. "This is the last time I shall ever set pen to paper, and may Almighty God, in a future world, judge me for the truth of the matter herein set forth. Signed, George E. Graham."[19]

Of course, there were those who still were not convinced by Graham's final statement. Editor George Sawyer, for instance, dismissed it as the "veriest twaddle, similar in import to the screeds that have, from time to time, issued from his pen." Sawyer claimed that the statement had been written at the behest of Mrs. Molloy's lawyers in case of Graham's "sudden taking off."[20]

Three letters were found in Graham's cell after he was taken out by the mob: one to his boys, one that was presumably from Cora, and one he had written to Cora.

Graham's letter to his boys was written on Monday evening, just hours before he was dragged from his cell. Obviously sensing that his death was imminent, Graham told Charlie and Roy that he was sending them his "very last message of love." He said that whatever else might be said about him, he wanted them to know that he loved them more than he ever imagined he could love anyone. He cautioned them not to turn against Cora Lee, assuring them that she had been unjustly dealt with by the law and that she always had their best interests at heart. The letter then ended abruptly, meaning it was probably not finished at the time Graham was lynched.[21]

The letter that was presumably from Cora was undated and unsigned, but it was written in a feminine hand and was addressed to "My Darling." The writer admonished George that it was his duty "to make life just as endurable as possible" for her. Much of the letter was vague as to exactly what she was talking about, but she seemed to be explaining that she had not forsaken George and that he had only been deceived into believing so. She signed the letter, "Yours lovingly and always the same."[22]

Graham's letter to Cora that was found in his cell, like his letter to his boys, was dated Monday evening of April 26, just hours before he was destined to die. It was headed "My Darling Wife" and began with an expression of sorrow that she was feeling bad. Graham told her that his lawyer was trying to get him released on bond from the bigamy charge so that he could have a preliminary examination in the murder case. He asked Cora whether she remembered the previous two Easter seasons (when they'd evidently been together). In an apparent reference to the *Washington Post* editor, Graham said Barrett had a long letter from him giving his "views of matters in general," and he mentioned a fee in connection with the letter, giving credence to Mrs. Molloy's claim that Graham was commanding payment for some of his statements. In reference to the murder case against him, Graham accused the prosecution of buying evidence, and he mentioned Peter Hawkins and Everett Cannefax, in particular, as having been paid to swear falsely. Graham claimed the case against him was a "pitiful, put up affair." He closed the letter, "With lots of love and many kisses (which I would like awful well to give in person) I am always, my own darling wife, your ever loving and faithful husband. G. E. G."[23]

Graham had also written a letter to Cora a few weeks earlier and given it to Newbill with instructions that it not be published until he authorized it or, as he told the editor, until "sensational developments would make opportune its publication." This letter, considerably longer than the one found in Graham's jail cell, was published in the next edition of the *Express*. It began,

> My Own Darling Cora: For the very, very last time I address you. When you receive this the heart that, whatever its waywardness, always throbbed with unutterable love for you will be stilled forever, and the soul will be *where?* What a tragic ending! What a horrid awakening from bright so a dream! Did either of us imagine that winter evening on which I first met you that our meeting could be so disastrous to each other. And yet, though, I have brought you nothing but shame, disgrace and ruin, you have been the only sunshine my miserable life has ever had.[24]

Graham begged Cora not to forget him or to break their sacred vows after he was gone, and he pledged to love her not only until death but even when he awoke in the next world. He promised to write a last statement to prosecutor Patterson reaffirming "the plain truth in this case," and "they *must,* they MUST believe it, and acquit you and Emma."[25]

He continued,

> Poor, dear Emma? . . . Why I was ever insane enough to make that "statement" I can't tell. I was goaded into it by the reports that were freely brought me about what you two said. . . . I dare not ask Emma to forgive me. . . . No mortal was ever so just, generous, patient, helpful, loving and unselfish as she has been with me, and no one has ever suffered so terribly for it as she has. Surely, if there be a God of Justice, her faults will all be lost sight of, and swallowed up in view of her great, loving, merciful heart. Before God, Cora, I believe I am possessed with a Devil at times, that impels me *on and on* to do things that I loathe and shrink from. I am *not* bad at heart. I detest meanness and cruelty, and yet at times I know I have been both mean and cruel beyond compare.[26]

Graham lamented that Cora had not answered his recent note with any word of love or forgiveness, but he knew how terribly she had suffered by her love for him. He asked Cora to say "goodbye" for him to Etta Molloy and Emma Lee, who had always been "good and true friends." He regretted that the question of Charlie and Roy's custody had been settled in favor of Abbie Breese because he had hoped that they might be placed under Cora's "gentle, restraining influence" rather than thrown among questionable associations.[27]

Graham said he was enclosing in the letter a ring of Mrs. Molloy's that he had been wearing. He wanted Cora to tell Emma to wear the ring in memory of him if she could ever find it in her heart to forgive him for his "base meanness to her, the truest friend man ever had."[28]

Graham's long letter was written over a period of days, and while he was writing it, he received from Cora the first note he had gotten from her since Sarah's body was discovered, despite the fact that he had written to her a dozen times. Graham had been told that Cora received all his letters and simply refused to answer them, but in her note, Cora explained that she had not received the letters. Graham said he had previously believed those who told him Cora refused to communicate with him, but now he thought they were just playing "dirty tricks" and he believed her "in preference to the whole world."[29]

In closing, Graham said he knew it was presumptuous to beg for mercy after his dastardly behavior, but he dared to ask both Cora and God to forgive him for "the most cowardly act" of his "cowardly life" in deliberately hurting Cora, from whom he had received "nothing but love, tenderness and sympathy." As a final request, he asked Cora to have him buried where she would ultimately be laid to rest because he couldn't bear to be separated from her. "I say a last, long Good Bye! I sign myself for the very last time, my precious, darling wife, my Codie girl, Your loving, faithful husband, 'George' E. Graham."[30]

In addition to Graham's "To all Whom it May Concern" statement, which was likely written partly in fulfillment of his promise to Cora to write a last letter to prosecutor Patterson exonerating her and Emma, Graham also wrote to Patterson on April 26, just hours before the lynching. He again complained of the unjust treatment he was receiving from the prosecutor and sheriff. The prisoner was upset, in particular, that the officers were preventing him from seeing Cora, and he asked that he be allowed to see her when she was brought from Bolivar with only those restrictions that were placed on other defendants.[31]

It was also revealed in the immediate wake of Graham's lynching that he had recently been corresponding with former Missouri lieutenant governor Charles P. Johnson of St. Louis, who was perhaps the most noted criminal lawyer in the state. Graham had written Johnson on April 2, asking to retain him as cocounsel with his Springfield lawyers in his murder case, and Johnson replied a few days later, putting his fee at $250. Graham wrote back on April 12, tentatively accepting the offer and promising that someone acting on Graham's behalf would soon be in touch with Johnson.[32]

On Wednesday, April 27, Mrs. Molloy went to Bolivar to be with Cora Lee, who was sick and despondent. Before leaving, Mrs. Molloy wrote to the *Springfield Leader*, claiming a ring belonging to her that had been found on Graham's finger after his body was cut down. This was the same ring Graham had told Cora he would enclose in his letter, but he had failed to do so. Mrs. Molloy explained that the ring was presented to her several years earlier by a reform club of Vermont as a souvenir of her work in that state and that Graham had playfully put it on his finger one day the previous summer and told her she could have it back when he died. Mrs. Molloy said she'd had a lot of her personal items taken by "relic hunters who made a public highway" of her house after Sarah's body was found, but that she'd like to have this one small token from her "boys" of Vermont returned to her. The *Leader* published her letter later that afternoon under the heading "Give Her the Ring."[33]

Both the *Leader* and the *Herald* editorialized against mob violence in the wake of Graham's lynching. The *Leader*, however, thought the *Herald* was hypocritical in its condemnation of Graham in death after having cultivated his friendship while he was alive. The *Leader* even laid part of the blame for the extralegal hanging at the doorstep of the rival newspaper, suggesting that by publishing Graham's "conceited attacks" on the people of Greene County, the *Herald* had produced "a feeling of disgust and irritation in the public mind which undoubtedly helped to swell the mob's spirit." Undeterred by the *Leader*'s criticism of the *Herald*'s sensationalizing of the Graham murder case, the publishers of *The Graham Tragedy and the Molloy-Lee Examination*, who were associated with the *Herald*, rushed an addendum to the pamphlet into print that gave a full account of George Graham's lynching.[34]

Considerable speculation arose in the wake of the lynching as to the identity of the mob, although no determined effort was ever made to discover the actors in the vigilante drama, and a grand jury charged with that task less than a week after the hanging failed to return any indictments.

Critics of Mrs. Molloy suggested that the lynching might have been instigated by her Springfield friends, specifically Judge Baker, to keep Graham from revealing additional incriminating information about her and that Graham's denials of the two women's guilt were orchestrated charades meant to shield the women from the justice they had coming.[35]

However, the available evidence and the heartfelt tone of Graham's final communications, particularly his ante-mortem letter to Cora, do not seem to support such a conspiracy theory. Instead, the lynch mob was probably organized in the Brookline area, and few, if any, of the vigilantes were likely drawn from among Baker's Springfield friends.

Ever since Sarah Graham's body was discovered, rumors of vigilante justice had been afloat, and most of the rumors emanated from Brookline. Just days after the discovery of Sarah's body, a large group of men had met in the Brookline area and drawn up a letter to prosecutor Patterson and Judge Geiger, containing a veiled threat of vigilante action if the prosecution of the murder case against Graham was delayed. Just a week before the lynching, a large body of horsemen had been seen near Brookline going through what appeared to be some sort of disciplined rehearsal, and Graham's lynchers seemed to be a well-organized body that came into Springfield from the west and departed toward the west. In addition, on Monday, the day before the lynching, lawyer Thomas Delaney initiated proceedings to get Graham released on bond from the bigamy charge. Many observers saw the move as just the type of legal maneuvering the letter to Patterson and Geiger had warned against, and they felt Delaney's petition might have been the immediate impetus for the mob action that occurred less than twenty-four hours later.[36]

Perhaps the strongest evidence that the lynchers were drawn primarily from the Brookline area were two letters written to editors of separate newspapers a few weeks after the extralegal hanging. Someone purporting to be a member of the "Three Hundred" headquartered at Brookline wrote to the *St. Louis Chronicle* threatening to destroy Springfield and execute both Cora Lee and Mrs. Molloy if their cases were continued or they were granted changes of venue. In response, another anonymous correspondent from Brookline fired off a missive to the *Springfield Herald* branding the *Chronicle* letter writer as a fraud and the threat contained in his letter as not representative of what the "Three Hundred" stood for. The latter correspondent said that the "Three Hundred" represented some of the best citizens of the county, that they would in no manner act precipitously, and that none of the men who participated in the hanging of Graham would lay a violent hand on a woman, whether guilty or innocent. However, in Graham's case they had acted after due deliberation to rid the county of "the most depraved specimen of human nature that ever invaded our soil."[37]

It is true that twenty years before the Graham affair, a prominent citizen of Springfield named James Baker had publicly supported a band of "Regulators" who briefly dispensed vigilante justice throughout Greene County in the spring of 1866. However, that man was a different James Baker. Judge James Baker had actually spoken against the group. So, there is little basis to dispute Mrs. Molloy's assurance to Graham in her "Poor Boy" letter that Judge Baker only wanted to see justice done and was adamantly opposed to mob violence.[38]

20

Mrs. Molloy's Statement

IN LATE April 1886, Cora Lee was still ill at Bolivar. A rumor reached Springfield that she had died, but the report proved to be a hoax. Cora was instead on the slow road to recovery, and on May 1, Mrs. Molloy returned to Springfield from her visit with Cora.[1]

In early May, Mrs. Molloy's Springfield friends asked the *Herald* to reprint some of the many letters of support she had received from her friends in other states. Editor George Sawyer agreed it was "simple justice to her" that some of the letters be made public, and he published a handful on May 8. Pointing out that a few of Mrs. Molloy's letters of support came from prisoners and ex-prisoners, he said that many Springfield people probably did not realize that Graham was not the only ex-convict "who had been the recipient of her kindness." Sawyer mentioned that the letters chosen for publication were just a small sampling of the hundreds Mrs. Molloy had received. Most of the letters, including the few that appeared in the *Herald*, were written before Graham's sensational allegations of immorality became public.[2]

Four of the letters printed in the *Herald* came from residents of Washington, Kansas. One was a general statement of support expressing the belief that Emma Molloy was an "honest, pure Christian woman" who could never be involved in a heinous crime like murder, and it was signed by a large number of Washington citizens, including Philip Darby. At least a couple of the letters from Washington were written to counter reports of Mrs. Molloy's supposed scandalous behavior in that town, which her enemies there had transmitted to Springfield. One of the letters, in particular, attacked "drunken Charley Barrett" and "his filthy lies." Editor Barrett, of course, was the man who'd first propagated the rumor that Mrs. Molloy and George Graham had spent the night together in a Kansas City hotel, and he had traveled to Springfield to report on the Graham murder case, carrying his slanderous allegations with him.[3]

The *Herald* also printed a letter that Judge Baker had received from Clement Studebaker of the Studebaker Wagon Company, who had known Mrs. Molloy in South Bend. Studebaker conceded that Mrs. Molloy was "impulsive, sometimes imprudent," but that she was always "anxious to promote good ends, earnest, enthusiastic, liberal, warm hearted and sincere." She might be "regarded as a little erratic," he said, as most reformers were, but he thought her entirely incapable of being involved in a murder.[4]

Mrs. Molloy's long-awaited public refutation of Graham's charges of immorality was placed in the hands of Sawyer on the evening of May 10. He published it in the *Herald* the next morning and also wired it to other newspapers across the country.[5]

Mrs. Molloy began not with a defense of herself but of Cora Lee. Not only was Cora innocent of complicity in Sarah's murder, Mrs. Molloy said, but also of knowing she was married to Graham illegally. Mrs. Molloy went on to suggest that any man who could declare his utter love for a woman in one breath and then, in the next, charge her with "criminality such as could only be practiced by the vilest woman," as Graham had done in Cora's case, was unworthy of credence. Had Cora been as loose in morality as Graham made her out to be, there would have been no reason for him to risk a bigamous marriage with her.[6]

Space would not allow a complete chronicling of her involvement with George Graham, Mrs. Molloy said, but she expected soon to release a history of her prison and reform work, which would give a completely different side of the story than what had thus far been given to the public. Perhaps then people would see how it happened that she was deceived by Graham, who, she noted, was a man of "no ordinary brain."[7]

Mrs. Molloy said she recognized that "intruding [herself] upon the public" while the proceedings against her were still going on was perhaps not advisable from a legal standpoint, but she had concluded nonetheless to issue a statement, not to try to convince her critics but for the sake of her Christian friends, who had stood beside her during her trouble despite the cost to their own reputations, and especially for her children, who had suffered so much because of the allegations against their mother. Lastly, she was issuing the statement to redeem her own life and character. She considered her life "a holy trust," or else she might have sought "the refuge of the grave" during "the merciless storm of persecution" that had been waged against her.[8]

She continued,

> It takes a lifetime to build character. It is the work of years to establish a good name, and for a woman thrust by life's emergencies into a public position as I have been, it is a battle inch by inch with all the odds against her, and such is the structure of society that the breath of a slander from the lips of ever so characterless a man, may in an hour demolish the work of all the years, or at least impair it so that she is forever crippled. I cannot wonder, stranger as I was to the people of Springfield, that the horrible occurrences of the past few months have made the public severe in its denunciations and dealings with me or that those who were my friends have silently stood aloof waiting to see the outcome, and demanding an explanation and refutation of all the charges made against myself and Cora Lee. I rather marvel at the pure gold of the true and unwavering friendship of the noble men and women, who, knowing so little as they did in the beginning of this trial, of my real inner life, have stood bravely by me in good and evil report.[9]

Mrs. Molloy thanked, in particular, Judge Baker and his wife, the other men who had signed her bond, and her lady friends within and outside the WCTU who had "stood like an iron wall" around her while "cold, gray eyes steel-bladed" pierced her through in the courtroom and who had shown her sympathy even as "the sneers of the thoughtless rabble" and "a sensational press" crucified her. It was for the sake of these people, she said, that she now positively denied the truth of Graham's slanderous allegations. She said she had wished to issue such a public denial as soon as Graham's statement appeared, but she had been advised that her mere assertions were not enough. She must establish the truth of her denials through affidavits positively stating her whereabouts on the dates Graham had charged her with criminal intimacy. She had accepted the advice because she remembered that "There are no two classes of people whom the world . . . so readily believe a scandal about" as "a minister of the gospel and a woman." Mrs. Molloy, who, of course, happened to be both, continued, "When the two characters are combined, and a scandal can be concocted sufficiently ingenious for the public to swallow, however nauseating and polluting it may be, it is devoured with an ecstasy of delight. It matters not that hearts may break or lives go out in grief, if but these human vultures of society may fatten upon the slain reputations of others."[10]

In issuing his statement, Graham had said that he was not motivated by any noble impulse, and Mrs. Molloy agreed that any man who would publicly acknowledge his shame in front of his children, even if his accusations had been true, was obviously not actuated by any high or holy purpose. Rather, she said, his main purpose was "a cowardly desire to shift some of the moral responsibility of his crime" onto others. He also acted out of spite, since he was still angry that Mrs. Molloy had not hurried home from Illinois to put up his bail when he was first arrested for bigamy.[11]

Mrs. Molloy denied that either she or Cora Lee had deserted Graham or urged mob action against him in the wake of their arrests, as he had claimed in his statement. Indeed, Cora's refusal to abuse Graham, Mrs. Molloy pointed out, had been used as a supposed proof of her complicity in Sarah's murder.[12]

As for Graham's "purported history of criminalities" between him and the two women, Mrs. Molloy pointed out that they, like the scandalous behavior his son had testified to in court, "were only known to him" and, therefore, for lack of witnesses, "could only be proven on his bare assertion or disproved on our denial." Expanding on the point of Charlie's testimony, Mrs. Molloy said that she, Cora, and Graham had never been in bed together nor engaged in any of the other "implied immoralities" to which Charlie, a self-confessed perjurer, had testified. She added that the word of a boy who at twelve years old had such a dirty mind that he could interpret her behavior toward Graham as anything other than "the innocent familiarities" that she showed every other member of the home should not be trusted to "condemn to the world wholesale a woman who has lived in the blaze of the public" for as many years as she had.[13]

The fact that Graham had given only the initials of the physicians who had supposedly performed abortions on Cora was a doubly sly provision, Mrs. Molloy said, because it not only made refutation of the charges virtually impossible but also protected the newspapers that published the charges against libel suits from the doctors.[14]

Turning her attention to Graham's claim that he had declared his "burning passion" for her on November 17, 1882, at Elgin, Illinois, Mrs. Molloy said she was still in La Porte, Indiana, at the time, having not yet moved to Elgin. She produced a letter, dated November 21, from Graham at Elgin to her at La Porte in which he was still making final housing arrangements for her to come to Elgin. Greeting her as "Mrs. Emma Molloy," Graham was businesslike in tone and evinced no special intimacy.[15]

Reminding readers that "slander, like death, loves a shining mark," Mrs. Molloy next refuted Graham's charges of criminal intimacy between herself and Jerome Talbott. She first pointed out that Talbott died at South Bend, not Elkhart, as Graham had said. She admitted that she and Ed Molloy had taken Talbott into their home and treated him during his final illness, but she denied that her friendship with Talbott was the cause of her divorce from Molloy. She and her ex-husband had parted on friendly terms and still held each other in high regard. Neither she nor Mr. Molloy had ever spoken of the other in detrimental terms, as far as she knew, and she had never known him to express jealousy while they were married. Although Talbott was an "unfortunate victim of drink," he was the "soul of honor, incapable of a mean act." She admitted that some people had criticized her for ministering to him during the last days of his illness, which was the only reason she could fathom as to why Graham had dug "ghoul like" into the grave of a man who had been dead for ten years to slander both her and the dead man.[16]

Addressing the charges Graham had leveled, accusing her, Cora, or both of them of rendezvousing with him at specific hotels on specific dates, Mrs. Molloy listed seven of the supposed trysting places and dates. She then refuted the charges by citing affidavits she had obtained from people she had been with at the time, backed up by her own diary entries. For instance, Graham had alleged that he and Mrs. Molloy shared a hotel room in Crestline, Ohio, on October 8, 1883. Mrs. Molloy said she was in Xenia, Ohio, on October 7, a guest of Mrs. H. L. Monroe. After speaking to a large audience that evening, she left on the morning train for

Mechanicsburg, accompanied by Rev. W. H. Gilburn and his wife. They spent a couple of hours in Springfield with Mother Stewart and arrived that afternoon in Mechanicsburg, where she was the guest of Mrs. Eliza J. Neer and her husband. Mrs. Molloy had a statement from the Neers swearing that Mrs. Molloy gave a speech that evening in Mechanicsburg and then spent the night in their home. The next morning, October 9, they accompanied her to the depot to see her off to Mansfield.[17]

Mrs. Molloy refuted several of Graham's other specific charges through affidavits similar to that of the Neers. In reference to her supposed assignation with Graham at the Union Depot Hotel in Kansas City when she was on her way from Washington to Springfield in the spring of 1885, Mrs. Molloy said the accusation had already been investigated and disproved by Fletcher Meredith, editor of the *Hutchinson Interior*, shortly after Charles Barrett first printed it.[18]

In addition, Mrs. Molloy said Graham had told editor Newbill of the *Express*, shortly after his "statement" was published, that it was a "wicked lie." Graham had explained that he was, in fact, registered at some of the hotels on the dates in question, but that he was with women other than Mrs. Molloy or Cora Lee.[19]

Mrs. Molloy continued,

I do not write this with the expectation of total recovery from this murderous assault. . . . When a woman's reputation is thrust under the Juggernaut of the American press by so vile a pen as was wielded in this case, it is impossible to wholly undo its work. Over the electric wires it has crept into homes where I was beloved as a sister from the Atlantic to the Pacific. . . . There are thousands who have read the charges who will never read the refutation. My case has been prejudged before a single witness on my side has been heard, or a shred of rebutting evidence given. I can only hope this statement may reassure my friends who have stood by me in the storm, and make the world a little more tender to the orphan children whose prospects have been so clouded in this great calamity. The thoughtless men who have hurled to the world this vile calumny, owe it to these children as well as to myself, that they give this refutation as wide publicity as they have the slander. As I think of their blasted lives, and look into their sorrowful faces, and into the grave of my usefulness and witness the humiliation of my parents, and brothers, and sister, whose pride has been the unspotted record of our family, I can but ask what has been gained by the publication of this filth to the world? It has been like opening a charnel house whose very breath has carried moral disease and death into thousands of homes.[20]

De Quincy in one of his essays treats of "murder as a fine art." Has it not become so in America, when the press lends its aid to a criminal guilty of the blackest crime, to continue his murderous work, and destroy the woman whose crime was her credulity in believing that "salvation could reach the uttermost"? George Graham gave his wife the blessed luxury of an immediate death. To the victims of his treachery and deceit, he has awarded a torture as exquisite in its anguish as it is slow in its consummation. The memory of that horrible murder will forever be a canker, blighting all joy; and his name so unjustly linked with mine in that awful crime, it seems to me was enough, without this *added* slander. It has been my earnest desire ever since I can remember, to do good in this world, and to live so that those who came into contact with me should be happier and better for that contact. Only God can know the soul-agony I have endured as I have read daily the false caricatures of that life, caricatures that contained not a shadow of truth, and I think of the little children whom I have loved all over this land who have thus been made to regard me as a monstrosity of vice and crime, of the thousands of friends who have been made cold and distrustful.[21]

At the end of her long letter, Mrs. Molloy appended a brief poem that read like a dirge of her despair, and then she concluded, "Even my last cry will be sneered at, I am aware." But, she reiterated, the letter was not written for those who gloried in her downfall but for her friends. "To them I wish to say, though I have made grievous mistakes, I have had most honest intentions and surely no one has suffered in this cyclone more than EMMA MOLLOY."[22]

As Mrs. Molloy predicted, her refutation was not as widely published as Graham's sensational allegations. Sawyer did, however, wire it to a few newspapers in midwestern cities like Chicago, Indianapolis, Kansas City, and St. Louis, and it was published in those places on the same day it appeared in the *Herald*. It was later reprinted in a number of other newspapers, including Springfield's other papers.[23]

In distributing the letter to the out-of-town newspapers, Sawyer noted that most Springfieldians had already concluded that it would be hard to prove Mrs. Molloy guilty of being an accessory after the fact to Sarah Graham's murder, and with the publication of her refutation, the pendulum of public opinion swung marginally farther in her favor. Almost all commentators agreed that her letter was eloquently written, and the majority were even willing to admit that she had offered strong evidence to refute Graham's specific charges of hotel assignations. If even a few of his accusations of criminal intimacy were false, several newspapers reasoned, they were probably all untrue.[24]

To newspapers that had supported Mrs. Molloy all along, her letter of refutation offered a confirmation of their faith in her. Noting that she had thoroughly demolished Graham's allegations against her chastity, the *Garnett Journal* opined, "The only mistake Mrs. Molloy has made in the matter from the beginning to the end is her unbelief in the doctrine of total depravity."[25]

Many observers, however, were still unwilling to give Mrs. Molloy the benefit of the doubt. The sharpest and most frequent criticism was that her refutation came too late. "It would have been proper for Mrs. Molloy to have denied Graham's allegations as soon as made," said the *Leavenworth Times*, "and not wait until he was hung by a mob. Her delay in this matter, coupled with the insinuation that comes from Springfield to the effect that Mrs. Molloy's friends were suspected with having a hand in Graham's lynching, will hardly satisfy a scrutinizing public." Indeed, in the same issue in which the *Times* offered the preceding comment, it published Mrs. Molloy's entire letter under the heading "A Little Late, Emma."[26]

Even those who were convinced that Mrs. Molloy was telling the truth and that George Graham "died with a lie on his lips" often still found a reason to fault Mrs. Molloy. Declaring Graham a "consummate liar," the *Huntington Daily Democrat* observed, "The woman who has been so strangely mixed-up in this case will have very hard work to explain how she ever came to be so intimately associated with such a person."[27]

In a similar vein, the *Weekly Atchison Champion* dismissed the argument of Mrs. Molloy and her defenders (like the *Garnett Journal*) that she took Graham under her wing because it was her Christian duty.

Calling such a defense "all twaddle," the *Champion* said the real reason was that "it was a folly of woman to fall into gush and sentimentality about scoundrelly men."[28]

Shortly after Mrs. Molloy's statement was made public, an editorial in the *International Record of Charities and Correction* suggested that Mrs. Molloy's downfall came about because of her lack of humility and her excessive ambition. Prison reform, the writer said, was no work for women. Working with prisoners and convicts was too dangerous for women to undertake. Mrs. Molloy "over-estimated her talents and her strength; she under-estimated the peril of the role which she had chosen."[29]

Perhaps the harshest reaction to Mrs. Molloy's letter of refutation came from Mary, very likely the same woman who'd compared Mrs. Molloy to Cleopatra in a letter to the *Herald* shortly after Mrs. Molloy and Cora were arrested. Mistakenly assuming that Mrs. Molloy had referred to herself, not to Jerome Talbott, as a "shining mark," Mary now fired off another biting, satirical letter to the *Herald* attacking the temperance revivalist for her immodesty and suggested that she should be more unassuming in the future. Noting that Mrs. Molloy had used her children to make an emotional appeal, Mary pointed out that she had avoided mentioning Frank by name, because she had "lost Frank's affection by her excessive attention to George E. Graham." Mary continued, "When such a shining light as Mrs. Molloy takes into her home and her affections, such a man as Graham, who never professed a change of heart, as I have heard, how can she blame the 'villainous press' for publishing the products of his brain?" Mrs. Molloy said in her letter that she was working on a book, and Mary concluded that she might write one also. It would be titled "The Life of Sarah Graham," it, too, would "read like a romance," and she would give the profits from the book to Roy and Charlie Graham.[30]

21

Mrs. Molloy's Desolation

ON MAY 11, the same day Mrs. Molloy's statement appeared in the newspapers, a Greene County Circuit Court grand jury jointly indicted George Graham and Cora Lee for the first-degree murder of Sarah Graham. The jury concluded that there were two potentially fatal wounds, a gunshot to the side and a blow to the head from a blunt instrument.[1]

Cora was brought to Springfield from Bolivar on May 24. Arraigned in the circuit court the next day, she pleaded not guilty. On May 29, she asked for a continuance until the November term on the grounds that she had not been able to properly prepare her defense because she had been sick and had been shuffled back and forth between Bolivar and Springfield. Also, she had still not completely recovered from her illness and could not go to trial without endangering her health and that of her unborn child. She needed more time to obtain the means to employ counsel and to line up rebuttal witnesses. On the evening of May 29, Cora was taken back to Bolivar, which was considered a safer place for her than Springfield, and her request for a continuance was later granted.[2]

On June 5, the grand jury indicted Emma Molloy as an accessory after the fact to murder and as an accessory before the fact to bigamy. This came as a mild surprise to many observers, since she had not been indicted at the same time as Cora Lee. Arraigned on June 12, Mrs. Molloy pleaded not guilty to both charges and was released on a cumulative bond of $1,100, $800 on the murder charge and $300 on the bigamy charge. Judge James Baker was again one of the primary bondsmen. Mrs. Molloy's release on bond briefly revived rumors of vigilantism, but no mob action was ever attempted against either her or Cora Lee.[3]

On June 14, Mrs. Molloy's lawyers filed motions to quash both indictments against her, citing defects in the language of the documents. For instance, the indictment against her for accessory to murder did not charge that the offense had been done "against the peace and dignity of the State." The motions to quash were granted on June 21, and Mrs. Molloy's bond was continued, pending her appearance at the November term to answer new indictments.[4]

About the time Mrs. Molloy was arraigned, she received thirty dollars from Frances Willard, WCTU president, as a token of love and support. Some Springfield citizens denounced Miss Willard's action, suggesting that it would damage the cause of temperance. Others, however, applauded the deed. One prominent Springfield businessman remarked that "not a scintilla of evidence had been adduced against Mrs. Molloy so far and the case should have been dismissed long ago; that a lot of pettifoggers were keeping up the excitement to get an office."[5]

Mrs. Molloy left Springfield in late June, announcing that she planned to return to Indiana to visit friends. However, she went first to Peoria, Illinois, where she "met with a very hospitable reception from the Christian ladies who refuse to believe that her relations with George Graham, the wife-murderer, was for any other purpose than to elevate that talented rascal from diabolism to usefulness."[6]

While she was in Peoria, Mrs. Molloy let it be known that once the charges against her in Springfield were settled, she planned to sue in US Court a number of newspapers that she thought had libeled her, starting with the *Peoria Journal*, which had rehashed "her Indiana record" when she first came under suspicion in the Sarah Graham case. The *Journal*, however, was undaunted. Upon hearing the rumor of Mrs. Molloy's proposed lawsuits, the Illinois newspaper denounced her in a scathing editorial for her "monumental gall" in commencing "to talk big" while still under indictment for murder. "We are ready to hear her twitter her little twit."[7]

Other newspapers across the country, especially in Springfield and Fort Wayne, greeted the Peoria report with a defiant note. Challenging Mrs. Molloy to include the *Springfield Leader* in her list of papers to be sued, editor S. K. Strother declared,

Before she gets through with her libel suits . . . , she will find that she is not before a court to answer to the charge of being accessory after the fact to the murder of Sarah Graham. She would fare a thousand times better in such a case than she will in a contest with the newspapers with her character the point at issue.

For despite Judge Baker's powerful support, the death of Graham and her own verbose self-exonerative statement, Mrs. Molloy's character is an ugly thing that should be hidden in obscurity and penitence.[8]

In early July, Mrs. Molloy went to South Bend to visit her father. She planned to stay there until the fall and to spend her time working on a book that would chronicle her life and vindicate her involvement with George Graham.[9]

Mrs. Molloy, who'd lost her first two children in infancy, was struck by tragedy again on July 22, 1886, when Frank, her only surviving biological child, drowned in a boating accident in La Porte, where his father still lived. The funeral was held in South Bend, and he was buried in the South Bend City Cemetery, near Emma's mother and other children, Lottie and Allie. "Verily the cup of sorrow of Mrs. Emma Molloy has been filled to overflowing," observed the *Fort Wayne Daily News*.[10]

In mid-August, Mrs. Molloy penned a poem for the *South Bend Tribune* describing her grief:

DESOLATE

There is something gone from my life!
The sunshine in dimples falls on me,
The river still dances past in glee,
Yet nothing is as it used to be
In the days agone, in my life.
There's something missing! Can you tell
Why it pains my heart to look in the sky
Where the fleecy clouds go sailing by,
And sun in his golden car rides high?
There's a sob in your deep-toned bell!
There's a weary wail in the wind;
The days are leaden, and joy has fled;
Hope lies prostrate, ambition is dead;
My life to despair seems strangely wed,

There's something I cannot find!
O, I miss a bright, sunny face;
A voice that in turmoil brought repose,
Lips that were fresh as the dewy rose,
Hands whose love-touch banis'd my woes
And a form of bewildering grace.
It is gone like the dream that's done;
And the long, long days creep slowly by
While I sit and listen, and smother my sigh
Lest I miss the touch of the angel nigh,
Whose absence has clouded the sky.
    Emma Molloy
South Bend, Aug. 17th, 1886.

The *Springfield Express,* in reprinting the poem, ventured that no matter what its readers' opinions of Mrs. Molloy might be in regard to the Graham murder case, no one who read the poem's "sad wail" could "fail to sympathize with a mother's bereavement."[11]

On September 3, Mrs. Molloy rushed out of her father's home in South Bend and charged down a hill into the nearby St. Joseph River. After plunging under water several times, she was rescued as she lay exhausted near the shore, and she was placed under a physician's care. Although many newspapers initially reported the incident as a suicide attempt, her hometown *South Bend Tribune* did not, and later reports clarified that Mrs. Molloy had been suffering from a "sick headache" and had dosed herself with ether, causing her to run into the water under the hallucination that she saw her son drowning. After she was rescued, she declared piteously that she had gotten hold of Frank's hand once, but that it had slipped from her grasp.[12]

At least one newspaper found cause to assail Mrs. Molloy, even in her despair, for not knowing her place as a woman. The *Holton Signal* conjectured that after Frank died, Mrs. Molloy probably wished she'd spent more time with him. As she stood on the bank of the river contemplating suicide, she no doubt regretted having spent so much of her life "away from husband, children and home. She thought more of politics than she did of those who ought to have been dearer to her than all else in the world."[13]

The *Springfield Daily Herald,* one of the newspapers that reported Mrs. Molloy's near-drowning as a suicide attempt, said the news would not surprise local residents who were familiar with Mrs. Molloy's mental state during the weeks immediately after her preliminary hearing, while she was still in Springfield staying with Judge Baker and Judge Howell. Although she "bore up bravely" and was usually composed during the examination, she broke down shortly after Graham's lynching and spoke openly of taking her own life, declaring that she would do so if it were not for the fact that suicide was morally wrong. She seemed unconcerned about the possible outcome of the legal proceedings against her, but she was deeply wounded by the stain on her character, distraught and incredulous that so many people were willing and eager to believe such "horrible things" about her. "Her disposition remained gentle," the *Herald* recalled, and she was perfectly rational except when it came to the subject of suicide. "To those who knew her best, the only surprise is that the death of her son Frank has not completed her cup of sorrow and caused her death before this time."[14]

In October, Mrs. Molloy committed herself to the Battle Creek Sanitarium in Michigan to regain her health. This was a resort that emphasized medicinal water, sunshine, exercise, rest, and proper diet rather than a mental health facility such as we might envision today.[15]

In mid-November, a Greene County grand jury returned a new indictment against Mrs. Molloy for accessory to murder, and she was notified to return to Springfield and prepare for trial. However, the trial was not immediately scheduled, and Mrs. Molloy instead visited Nebraska, where Ida Lee and her husband lived, before returning to Indiana.[16]

Cora Lee's trial was set for December, but it was postponed by the consent of attorneys on both sides. Judge Geiger had died, and the man appointed to complete his term was due to leave office at the end of the year. Furthermore, Judge Hubbard had been elected to replace Geiger as permanent judge of the Twenty-first Judicial Circuit, encompassing Greene and surrounding counties, but he couldn't hear Cora's case because he'd been involved in prosecuting her. Judge Charles C. Bland of the Eighteenth Judicial District east of the Greene County area was assigned to hear Cora's case in Springfield in early January.[17]

When Cora's case was called on January 7, she entered the courtroom dressed in mourning but with her veil thrown back to reveal a careworn face. When the state moved for a continuance on the grounds that a key prosecution witness, Lewis West, was missing, Cora was so anxious for her trial to commence that she broke into tears, according to one correspondent. The prosecution's motion was granted, and the trial was rescheduled for the May 1887 term. Cora Lee was granted bail, the bond being fixed at $7,000, but she was returned to jail until she could come up with the money. This time she was taken not back to Bolivar but to the Laclede County Jail in Lebanon, located in Judge Bland's district.[18]

On the morning of February 9, Cora was brought back to Springfield, where she gave the required bond. Her bondsmen were Judge Baker, Judge Howell, and banker Fred Rexinger of Bolivar.[19]

Ever since Sarah Graham's body was found, certain detectives, allegedly hired by Mrs. Molloy, had been pursuing George Graham's self-serving theory that the clothes found at the bottom of the well on the Molloy farm belonged to Sarah Graham, put there as a frame-up by Timothy Breese, but that the dead woman herself was not Sarah. According to George's outlandish story, Sarah had instead gone to Washington Territory to be with her brother, who was stationed at an army post near Vancouver. Now, almost a year later, word filtered back from the West that the detectives had turned up evidence that a woman very much resembling Sarah Graham had indeed been in regular contact with Stephen Gorham and that she was hiding out somewhere in Wyoming. Embracing the dubious report like a drowning person desperately clinging to a piece of flotsam, Mrs. Molloy suddenly left Indiana for the West Coast about January 1, 1887, to investigate the new leads. Or so said an article that appeared in the *Boston Globe* in early February. When the fantastic story reached Springfield, prosecutor Patterson and most other observers dismissed the notion that the woman found in the Molloy well was someone other than Sarah Graham as a ridiculous yarn that had long ago been discredited. Most people in Fort Wayne, including Graham's own stepmother, also greeted the news with ridicule.[20]

Mrs. Molloy might have gone west at least partly in pursuit of a farfetched theory, as her critics suggested, but she also used the occasion to resurrect her career as an orator. Beginning in early January, she conducted a revival campaign in the Vancouver area "with temperance and woman suffrage thrown in for effect," and the available evidence suggests that the revival was arranged well before she left Indiana.[21]

She returned to Springfield on February 14 looking "bright and cheerful." She was arraigned on the new charges against her later the same day. Judge Howell insisted on an immediate trial, saying his client had traveled 3,000 miles and spent $100 to get to Springfield, but the state's request for a continuance was granted. Mrs. Molloy was released under bonds of $500 in the bigamy case and $800 in the accessory to murder case, with Howell and Judge Baker among her bondsmen. She stayed in Springfield for a couple of weeks, visiting friends and working on the book about her life. She stated that she'd been well received in Vancouver, the story of her trial having made no impression on the people there, and during her stay in Springfield, she received well wishes from all across the country, including from noted women's rights activists Belva Lockwood and Mary Livermore. On February 27, Mrs. Molloy left for the Northwest to resume her series of revivals. Cora Lee accompanied her as far as Omaha, where Cora's sister Ida lived.[22]

Mrs. Molloy's declaration that she'd been well received in Vancouver was generally true. Endorsements from prominent people had preceded her arrival in early 1887, and the two ministers who engaged her had investigated her background, including the criminal charges against her, before booking her. One of the people who wrote letters of recommendation was Judge Baker, who told the preachers that the persecution of Mrs. Molloy was the work of "a Missouri mob in the interest of the liquor traffic." Baker said Graham's slanderous charges of immorality were extorted from him by the mob under a threat of lynching and that when Graham refused to incriminate the women in the murder, the mob went ahead and hanged him anyway. So, the ministers had put their faith in Mrs. Molloy, and her campaign stirred little controversy at first. That changed, however, about the time she returned from Springfield and a notice appeared in the *Portland Morning Oregonian* of her alleged Missouri crime. The same two ministers and their congregations rose to her defense, and the *Oregonian* finally admitted that Mrs. Molloy was probably not guilty of abetting murder. However, the newspaper thought she was "a foolish kind of woman" with "a great gift of tongue," whose "work" was an ephemeral, worthless harlequinade.[23]

Writing to a friend in Indiana in mid-March, Mrs. Molloy blamed the controversy she faced in Washington on the publisher of the sensationalist pamphlet that had been released about the time of Graham's lynching.

The publisher had, "with commendable fidelity to the interest of the whiskey ring," flooded Vancouver with copies of the tract. Despite the efforts to discredit her in Washington, Mrs. Molloy said she was having "nice work" there with sixty-seven conversions just within the preceding week. She also decried the fact that her trial had been postponed for no better reason than the absence of state witness Lewis West, who was missing only because he "got drunk and gouged a poor man's eye out" and fled to avoid prosecution.[24]

22

Cora Lee's First Trial

CORA LEE'S trial finally came up in Springfield in early June 1887 before Judge Bland. Joseph Dodson was now the Greene County sheriff, and the defense objected to his selecting the jury, since he had testified against Cora at her preliminary hearing. Next in line for the task was coroner Eli Paxson, but the prosecution objected to him on the grounds that he was too much under the influence of Cora and her attorneys. A. J. Potter, former sheriff, was then selected as an elisor to fill out the venire. He had considerable difficulty doing so, because many prospective jurors admitted they'd already formed an opinion.[1]

But the jury was finally selected, and the defense's plea in abatement, arguing that a new indictment should be brought because Cora's codefendant was dead, was overruled on Monday morning, June 13. Testimony got under way later the same day with a large audience in attendance. Many of the state's witnesses during the trial, including Charlie Graham, were the same as those who had testified at the coroner's inquest or the preliminary hearing, and their testimony generally coincided with what they'd previously said.[2]

Prosecutor Patterson called a number of new witnesses to try to establish his theory that Cora Lee had driven to Springfield on the evening of September 30, 1885, to pick up George and Sarah Graham and that she and George had killed Sarah sometime during the return trip to the Molloy farm. Several people, who were either camped or passing along the Brookline-to-Springfield road on the evening in question, testified that they had seen a woman in a black veil driving a spring wagon hitched to a gray pony headed toward Springfield about sundown. One of the campers was Sarah West, wife of the missing Lewis West. A couple of other witnesses said they'd seen a veiled woman in Springfield that night matching the description of the woman seen on the Brookline road. None of the witnesses could say for sure who the woman was, but at least two said they recognized the pony as belonging to the Molloy family. Most were also not positive of the date, but J. L. Gardner and R. P. Norman claimed that they were. The defense, on cross-examination, impeached Gardner as a drunken, unreliable witness who had allegedly threatened to lynch both Cora Lee and Emma Molloy.[3]

Margaret Dyer, her niece Mattie, and Mattie's sister told the court that Cora, who was guarded at the Dyer home in Springfield on the night after she was arrested, had mentioned in casual conversation that she had gone for the mail on the evening before Sarah Graham was killed, hoping to receive a letter from George, and she had gotten back home between 8:00 and 9:00 P.M. The women could not say for sure whether she meant that she had come to Springfield, although they thought so. When one of the young women asked Cora whether she wasn't scared to be out after dark alone, she said no because George had left his pistol with her for protection. Cora also added that she would not have believed George capable of murder if he had not confessed because he would not hurt a helpless animal.[4]

In a somewhat surprising move, Mrs. Molloy, who'd arrived in Springfield just in time for the trial, was called as a prosecution witness. The line of questioning predictably turned to the romantic relationship between Cora Lee and George Graham. Mrs. Molloy said she had never heard Cora express any affection for Graham until after Sarah left Kansas to return to Fort Wayne. She admitted, however, that she, her son, Cora, and George Graham stopped at the same hotel in Atchison, Kansas, in June 1884, and the hotel register was produced showing that all four shared the same room. In speaking of the living arrangements at Washington, she emphatically denied that she had ever gotten out of her bed to get in bed with George Graham, and she never knew Cora Lee to do such a thing. "My boy was sixteen years of age," she said, "and I am not a beast or an idiot."[5]

Mrs. Molloy said she believed George and Sarah were married when they were living with her in Washington, but that she also believed Graham's later "confession" that he and Sarah had been living in sin, especially after he produced a copy of the divorce decree. She said she and Sarah had never exchanged unkind words, and she did not believe that Timothy Breese had anything to do with putting Sarah's body in the well.[6]

Sam Clarke, former editor of the *Washington Post,* testified that Cora Lee showed him a picture of George Graham when he first met her in early 1884 and referred to Graham as "her fellow." Clarke said he always thought Cora and George were "a little bit spoony." He added that he knew Cora, George, Mrs. Molloy, and Frank Molloy had gone to the hotel in Atchison together in June 1884 because he had accompanied them and had registered at the same hotel. He'd seen Graham and Cora go to the same room, but on cross-examination he admitted that he was in the room with them and did not see Graham and Cora go to bed together.[7]

David Fisher, a former waiter at the Laclede Hotel in Independence, Missouri, swore that George Graham and Cora Lee registered at the hotel on April 26, 1884, as husband and wife and shared the same room. Emma Molloy accompanied them, but she stayed in an adjoining room. The defense suggested on cross-examination that Fisher's testimony was a case of mistaken identity, but he stuck to his story.[8]

The state tried to show that when Cora first came to Springfield, she purchased a train ticket in Kansas City under the name Mrs. George Graham. The ticket agent of the Union Depot in Kansas City testified to that effect, but the railroad officer whose duty it was to maintain the records said he didn't know anything about it.[9]

After the state rested, Cora's attorneys called several people to rebut the testimony of the prosecution witnesses who said they'd seen a veiled woman along the Springfield-Brookline road on the evening before Sarah Graham was murdered. The defense witnesses testified that they had been on the same road on the evening and near the time in question and that they had not seen such a woman. They had also not seen the prosecution witnesses who were camped along the road when the mysterious veiled woman passed.[10]

Cora's attorneys admitted that the state witnesses might have seen a veiled woman near the time in question, but they suggested that the date was Monday, September 28, not Wednesday, September 30. Arguing that Sarah West and the other state witnesses were simply mistaken as to the date, the defense called witnesses who had traveled along the Springfield-Brookline road on September 28 and who had seen Mrs. West and her husband camped between the two towns on that date.[11]

In addition, the defense called S. I. Haseltine, station agent at the Dorchester train depot, to the stand, and he testified that George Graham and a woman whom he identified from a picture as Sarah Graham had gotten off at the Dorchester station with him on the night of September 30. On cross-examination, the prosecution called detective Ed Davis to the stand, and he said Haseltine had told him shortly after Sarah's body was found that no one besides himself got off at Dorchester that night. However, another defense witness, railroad brakeman Thomas Hayden, supported Haseltine's testimony. Upon being recalled, Haseltine admitted he'd lied to Davis at first because he did not want to give testimony in court that might hang a man, but now that Graham had been lynched anyway, there was no reason not to tell the truth.[12]

Emma Lee took the stand and reiterated the testimony she'd given at the inquest. She said that Cora had gone to Brookline for the mail on September 30, 1885, that she got home in time for lunch, and that she stayed home the rest of the day. That night, Cora, Emma, and Etta slept together in the same bed, and Cora never got up until Graham came home in the wee hours of the morning. Etta Molloy also testified for the defense, corroborating what Emma Lee had said.[13]

Florence Warner, who'd been employed as a clerk with the *Morning and Day of Reform* in Washington for five months, testified that she'd never witnessed any unbecoming behavior between George Graham and Cora Lee.[14]

Taking the stand in her own defense, Cora Lee confirmed her movements on September 30, 1885, as previously related by her sister Emma. Contrary to the prosecution's accusation that Cora had rendezvoused with Graham in Independence, Missouri, on April 26, 1884, she said she was in Leavenworth on that date. She had never even been to Independence. Cora said that the first time Charlie told her his mother had come from Fort Wayne to St. Louis was in January 1886, about the time of the forgeries, and that he did not tell her that Sarah had come all the way to Springfield until the day her body was discovered. In an ef-

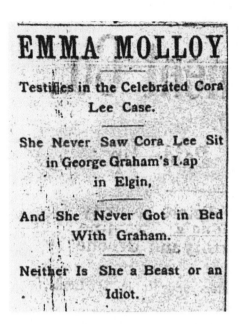

EMMA MOLLOY

Testifies in the Celebrated Cora Lee Case.

She Never Saw Cora Lee Sit in George Graham's Lap in Elgin,

And She Never Got in Bed With Graham.

Neither Is She a Beast or an Idiot.

Headline about Emma Molloy's testimony at Cora Lee's first trial (From the *Springfield Leader,* June 15, 1887)

fort to impeach Mattie Dyer's testimony, Cora said she'd never told the Dyers she came to Springfield on the night of September 30, 1885. She added that she had heard Mattie remark that she wished Cora would be hanged, and Mattie, upon being recalled, admitted that she'd made such a comment.[15]

The defense also tried to impeach the testimony of Everett Cannefax, the man who'd said he'd seen Cora with Graham near the well shortly after the murder. Cannefax had reportedly told a washerwoman named Mrs. Egbert that he intended to help the prosecution all he could and that he'd like to knock Judge Howell down some time. Cannefax denied having made the comment, but Mrs. Egbert took the stand to verify it.[16]

Emma Molloy was recalled to the stand to answer an insinuation from the prosecution that Cora Lee wore black because she was in mourning for George Graham. Mrs. Molloy said Cora had always worn black ever since her father died when she was a young girl.[17]

Closing arguments in the case began on Tuesday, June 21. Prosecutor Patterson reviewed some of the evidence, such as Sam Clarke's statement that Cora had referred to Graham as "her fellow" long before they were married, and he emphasized to the jurymen their "sad duty" to follow the evidence and find Cora guilty of murder. The defense's response began on

Tuesday evening and continued into the next day. Defense attorney Howell admitted that the state had presented a lot of so-called evidence, but it was "mostly chaff and little wheat." Prosecutors had proved that a woman's body was found in the Molloy well, and they had also proved that an unidentified veiled woman had passed along the Brookline-Springfield road near the presumed date of the woman's murder. That was about it, Howell concluded. The defense, however, had offered testimony proving that Cora was home all night at the time of the crime.[18]

On Wednesday, curious spectators filled the courtroom "to its utmost capacity" in eager anticipation of a verdict. Patterson's closing statement on Wednesday afternoon was interrupted two different times by applause from the rowdy audience, but Judge Bland quickly called for order. The case was given to the jury at 4:00 P.M. They came back at 9:00 P.M. and reported that they had not yet reached a verdict. Bland adjourned the court for the day with instructions for the jury to continue deliberations. When the jury once again reported on Thursday morning that they could not agree, Bland declared a mistrial and dismissed the jurors. It was later reported that the jury was split eight for conviction and four for acquittal from the beginning and that the divide did not change throughout deliberations.[19]

Mrs. Molloy's trial was scheduled to begin the next day, Friday, June 24, but her attorneys asked for a continuance on the grounds that she needed time to secure certain witnesses, particularly Mrs. S. L. North of Leavenworth, whose testimony would disprove David Fisher's allegation that she and Cora spent the night with Graham in an Independence, Missouri, hotel on April 26, 1884. Mrs. Molloy did not know that this witness would be necessary until Fisher testified at Cora's trial. Judge Wallace, who'd been brought in from Lebanon to hear Mrs. Molloy's case, overruled the motion.[20]

Having been denied a continuance, Mrs. Molloy on Saturday asked for a change of venue to somewhere outside the Twenty-first Judicial Circuit, which encompassed Springfield and surrounding counties. She said she had only recently learned how pervasive the prejudice against her was in the Twenty-first Circuit, which was the jurisdiction of Judge Hubbard, cocounsel for the state during the preliminary hearing.[21]

Judge Baker was among those who testified for Mrs. Molloy at the hearing to consider her request for a change of venue. He said he had been "hooted at" and ostracized by the people of the Twenty-first Judicial

Circuit because of his friendship with Mrs. Molloy, and even Judge Hubbard admitted that there was considerable prejudice against Mrs. Molloy in Greene County. She was accordingly granted a change of venue, but only to neighboring Christian County, which, like Greene, was within the Twenty-first Judicial Circuit. Her trial was not immediately scheduled, but it was later slated for October 1887. Meanwhile, Cora Lee's new trial was set for the November 1887 term in Greene County.[22]

Still under bond, Mrs. Molloy and Cora Lee left Springfield around July 1, 1887. Mrs. Molloy was thought to be bound for the West Coast to resume her evangelical work, while Cora had obtained a job in Omaha as a nurse.[23]

23

Cora Lee's Second Trial

Upon leaving Springfield, Mrs. Molloy, instead of immediately traveling back to the West Coast to resume her evangelistic work, began hunting up evidence to support her case when it came to trial. She spent a few weeks in the Kansas City area and then traveled to Leavenworth to solicit a statement from Mrs. North swearing that Mrs. Molloy had been with her at the time David Fisher claimed she had been at an Independence, Missouri, hotel. It was for this purpose, of course, that Mrs. Molloy had sought a continuance before she was granted a change of venue.[1]

Later, Mrs. Molloy traveled to Washington, Kansas, on behalf of herself and Cora Lee in search of depositions from her friends there. Mrs. Molloy was accompanied by one of her attorneys and by Fred Rexinger, the Bolivar banker who'd befriended Cora, while J. W. Rector, Washington attorney and sworn adversary of Mrs. Molloy, represented the state during the taking of depositions. The *Washington Register* reported that Mrs. Molloy had trouble finding witnesses who would vouch for her character and that she therefore broke off the interview process earlier than expected. The *Register* accused Mrs. Molloy of intimidating some of the witnesses who would have otherwise offered unfavorable testimony and of caring more about her own reputation than she did about Cora Lee's fate. Even those deponents who gave statements favorable to Mrs. Molloy, the *Register* insinuated, were lying to shield a woman they considered their friend. The rival *Washington Republican,* however, replied the next week defending the character of those who had vouched for Mrs. Molloy and accusing the *Register* of deliberately seeking to pull down rather than build up "a regard for truth and decency." The *Republican* reminded its readers that the rumors of Mrs. Molloy's supposed immorality during her stay in Washington did not begin until after the *Washington Post* published its "Kansas City expose."[2]

While Emma Molloy and Cora Lee were collecting depositions in their defense, prosecutor Patterson was also busy taking depositions to use against Cora. For instance, in late August he traveled to Omaha, where Cora was now staying with her sister.[3]

Mrs. Molloy's trial, originally scheduled for October 1887, was postponed until the February 1888 term of the Christian County Circuit Court. Meanwhile, Cora Lee's second trial in Greene County was reset from November 1887 to January 1888.[4]

Cora Lee returned to Springfield from Omaha in early January. She refused to see a newspaperman when he called on January 9 at the home where she was staying. A week later, she appeared in court during jury selection accompanied by her attorneys and her sister Emma. Cora was wearing a black, fur-trimmed, velvet cloak with lavender flowers edging its hood. During the examination, she took notes and perused papers relative to her case, lending aid to her lawyers whenever possible. Most of the potential jurors were dismissed because they admitted they'd already formed an opinion in the case. Several of those ultimately selected were newcomers to the county and were, therefore, not in the area "to feel the influence of public sentiment" or to read the local papers during the case's sensational early stages.[5]

The trial began on Thursday, January 19, with opening statements. Prosecuting attorney Patterson briefly reviewed Graham's history of crime, including his bigamous marriage to Cora Lee, and he said the state planned to prove that Cora was an active participant in the murder of Sarah Graham. Judge Howell countered that the defense would prove Cora Lee not guilty by showing that she came to Springfield on Monday, September 28, 1885, not on Wednesday, September 30, as the state claimed. Among the early witnesses were John Potter, the former postmaster, and constable William O'Neal. Mrs. Molloy was not present when the trial began, but she was expected any day from Port Townsend, Washington, where she had been conducting another revival.[6]

Like Potter and O'Neal, many of the other witnesses had also testified at previous proceedings in the case. Charlie Graham, for instance, gave much the same testimony he'd given before, accusing Cora and

Mrs. Molloy of scandalous behavior with his father. On cross-examination, the defense suggested that Charlie's father had instigated him to
lie about Cora and Mrs. Molloy, but Charlie denied the charge. He did
admit, though, that he was taught to always do what his father told him.[7]

Cora's lawyers also extracted a few other admissions from Charlie that
tended to help their client's case. Contradicting his testimony at earlier
proceedings, Charlie said he saw a pistol in his father's possession in St.
Louis. He said his mother and father had mentioned the prospect of having to walk several miles as a reason why he and Roy were left at Fay's
Boarding House on the night of September 30, 1885, the suggestion being
that Graham had not arranged for Cora Lee or anyone else to meet them
in Springfield. Although he'd previously said he first told Cora about his
mother coming to Springfield near the time of his father's forgeries, he
now said he couldn't be sure and that it might have been at the time his
mother's body was discovered. He also admitted that Abbie Breese, with
whom he had been staying, didn't like Cora and wanted to see her convicted. He did, too, he said, but only if Cora was guilty.[8]

Sam Clarke, who had published the *Morning and Day of Reform* for
Mrs. Molloy during much of the time it was located in Washington, reiterated his previous testimony that he'd heard Cora refer to Graham as
"her fellow" long before Sarah and George split up, but he admitted he
did not witness any improper relations between Graham and Cora during
the time he published the temperance newspaper. However, R. D. Williamson, who had worked in a room adjoining the editorial office, said he
once looked through a hole in the wall and saw Graham lying on top of
Cora Lee.[9]

Reverend Plumb's wife, Elizabeth, said she had once seen Graham
lying on the same bed with Emma Molloy and Cora Lee during the time
that the two women were staying at the Plumb residence prior to Cora
and Graham's marriage. Mrs. Molloy, who was sick in bed at the time,
explained that she'd let George lie down because he was so tired. Mrs.
Plumb said she'd allowed for the behavior because of Mrs. Molloy's
sickness, but that she didn't feel the same toward Cora and Mrs. Molloy
after that incident.[10]

As was the case during the first trial, much of the prosecution testimony was aimed at proving Cora Lee came to Springfield on the evening
of September 30, 1885. For instance, R. P. Norman testified, as he had

previously, that he saw a veiled woman on the Brookline-to-Springfield road on the evening in question driving a spring wagon drawn by a gray pony that belonged to the Molloy farm. The prosecution introduced a few new witnesses to support the testimony of previous witnesses like Norman. Notable among these was Lewis West, who backed up his wife's earlier statement that the couple had camped along the road on or about September 30, but, like his wife, he couldn't be sure of the date. West said that not only did a veiled woman drive a gray pony along the road to Springfield early on the evening in question but that two women and a man also passed in the opposite direction between 11:00 P.M. and midnight in a wagon pulled by the same pony. West said the reason he hadn't come back to Springfield sooner was that he wasn't aware he'd been indicted for putting a man's eye out. Another dubious witness was M. L. Zittle, who said he saw Mr. and Mrs. West camped along the Brookline road on September 30, and that he was sure of the date because he'd shot a man in Springfield two days earlier.[11]

David Anderson offered several tidbits of damaging testimony. He confirmed he'd sold Mrs. Molloy a gray pony matching the description of the one that had allegedly been seen on the Springfield road on the night of September 30. He said Cora appeared dangerous on the day he was there when she returned to the house with a pistol after Timothy Breese and Constable O'Neal had passed in a wagon. And he said that when Mrs. Molloy had called him to her house to discuss Graham's forgeries, she told him or led him to believe that Graham was in Kansas, but he later learned that Graham had been in the next room. However, Anderson also offered an explanation for Mrs. Molloy's agitation on the day she went to Brookline to retrieve Charlie's letter, saying that she was afraid Charlie had told his Indiana relatives about Graham's forgeries.[12]

The Dyer women largely confirmed the testimony they'd given at the first trial. They added that Cora had said she didn't think Graham shot Sarah because he'd left his pistol with her, and all the women agreed that Cora had said she got home between 8:00 and 9:00 P.M. on the night in question.[13]

After the prosecution rested, Cora's lawyers outlined their defense for the jury. They planned to show that Cora's reputation had always been impeccable prior to her association with George Graham, and they intended to refute the testimony of prosecution witnesses like R. D.

Williamson, who had attacked her character. The defense attorneys also sought to show that Cora's trip to Springfield had occurred on September 28 instead of September 30, and they wanted to establish their own theory of the crime—that George and Sarah Graham had taken a train from Springfield to Dorchester on the night of September 30 and that George had killed Sarah as they approached the Molloy farm on their cross-country walk from Dorchester.[14]

Civil engineer E. W. Newton was called to the stand as the first defense witness. He produced a plat of the Dorchester area showing a path leading from the train depot directly to the gate on the east side of the Molloy farm. He also displayed a plat of the farm showing that trees and brush surrounded the gate on all sides except the east and that the crime, therefore, could have been committed near the gate and yet be completely out of sight of the house three hundred yards away.[15]

Albert Crosby, a former associate of R. D. Williamson, came to the stand to refute Williamson's testimony that he'd seen Graham on top of Cora Lee in the Darby building at Washington, Kansas. Williamson had claimed Crosby witnessed the same behavior, but Crosby said he had not done so. He also testified that Williamson had a bad reputation in Washington and was not trustworthy. Philip Darby also said Williamson's reputation was bad, and he explained that the so-called peephole did not even go all the way through the wall.[16]

The question of when Mr. and Mrs. West had camped along the Brookline-to-Springfield road was, of course, a major point of contention, since they were two of the state's star witnesses. Cora's attorneys, as they had done at the first trial, called several people who had passed along the road on September 30, 1885, but who had not seen Mr. and Mrs. West. Several other defense witnesses testified that they'd seen the couple camped along the road two days earlier, on September 28, 1885.[17]

Several people who'd previously known Cora Lee testified to her good character, and her lawyers read deposition after deposition vouching for her virtue when she lived in Indiana and Illinois. Typical of the many glowing endorsements were those of George H. Service and Frances Covey. Service, a businessman who had known Cora as a girl and young woman in New Carlisle, said her reputation in her hometown was "without spot or blemish." Mrs. Covey, who lived near the Molloy family in Elgin, said Cora was industrious and her character was "the very best."[18]

Sketch of Cora Lee at the time of
her second trial (*Chicago Tribune,*
January 29, 1888)

Emma Molloy arrived in Springfield from Port Townsend, Washington, shortly after Cora's second trial began, but she did not appear as a witness. However, both Etta Molloy and Emma Lee did. They repeated essentially what they'd said at the coroner's inquest and again at Cora's first trial—that the three young women went to bed about 9:00 P.M. on the night of September 30, 1885, all sleeping in the same bed, and that Cora did not get up until George came home in the wee hours of October 1. The *Springfield Leader* remarked that Emma Lee was "by far the cleverest witness yet introduced by the defense," and that Emma Molloy's absence was "a subject of comment."[19]

Cora Lee also testified once again in her own defense. She confirmed the testimony of her sister and Etta about the night of September 30, said she knew nothing about the murder of Sarah Graham, and repudiated Charlie's testimony about her, Mrs. Molloy, and George Graham being in bed together.[20]

Closing arguments began on January 27 and continued the next day. In wrapping up the case for the defense on January 28, O. H. Travers argued that if Charlie Graham would perjure himself at the behest of his father, he might do the same at the instigation of his aunt. This brought Abbie

Breese to her feet. "Do you mean to say I would have Charlie lie?" she demanded. Travers responded, as Timothy Breese drew his wife back to her seat, that he was making no insinuations except what followed from the evidence. He assured a teary-eyed Mrs. Breese that he sympathized with her in the loss of her sister, but that his client was not guilty of Sarah's murder.[21]

Taking the floor after Travers, prosecutor Patterson spoke for several hours, closing the state's case at about 5:00 P.M. on January 28. Judge Bland, who had previously reprimanded the prosecution for spending too much time putting forth presumptions rather than submitting evidence, stressed in his instructions to the jury the one presumption that warranted consideration—the presumption of the defendant's innocence. He cautioned the jurymen that in order for them to find Cora Lee guilty, the evidence not only had to point to such a finding beyond a reasonable doubt but that it also had to exclude any other reasonable explanation.[22]

The jury retired to deliberate, and most people, including the judge, left the courtroom with the expectation that the jury would be out a long while. But they were back in seven minutes, and the judge and the spectators quickly filed back into the room. The jury had reached a unanimous verdict of not guilty on the first vote.[23]

When the judge read the verdict, Cora received it with outward calm at first, but then she beamed with joy and broke into tears as her friends rushed to congratulate her. Still sobbing with joy, she thanked the members of the jury and shook hands with them as they filed out of the courtroom. Mrs. Molloy also "gave evidence of great happiness over the result of the trial."[24]

Interviewed shortly after leaving the courtroom, Cora said it was only a knowledge of her innocence and the support of her friends that had "buoyed up her often-failing spirit" and made life bearable during her two-year ordeal. She said she had no bitter feelings toward anyone and that she thought prosecutor Patterson had only done "what he believed to be his duty." She thanked Judge Bland, the jury, her bondsmen, and all her friends. That evening "a general rejoicing" took place at the Springfield residence of Mrs. C. W. Eversol, where Cora and Mrs. Molloy had been staying.[25]

Although the speed with which the jury returned a verdict came as a surprise, the verdict itself did not. A couple of days before the trial ended, the *Springfield Daily Republican* opined that it was "almost beyond question" that the defense had raised "a very strong reasonable doubt" in the Cora Lee trial. Echoing the same sentiment after proceedings concluded, the *Herald* pointed to the "various theories" and the "contradictory evidence" in the case, while the *Leader* said "it was evident at the beginning of the trial that time had mellowed the feelings and recollections of the 'maddening crowd.'"[26]

Commenting on the outcome of Cora's trial the day after it ended, the *Daily Republican* attempted to put the case in perspective:

> The verdict will, of course, not be disturbed, and so far as human tribunals go, the dreadful details of Sarah Graham's murder must remain a mystery unrevealed and unattached to any skirts save those of her bigamous husband. Whether or not the general opinion of the thousands who have read the narrative of witnesses on this trial will be one of acquiescence in the justness of the verdict rendered, is another matter. With that event, the *Republican* has nothing to do and but little to say. It is easy, as well as natural, to speculate upon impressions, but not so wise nor easy to do so in a capital criminal case where circumstantial evidence is made to take the place of cold facts in forming human judgment. The jury has said without a dissenting voice, upon a single ballot, with no contentious deliberation, that Cora Lee is not guilty of being an accessory to the murder of Sarah Graham. Let this settle the case for the public mind. It is for such purposes that criminal laws are framed and that the right of trial by jury is so strongly fortified in civilized society.[27]

But, of course, the not-guilty verdict failed to completely "settle the case for the public mind" or to remove Cora from the deprecatory eye of gossipers. In early February, when she and her sister Emma stopped in Kansas City on their way to Nebraska, women in the ladies' waiting room at the train depot crowded around Cora and "stared persistently" when they realized who she was. A *Kansas City Star* reporter approached her and addressed her as Miss Lee, but she corrected him, saying her name was Mrs. Cora Graham, not Miss Cora Lee. Cora didn't know why people persisted in making that mistake. "I'm tired of being interviewed and stared at," she continued. "Any one would think I was a wild beast from the manner in which women look at me." She said she felt vindicated, however, by the recent verdict. She was only twenty-seven years old, and she thought life still had "something good in store" for her.[28]

24

Mrs. Molloy's Redemption

EVEN AFTER Cora Lee was found not guilty, some people still clamored to see the great evangelist Emma Molloy put on trial, but most observers expected her case to be nol-prossed (not further prosecuted), since the state's evidence against her was much the same as that which had been presented at Cora's trial. And the general forecast proved true. On March 3, 1888, in the Christian County Circuit Court at Ozark, the prosecution officially dropped the charges against Mrs. Molloy in both the accessory to bigamy case and the accessory to murder case.[1]

Mrs. Molloy had spent much of the past year crisscrossing the nation, collecting testaments to her character and statements swearing she was not where her accusers, including George Graham, had said she was on certain dates. She had amassed deposition after deposition to present at her trial, just as Cora had done. Many of the statements were from prominent people, like the assistant warden of the Indiana State Prison North. As one newspaperman observed, "Mrs. Molloy was amply prepared to meet any charges of immorality her accusers might have brought against her." But the documents proved unnecessary.[2]

Shortly after her case was nol-prossed, Mrs. Molloy, accompanied by her daughter, Etta, left the Springfield area, bound for Port Townsend, where she planned to live and to take charge of the Seamen's Bethel, a mission ministering to sailors. Commenting on her departure, the *Springfield Express* said she was leaving numerous friends in Springfield who had "stood by her all along and denounced [her] prosecution as a persecution."[3]

On her way to Washington Territory, Mrs. Molloy stopped in Kansas City to visit Fred Rexinger and his wife. Interviewed by the *Kansas City Times*, she said she intended to devote the rest of her life to religion and temperance, and she informed the reporter that Cora Lee was working as a nurse in an Omaha hospital. David Fisher, the man who'd testified that Mrs. Molloy had spent the night at an Independence hotel with George Graham and Cora Lee, had recently been arrested for a criminal assault on a married woman, and Mrs. Molloy remarked that he was "simply a representative of the class of witnesses who swore against her." Mrs. Molloy said that Fisher had never seen her before in his life until he came to Springfield, where she was pointed out to him so that he could identify her in court.[4]

She also mentioned Lewis West, "who had in a drunken fit gouged a man's eye out" and run away "to escape the penitentiary." Mrs. Molloy said he came back under a promise that if he swore against Cora Lee, he would not be prosecuted. Peter Hawkins, the black man who had worked on the Molloy farm, was another witness who, according to Mrs. Molloy, had sworn falsely against her and Cora. He had not appeared at Cora's second trial, Mrs. Molloy said, because he'd shot someone at a dance and was serving a long prison term.[5]

In reference to the Union Depot Hotel affair first alleged by editor Charles Barrett of the *Washington Post*, Mrs. Molloy said she had proved by the hotel proprietor and by depositions that Graham had stayed at a neighboring hotel, the Morgan House, by himself that night. "The whole truth of my case," she added, "is that Prosecutor Patterson persecuted, rather than prosecuted, me. . . . This man Patterson had piles of hotel registers in court to endeavor to prove that Cora and I had been with Graham at hotels throughout the country, but he did not dare to refer to them, as I had plenty of proof that I was far away in every instance."[6]

Mrs. Molloy's decision to reestablish herself in the Northwest was, of course, not universally applauded, especially at first. The *Portland Morning Oregonian*, for instance, thought Cora's recent trial had unmistakably shown Mrs. Molloy to be "a person of lewd habits."[7]

However, the famed revivalist found many friends in Port Townsend, and she was generally well received there. Taking up her work with the American Seamen's Friend Society, she preached, gave temperance speeches, and counseled sailors as resident chaplain at the Seamen's

Bethel. She also arranged entertainments and sometimes gave her own dramatic readings or played the guitar.[8]

She attended the Methodist Church in Port Townsend, sometimes preaching there when the minister was absent, and she became president of the local WCTU. Having found a home in Port Townsend, she built a house there in the fall of 1888 with the help of her friends. In late 1888, her daughter, Etta, married Decatur Blakeney and moved to Oregon, but mother and daughter continued to visit each other regularly.[9]

In early January 1889, Emma married Morris Barrett, an old friend and cousin of hers, and she was afterward known as Emma Molloy-Barrett. Morris Barrett moved to Port Townsend and worked as a printer on the *Port Townsend Leader,* and Emma later briefly edited a temperance column for the *Leader.*[10]

Emma not only helped bring temperance speakers to Port Townsend, but she also resumed her own traveling temperance and religious work. Nearly everywhere she went, her efforts were met with more enthusiasm than criticism as the scandal surrounding the Sarah Graham murder case gradually subsided. In early January 1889, just after her marriage to Morris Barrett, she held a series of revival meetings at the Methodist Episcopal Church in Salem, Oregon. Midway through the revival, the *Salem Statesman Journal* reported that Mrs. Molloy-Barrett preached "with great fervor and eloquence" and that the building had been "filled to overflowing" on the first two nights. A couple of weeks later, she preached at Harrisburg, Oregon, where she attracted the largest crowd in the town's history.[11]

Over the next several years, Emma settled into a pattern of spending the milder months in Port Townsend while traveling throughout the Northwest to evangelize during the remainder of the year. Although never ordained or officially appointed as an evangelist by the Methodist denomination, she preached mainly in Methodist churches.[12]

About 1893, Morris Barrett was paralyzed from a stroke. He and Emma took in a new foster daughter, Bessie Birekes, to help care for him and to do other household chores.[13]

After Morris Barrett died in January 1903, Emma continued her evangelistic work. In late 1906, she rented her home in Port Townsend and set out on an extended revival tour of Nevada and California. Emma was on a stagecoach ride in northern California in early May 1907 when the stage was disabled and she sat up all night in wet clothes. She arrived in Cedarville tired and ill, but after a very brief rest, she arose from her sick bed to give her scheduled sermon. Returning to bed, she went into a coma and died from pneumonia on May 14 at the age of sixty-seven.[14]

At her funeral, she was praised for her great religious and temperance work. She was buried at the Red Man Cemetery in Port Townsend beside Morris Barrett. In her will, she directed that all her papers be burned. This directive was apparently followed, as most of her correspondence and papers, including the autobiography she was working on, did not survive. Among the heirs to her money and personal belongings were her daughter, Etta Blakeney, and her foster daughter Cora Lee Juel.[15]

Cora Lee had married Ed Juel in Nebraska in 1889, about the same time Emma Molloy married Morris Barrett. Ed died in 1894, and at the time of the 1900 census, Cora was living with her mother in Nehama County, Nebraska. She later moved to Washington and then to Wyoming, where she lived with her sister, Ida. She returned to Washington and died there in 1943.[16]

Charlie Graham grew to manhood in Indiana, married a woman named Sarah, and had a large family, including a boy named Roy. Charlie lived most of his adult life southwest of Fort Wayne in Tipton County, where he was apparently a law-abiding citizen.[17]

Although the controversy surrounding the Sarah Graham murder diminished with the passage of time, the case was not altogether forgotten, especially in Springfield and Fort Wayne, and current events, such as the death of one of the players in the tragic drama, occasionally brought it back to the public consciousness. In 1891, when Marquis Gorham died in Fort Wayne, a brief story issued from that place recounting the "great sensation" his daughter's murder in Missouri had caused five years earlier. Similarly, when John A. Patterson died in Springfield near the beginning of 1923, the *Fort Wayne Sentinel* and other newspapers published a detailed summary of the most remarkable case of Patterson's career as a prosecutor. In 1930, the *Springfield Leader* printed a story titled "Old Timers Still Shudder at Memories of Graham Murder," in which J. G. Newbill, former editor of the *Springfield Express*, recalled the case in detail, especially the part he had played in the drama. Newbill remembered Sarah Graham's murder as the most "outstanding crime" in Springfield history. For many years, the case had been "on

Sarah Graham's headstone at Springfield's Maple Park Cemetery (Photo by the author)

everybody's tongue," he said, but it was now "all but forgotten" because "that was a long time ago—over 40 years."[18]

In 2004, Clifford Gorham, a collateral descendant of the Marquis Gorham family, was living in Springfield, Missouri, when he first learned of the murder of his distant relative there many years earlier. After researching the case, he decided to place a headstone on Sarah's grave, not just in tribute to her but also in homage to the citizens of Springfield who'd taken care of her body and shown kindness to her sister and other family members during their time of tribulation. The *Springfield News-Leader* carried a feature story about his plans, briefly recounting the murder case, and then on September 30, 2004, the 119th anniversary of Sarah's death, Gorham placed the headstone on her grave in the southwest quadrant of Maple Park Cemetery.[19]

25

Unanswered Questions

So, WHO was guilty of what? This is the question we are left with, even now, almost 135 years after Sarah Graham's nude and decomposing body was found at bottom of an abandoned well on the Molloy farm five miles southwest of Springfield.

Although the murder charge against George Graham was never adjudicated in a court of law, he undoubtedly killed his first wife. He denied the charge at first and even put forth a far-fetched notion that the body found on the farm was not Sarah's but instead had been planted there by Timothy Breese as a frame-up, but no one believed his incredible story. He later confessed to the murder, and he reiterated the confession on multiple occasions. Graham's implausible conspiracy theory was briefly revived near the beginning of 1887 when Mrs. Molloy traveled to the West Coast, reportedly in a desperate search for Sarah Graham. But the main reason for Mrs. Molloy's trip to Washington Territory was to conduct a series of revivals that had been arranged before her departure, and at Cora Lee's first trial a few months later, Mrs. Molloy said she did not believe Breese had planted evidence.

Even in the rowdy town of Springfield, Missouri, where Wild Bill Hickok had killed Dave Tutt in the first quick-draw gunfight of the Wild West era, plenty of people opposed mob violence. But nobody thought the vigilantes who strung George Graham up to an oak tree in the northwest part of town in the spring of 1886 got the wrong man.

Whether Cora Lee aided and abetted murder and whether Mrs. Molloy was an accessory after the fact are more debatable questions than whether Graham killed his wife. However, a dispassionate examination of the available evidence suggests that both women were not guilty of the charges that were brought against them.

Graham himself insisted that neither Cora Lee nor Emma Molloy knew anything about the murder. Although he was a chronic liar, the fact that he never wavered in his denial of the women's guilt lends at least some credence to the statement.

The main specification in the accessory to murder charge against Mrs. Molloy was that she had harbored and concealed Graham with the intention of helping him avoid arrest and prosecution for killing Sarah Graham. However, this allegation does not comport with what we know about Mrs. Molloy's actions in January 1886 because she was the one who convinced Graham to return to Springfield after he fled in the wake of his forgeries. If she had known that Sarah Graham was lying dead at the bottom of a well on her farm and she had been inclined to help George avoid prosecution, she no doubt would have counseled him to run for his life, not return to Springfield.

There seems to be little doubt that Mrs. Molloy did help conceal Graham after he came back to the farm in late January. When neighbor David Anderson came to her house to talk about the forgeries, Mrs. Molloy led him to believe that Graham had not yet returned from the Kansas City area when he, in fact, was in the next room, and later the same day, she told Constable O'Neal she planned to bring Graham back when he was, of course, already back. The deceit was likely at Graham's insistence because he was terrified of being arrested at this point. But even if Mrs. Molloy acted strictly on her own to shield Graham, one has to ask what she was shielding him from. According to Mrs. Molloy and Cora Lee's side of the story, Graham had convinced them that the Breese and Gorham families held a grudge against him and were trying to have him arrested on a trumped-up bigamy charge. So, even though Mrs. Molloy obviously protected Graham after his forgeries, it does not follow that she was hiding someone she knew to be a bigamist and a murderer. Instead, she might only have been shielding him from what she saw as a rush to judgment.

Mrs. Molloy's telling Charlie when he returned from Brookline on January 20, 1886, that he might have signed his father's life away was also cited, like her hiding Graham at her house, as evidence of her guilty knowledge of the bigamy and the murder. Specifically, Mrs. Molloy was reported to have said that Charlie might have signed something saying he had seen his father kill his mother. The *Fort Wayne Sentinel* was among editorial observers who thought this statement proved conclusively that Mrs. Molloy was guilty of being an accessory after the fact to murder. It is a leap of logic, however, to draw such a conclusion because Mrs. Molloy's statement does not necessarily mean she knew George Graham had killed his wife. It suggests only that she was aware such insinuations were going around.[1]

The letters exchanged among Graham, Mrs. Molloy, and Cora Lee during the days and weeks leading up to the discovery of Sarah's body, which Judge Baker cited in his defense of Mrs. Molloy, constitute strong evidence of the two women's innocence of conspiracy in the bigamy and the murder. Recall, for instance, that Graham was still denying the bigamy in one of his letters to Mrs. Molloy just a couple of weeks before Sarah's body was discovered.

Indeed, as Judge Baker argued, Graham's attempt to hide the bigamy from Cora Lee and Mrs. Molloy was the most probable motive for the murder of his first wife. And he continued trying to hide both crimes from them after the murder. He told Charlie and Roy, when he took them out to the farm, to say, if asked, that their mother had been left in St. Louis. He instructed Charlie not to tell Cora or Mrs. Molloy about the letter he and Charlie wrote to Sarah's relatives in the fall of 1885 to assure them that Sarah was all right and was staying in a Springfield boardinghouse. If Graham was concealing from Cora and her foster mother the fact that Sarah had come to Springfield, he must also have been hiding from them the fact that Sarah was dead.

Cora's burning of the letters on the evening after Sarah's body was found was cited as evidence that she was covering something up. Yes, she no doubt was destroying letters she didn't want the general public to read, but who hasn't written something in a letter, an email, or a text message that we wouldn't want the whole world to be privy to? Because the letters contained what Cora considered private exchanges does not mean they contained information that would incriminate her in bigamy or murder.

In its case against Cora, the prosecution also pointed to Charlie's testimony that he told Cora in mid-January about his mother coming to

Springfield and she reacted by warning him, for God's sake, not to tell anyone his mother came to Springfield. At Cora's second trial, Charlie admitted he couldn't be positive whether his conversation with Cora about his mother coming to Springfield occurred in January or in February at the time his mother's body was found. But even if Charlie's initial testimony was accurate, it does not show that Cora had guilty knowledge of Sarah's death. If we consider the defense side of the story that Cora did not realize her marriage to Graham was bigamous, then her statement to Charlie shows only that she was alarmed by the news and wanted to protect a husband whom she believed to be innocent of the allegations that were being whispered against him.

Another key piece of state evidence was the fact that Sarah's Bible and other belongings were openly displayed in the Molloy home. This supposedly constituted evidence that Cora and Mrs. Molloy knew Sarah was dead, but the circumstance was easily explained by defense testimony that Graham, when he brought the items to the Molloy farm, said Sarah had told him to take them because she didn't want anything he had given her.

The prosecution used John Brumley's testimony that Cora told him to cut wood on the side of the trail away from the well to suggest that Cora knew Sarah's body was in the well. Since Graham managed the farm, such an instruction more than likely came from him and Cora only relayed the message to Brumley. Even if Cora told Brumley on her own where to cut wood, she may have had other valid reasons besides concealing a body as to why she might have wanted him to cut wood south of the trail.

The state suggested that Graham was lying about the murder weapon to protect Cora, but that is not the only plausible reason he might have insisted that Sarah had been killed with a knife instead of by gunshot. Perhaps he was thinking ahead to the prospect of his own murder trial and was trying to mitigate his guilt. He probably reasoned that a murder committed with a knife during an argument would seem less calculated than a gunshot wound.

In the face of overwhelming evidence and expert testimony, Cora's lawyers accepted the idea that Sarah had been killed by gunshot. This admission allowed the prosecution to advance one of its strongest arguments against Cora because Graham had left his pistol with Cora when he departed for St. Louis to pick up his sons. She, therefore, must have participated in the murder of Sarah Graham on the night George returned, or at least she knew about it. This argument fell apart when Charlie admitted at Cora's second trial that he'd seen his father with a pistol in St. Louis.

At the very least, one can conclude that the prosecution fell far short of making its case against Cora Lee. All the state's evidence was purely circumstantial, and it was not even very convincing circumstantial evidence. All of it can just as readily be explained in a context that tends to exonerate the defendant rather than incriminate her.

The prosecution's case suffered from an ill-defined and inconsistent theory of the crime. Although the defense eventually yielded to the idea that Sarah Graham was shot, no bullet was ever recovered and no exit wound was found on the body. Where Sarah was killed was even less certain than how. Prosecutors at first explored the idea that George Graham and his first wife had taken a train out of Springfield and gotten off at either Nichols Junction or Dorchester, where Cora was waiting to pick them up. Sarah was then killed on the way back to the farm. At another time, they theorized that Sarah was taken all the way to the Molloy house and killed there rather than along the road. Even some of their own witnesses occasionally offered testimony favorable to the defense. For instance, although Peter Hawkins claimed Cora Lee had gone out in a spring wagon on the evening in question, he admitted she was home in bed long before he heard shots coming from the direction of the well.

In the end, the prosecutor, after hunting up sufficient witnesses, settled on the theory that Cora had driven to Springfield on the night of the murder to pick up George and Sarah. As defense attorney H. E. Howell suggested, the state's case boiled down to the fact that a veiled woman driving a pony that looked like the Molloy pony was seen on the road between Brookline and Springfield on approximately the night of September 30, 1885.

Although the jury in Cora's first trial, when prejudice against her was still running high, split eight to four in favor of conviction, a second jury seven months later, after passions had cooled somewhat, brought in a unanimous verdict of not guilty after only seven minutes of deliberation. There is no reason now, a century and a third later, to think they got it wrong.

If Etta Molloy and Emma Lee had been allowed to testify at Cora Lee and Emma Molloy's preliminary hearing, their testimony might have persuaded the justices hearing the case to hold Cora only as an accessory after the fact rather than as an active participant in the crime. Furthermore, if Cora and her foster mother had been accorded the presumption of innocence that defendants in criminal cases are supposedly guaranteed under the law, neither would have been indicted at all. But the justices yielded to the vengeful howls of an outraged public and a crusading editorial corps who were only too eager to prosecute the downfall of a successful female temperance revivalist, and Cora Lee and Emma Molloy were dragged through almost two years of judicial hell.

Although Graham's guilt in the murder of his first wife is virtually certain and Cora Lee and Emma Molloy's innocence of being accomplices in the crime is highly likely, the question of whether the charges of immorality brought by Graham and others against the two women is more vexing. Valid points exist on either side of the argument, but the weight of evidence again tilts in favor of the women. Without claiming sainthood for them or even complete chastity, we can suggest that they were probably not guilty of the most sensational charges leveled against them. Since George Graham was Cora Lee and Emma Molloy's primary accuser, perhaps the first question to consider is who one should believe in a "he said, she said" dispute or, in this case, a "he said, they said" dispute. Should we believe George Graham, a man who, even before he murdered his first wife, had been to state prison three times, had been charged with numerous other crimes that were not prosecuted, had been judged insane in a court of law, and was obviously an inveterate liar? As the *St. Louis Globe-Democrat* observed at the time Graham was lynched, he had established a reputation as a man who "never told the truth if he could in any way avoid it."[2]

Or should we believe Cora Lee, a young woman who had an impeccable reputation for honesty and virtue in her hometown and whose character had never been impugned until her name was dragged into the gutter by her own low-life husband? As Judge Baker pointed out, why would anyone believe a man who was willing to do such a dishonorable thing as to besmirch his own wife's reputation in public when the only immorality she'd supposedly committed was to have sex with him before they were married?[3]

And while Mrs. Molloy's morality had been called into question on at least a couple of occasions before she came to Springfield, her reputation for honesty and virtue was still much better than George Graham's. Her word, like Cora's, was certainly more credible than his.

Another point that strongly suggests Graham's salacious charges against Cora Lee and Emma Molloy were not true is the apparent closeness and lack of jealousy between the two women. Emma and Cora never behaved toward each other as anything other than loving mother and daughter during the time that Graham claimed to be bedding both of them, throughout the two-year ordeal that followed their arrest, nor even in later life after the murder case was settled. It seems hardly plausible that Cora Lee would have abided her lover and husband-to-be carrying on with her foster mother while simultaneously claiming to love only her. Regardless of whatever else might have been said against Cora Lee, she was not a whore.

Just as the letters cited by Judge Baker tended to show Mrs. Molloy and Cora Lee's lack of guilty knowledge of Sarah Graham's murder, some of them also evince a lack of intimacy between Graham and Mrs. Molloy. Graham's letters have the tone of a young man looking to a mother figure for help and advice, and hers have the tone of a woman anxious over the difficulties her wayward son has gotten into.[4]

Even Mrs. Molloy's "My Poor Boy" letter, which ironically was cited as proof of an intimate relationship between her and Graham, suggests that any such intimacy was more familial than passionate. One can infer from the letter that Graham might, indeed, have possessed knowledge that could have been embarrassing to Mrs. Molloy if it were to become public, but nothing in the letter leads to the conclusion that they were lovers.[5]

In answer to Graham's charges that he rendezvoused with Mrs. Molloy at hotels in various cities, Mrs. Molloy produced affidavits and other evidence showing that she could not have been where Graham said she was on several of the given dates. Perhaps even more convincingly, extant newspapers prove in at least a couple of instances that Mrs. Molloy was where she said she was, not where Graham said she was, on certain dates. For instance, contemporaneous newspaper accounts in the *Xenia Daily Gazette* and the *Wellington Enterprise* largely confirm Mrs. Molloy's version of events in her refutation of Graham's charge that he met her in a hotel at Crestline, Ohio, on October 8, 1883. As several observers pointed out at the time Mrs. Molloy issued her refutation, if Graham's charges were proven untrue in even one or two instances, none of them were probably true.[6]

According to Mrs. Molloy, Graham later admitted to editor J. G. Newbill the falsity of his scandalous charges. He supposedly said that while it could be shown that he stayed in the designated hotels with a woman on many of the dates in question, the woman in each case was neither Cora Lee nor Mrs. Molloy. Although Graham's retraction cannot be definitely confirmed, it makes sense because Newbill was also the person to whom Graham handed his ante-mortem letter to Cora, and in that letter he expressed deep regret for having written his sensational statement.

Many critics of Mrs. Molloy insinuated that Graham's charges of immorality against her must have been true since she waited until after he was dead to refute them. First of all, such a specious argument is unfair unless one assumes, as a few of Mrs. Molloy's most cynical detractors did, that she was actually in on the conspiracy to lynch George Graham. Otherwise, how was she to know that her statement of denial would come after his death? At any rate, it is not true that Mrs. Molloy waited until after Graham was dead to deny his charges. She denied them as soon as she learned of them, although she did not issue a formal, written statement refuting the charges until a couple of weeks after Graham was lynched. Her reason for not issuing such a statement as soon as she found out about Graham's charges, she said, was that she did not want to do anything that might instigate mob violence against him. This, of course, was not a groundless concern, but the other, perhaps more important, reason that Mrs. Molloy did not issue an immediate written statement is that she was taking time, based on legal advice, to gather evidence that would disprove Graham's charges rather than simply denying their truth.

Graham learned, shortly after his statement charging Emma Molloy and Cora Lee with immorality became public, that Mrs. Molloy had denied the charges and had suggested he only wanted to ruin her. He responded that if had really wanted to ruin her, he could have just as easily implicated her in Sarah's murder. This is perhaps the strongest argument against the virtue of Mrs. Molloy and Cora Lee. Why would Graham lie about adultery and not murder? There is no really good answer to this question. Perhaps he was bribed to make his sensational statement, as

Mrs. Molloy suggested, or frightened into it, as Judge Baker said. Or maybe, as the *Goshen Weekly News* suggested, Graham simply wanted to make the women look worse than they were in order to take some of the blame off himself. He was angry at the women for what he saw as their desertion, but perhaps not angry enough to directly implicate them in murder. However, considering George Graham's long history as a villain and a liar, maybe it's entirely pointless to speculate about the motivation behind anything such a man ever did or said.[7]

If George Graham was Cora Lee and Mrs. Molloy's primary accuser in charging them with immorality, his son Charlie was their secondary accuser. At his father's prompting, Charlie had lied to the members of the Molloy household throughout the fall and early winter of 1885–86 about the whereabouts of his mother, and he repeated the same lie on the witness stand when his father was charged with bigamy. It is not unreasonable to think he might also have been lying or at least exaggerating in his stories about seeing his father in bed with Mrs. Molloy and Cora Lee, a charge that both women vehemently denied.

But even if Charlie was telling the truth or exaggerating only slightly, it does not follow that his father and the two women were engaged in a ménage à trois. If Mrs. Molloy occasionally sat on Graham's lap (although she also denied this), it does not necessarily mean that she and Graham were lovers. Rather these acts might merely have been part of a pattern of familiarity that Mrs. Molloy exhibited toward other members of the family as well. Charlie's own testimony suggests that if indeed Mrs. Molloy engaged in such behavior, she scarcely tried to hide it. When the two families lived at Washington, for instance, the doors separating bedrooms were usually left open, and members of the household came and went frequently. The preponderance of evidence suggests that any affection between Mrs. Molloy and George Graham was more of the nature of a mother-son relationship than a romantic one.

The *Fort Wayne Daily News* and other critics claimed that, at the very least, Emma Molloy was guilty either of knowingly allowing Sarah and George to live in open adultery in her household in Washington or of allowing Cora to marry a man whom she knew was already married. But this ignores a third alternative—the one that Mrs. Molloy and Cora advanced—that they thought George and Sarah were legal husband and wife when they lived in Washington, but that they also believed George's later "confession" and forgave him when he said he and Sarah had not been married at the time.[8]

Judge Baker and other temperance friends of Mrs. Molloy suggested that the attempts to implicate her in the murder of Sarah Graham and the attacks on her character were the work of the liquor traffic. Brewers, distillers, saloon keepers, and common drunks alike saw the Sarah Graham murder case and the controversy surrounding it as an opportunity to hush a powerful voice against them. Some friends of Mrs. Molloy, like Reverend Munsell, added that she was also targeted because she was a woman. Mrs. Molloy herself made both points in her long refutation of Graham's charges against her. The public liked nothing better, she said, than to witness the downfall of a preacher or a woman, and she happened to be both.

This argument that the righteous indignation Mrs. Molloy encountered during the proceedings of the Sarah Graham murder case was stirred up by the liquor industry and by opponents of women's equality was true to a large extent. But at least some of the outrage did not stem specifically from the fact that Mrs. Molloy was a female temperance revivalist. She could just as well have been a male campaigning for the removal of swear words from one's everyday vocabulary. Those who set themselves up as arbiters of morality for others also set themselves up as inviting targets. So, Mrs. Molloy was attacked not just because she was a female evangelist and temperance lecturer but also, in a broader sense, because of what many observers saw as her self-righteous hypocrisy.[9]

However, it is true that, particularly during the Victorian Era, women were held to a higher moral standard than men, and even a woman's working outside the home was thought unseemly. Therefore, Mrs. Molloy's occupation and her sex definitely inflamed the storm of controversy she faced.

And the stain of scandal no doubt attached to Mrs. Molloy more readily and more permanently than it would have if she had been a man or a lowly washerwoman. She was tried and convicted in the court of public opinion before she was even arrested, and a "judicial mob," as she and Judge Baker characterized the officials overseeing her preliminary hearing, rushed to indict her. The highfalutin Mrs. Molloy was, as one of her Washington, Kansas, critics charged shortly after she was arrested, a base and brazen hypocrite, and for many people, nothing was going to change that view of her. Accordingly, neither Mrs. Molloy's statement denying Graham's charges of immorality nor Graham's ante-mortem letter to Cora expressing remorse that he'd made such outlandish charges was given the widespread publicity that Graham's original sensational statement was given. But even if Graham had issued a written formal retraction, many people would not have believed it anyway because they'd already made up their minds.

Emma Molloy was a controversial figure even within the temperance movement of the late nineteenth century. Despite her strict religious upbringing, her views on subjects like women's rights and prison reform were liberal to radical. She divorced twice and led an independent, unconventional life.

And she was not without her moral weaknesses. She was not above fudging the truth or deceiving people if it served her purposes. Thus she let David Anderson and others think George Graham was still in the Kansas City area when he was already home, and when Fannie Scott asked, near the time Graham and Cora Lee married, how long Graham had been widowed, Mrs. Molloy said three or four years. Although such a response might, given the circumstances, be understandable, it was still an untruth.

Mrs. Molloy was roundly criticized for suggesting, during the search for Sarah Graham, that she might be found in a St. Louis brothel. This possibility was first suggested by George Graham, and Mrs. Molloy merely passed it on to a group of men with whom she was meeting to discuss Sarah's probable whereabouts. However, Mrs. Molloy's overall low opinion of Sarah was seemingly unwarranted, and it serves as an example of her holier-than-thou attitude that many people found distasteful.

Perhaps Mrs. Molloy's most obvious shortcoming was her naive gullibility, at least where George Graham was concerned. She was a poor judge of character, and her misplaced faith in Graham, even after he'd repeatedly proved himself unworthy of such faith, ultimately led to her disgrace. As editor James Hagaman of the *Concordia Blade* said in July 1886, Mrs. Molloy could be faulted, if for nothing else, for giving Graham "a certificate of good character."[10]

But none of these failings, from her self-righteous martyrdom for the cause of temperance to her tendency to fudge the truth for expediency's sake, make her a murderer. They don't even make her an adulteress.

Epilogue

THE OLD J. B. Cooper farm on the western outskirts of Springfield, about three miles from the village of Brookline, is still mostly intact, looking much as it did 135 years ago when the Emma Molloy family moved in. The house and outbuildings have been redone, but the lay of the land is the same. The deep hollow in the northeast part of the property, where George Graham dumped the body of his wife, Sarah, in an old abandoned well in the fall of 1885, is still there. The paved road along the eastern edge of the property still steeply inclines just as it did when it was a dirt trail carrying the horses and buggies of investigators who arrived at the farm in February 1886 to search the premises for the missing woman. Less than a quarter mile to the east, Wilson Creek, which lent its name to the first major battle of the Civil War west of the Mississippi, still meanders through the countryside from north to south on its way to pass through the battlefield and empty into the James River.

But the rest of the area around the farm little resembles how it looked in the mid-1880s. Brookline, a once thriving railroad village, is now scarcely discernible as a distinct place—having been annexed into the neighboring town of Republic in 2005—and the sprawling growth of Springfield has transformed much of the immediate vicinity of the Cooper farm from sparsely populated countryside into suburban housing additions. Hundreds of people every day pass by the old farm place on West Farm Road 150 or hike along the Wilson's Creek Greenway Trail just to the east, and most, if not all, are unaware that the location was once the site of a shocking murder that made headlines across the United States.[1]

Notes

Prologue

1. In writing the prologue, I've relied largely on my overall knowledge and understanding of the Sarah Graham murder case, but I did consult several specific sources, especially Holcombe's Greene County history and the preliminary hearing testimony of Isaac Hise and A. J. McMurray in the G-M-L file.

1. The Agreeable, Intelligent, and Interesting Emma Molloy

1. Pickrell, *Emma Speaks Out,* 3–4; Anderson and Cooley, *South Bend,* 238–39.
2. Pickrell, *Emma Speaks Out,* 3–4; Anderson and Cooley, *South Bend,* 238–39; Hiatt, *The Ribbon Workers,* 285.
3. Pickrell, *Emma Speaks Out,* 5, 6, 138.
4. "Indiana Marriages, 1811–2007"; Pickrell, *Emma Speaks Out,* 8; "Emma Molloy: Interesting Letters Unearthed," *SDL,* Dec. 9, 1886.
5. Hiatt, *The Ribbon Workers,* 286–87; Pickrell, *Emma Speaks Out,* 8–9.
6. Pickrell, *Emma Speaks Out,* 10; Hiatt, *The Ribbon Workers,* 288–90; "Died," *Madison Wisconsin State Journal,* Oct. 24, 1863; "Died," *Madison Wisconsin State Journal,* Aug. 18, 1864.

7. "Guitar Instruction," *Madison Wisconsin State Journal,* May 12; "Guitar Instruction," *Madison Wisconsin State Journal,* June 20, 1865; Pickrell, *Emma Speaks Out,* 9, 11–12.

8. "Indiana Marriages, 1811–2007"; Pickrell, *Emma Speaks Out,* 12–14, 140.

9. "She Wields a Vigorous Pen," *Goshen (IN) Democrat,* June 17; "Neighborhood Items," *Goshen (IN) Democrat,* Dec. 2, 1868; Pickrell, *Emma Speaks Out,* 14.

10. "About Home," *Plymouth (IN) Weekly Republican,* Mar. 25, 1869; "She Wields a Vigorous Pen," *Goshen Democrat,* June 17, 1868; "Local Brevities," *Goshen (IN) Democrat,* Sept. 15, 1869.

11. Pickrell, *Emma Speaks Out,* 15–16; "Free Love," *South Bend National Union,* May 5, 1870, in Emma Barrett Molloy Collection.

12. Pickrell, *Emma Speaks Out,* 16.

13. "The Lecture," *Goshen (IN) Democrat,* Feb. 16, 1870; Pickrell, *Emma Speaks Out,* 16–17.

14. "City News," *Goshen (IN) Times,* Feb. 10, 1870.

15. "Local Department," *Plymouth Marshall County Republican,* Mar. 31, 1870; "Local Department," *Plymouth Marshall County Republican,* Apr. 7, 1870; Pickrell, *Emma Speaks Out,* 18.

16. "Among the pleasant acquaintances . . ." [first line; no title], *Kokomo (IN) Tribune,* May 23, 1871.

17. Pickrell, *Emma Speaks Out,* 19.

18. "Mrs. Molloy's Lecture," *Rochester (IN) Union Spy,* Mar. 10, 1871.

19. "City and County," *Goshen (IN) Times,* Jan. 18, 1872; "City and Country," *Goshen (IN) Democrat,* July 3, 1872; "An Address to the Women of America," *Elkhart (IN) Observer,* Aug. 21, 1872.

20. Pickrell, *Emma Speaks Out,* 21; "Cora Lee's Trial," *SE,* June 17, 1887.

21. Pickrell, *Emma Speaks Out,* 22–23.

22. Pickrell, *Emma Speaks Out,* 23; "Personals," *Goshen (IN) Democrat,* June 17, 1874.

23. Fletcher, *Gender,* 79; *History of St. Joseph County,* 584; Pickrell, *Emma Speaks Out,* 25; Hiatt, *The Ribbon Workers,* 292–93.

24. Hiatt, *The Ribbon Workers,* 5–10. See Fletcher, *Gender,* for a discussion of gender bias and the role of women in the temperance movement.

25. "Mrs. Molloy's Temperance Lecture," *Plymouth Marshall County Republican,* Apr. 9, 1874; "Another Falsehood Pinned," *Elkhart Observer,* Aug. 19, 1874; "Riot at Westville," *Elkhart Observer,* Sept. 30, 1874.

26. Pickrell, *Emma Speaks Out,* 27, 29; "Abstinence Apostles," *Indianapolis Journal,* June 11, 1875; Fletcher, *Gender,* 83.

27. Pickrell, *Emma Speaks Out,* 29–30.

28. "Emma Molloy: Interesting Letters Unearthed," *SDL,* Dec. 9, 1886.

29. Fahey, *Temperance and Racism,* 102; "City and Country," *Goshen (IN) Democrat,* Nov. 24, 1875.

30. "Mrs. Molloy," *Goshen (IN) Times,* June 22, 1876; Pickrell, *Emma Speaks Out,* 31.

31. Pickrell, *Emma Speaks Out,* 31–32.

32. "Hon. J. Talbott," *Plymouth Marshall County Republican,* Sept. 28, 1876.

33. "A Female Teetotaller Stirs a Tempest in a Teapot," *Nashville Tennessean*, June 3, 1877; "Mrs. Emma Molloy, our somewhat . . ." [first line; no title], *Goshen (IN) Times*, June 13, 1877; "Illness of Mrs. Molloy," *Montpelier (VT) Green-Mountain Freeman*, June 13, 1877.

34. Pickrell, *Emma Speaks Out*, 33; Hiatt, *The Ribbon Workers*, 304; "Complimentary Farewell to the Indiana Temperance Missionary, Mrs. Emma Molloy," *Boston Post*, Sept. 5, 1878; "Neighboring Notes," *Plymouth Marshall County Republican*, Aug. 29, 1878; "Mrs. Emma Molloy appears to be meeting . . ." [first line; no title], *Burlington (VT) Free Press*, Nov. 2, 1878.

35. Pickrell, *Emma Speaks Out*, 36–38.

36. Coker, *Liquor*, 202; Pickrell, *Emma Speaks Out*, 38; "Ex-Convicts' Aid Society," *Indianapolis News*, Feb. 13, 1880.

37. Pickrell, *Emma Speaks Out*, 38.

2. George Graham, the Irrepressible

1. "Ohio Marriages, 1800–1958;" "Graham's Glories," *FWDG*, Apr. 12, 1873; "Local News," *FWS*, July 14, 1884; United States Census, 1860.

2. "Graham's Glories," *FWDG*, Apr. 12, 1873.

3. "Graham's Glories."

4. "Graham's Glories."

5. "Graham's Glories."

6. "Graham's Glories."

7. "Graham's Glories."

8. "Graham's Glories"; Convict Register, Illinois State Penitentiary. According to what Graham later told the *Daily Gazette*, Gov. James M. Palmer visited the penitentiary shortly after Graham was admitted, George "succeeded in making him believe he was a persecuted and to-be-pitied individual," and Palmer soon granted the young man an unconditional pardon. Illinois prison records do not bear this out.

9. "Graham's Glories"; United States Census, 1860 and 1870.

10. "Indiana Marriages, 1811–2007."

11. "Graham's Glories."

12. "Graham's Glories"; "Graham's Gall," *Fort Wayne Weekly Sentinel*, Nov. 26, 1879.

13. "Graham's Glories."

14. Thornbrough, *Indiana in the Civil War Era*, 263; "Graham's Glories"; "Graham's Gall," *Fort Wayne Weekly Sentinel*, Nov. 26, 1879.

15. "Graham's Glories."

16. "In the Courts," *FWS*, Sept. 5, 1872; United States Census, 1870.

17. "The Law Courts," *FWS*, Apr. 11, 1873; "Graham's Glories"; "Graham's Gall."

18. "Graham's Glories."

19. "Graham's Glories."

20. "Graham's Glories."

21. "George Graham Reforms," *FWDG*, Apr. 22, 1873.

22. "George Graham Reforms."

23. "Graham's Reformation," *FWDG*, Apr. 28, 1873; George Graham pardon papers.

24. "The Law Courts," *FWDG*, May 9, 1873; George Graham pardon papers.

25. "City Personals" and "Legal Lessons," *FWS*, May 30, 1873; Descriptive List of Convicts, Indiana State Prison North.

26. "Personal Paragraphs," *FWDG*, Aug. 28, 1873; "Divorce Doings," *FWDG*, Sept. 18, 1873.

27. "Among the Convicts," *Fort Wayne Journal-Gazette*, Oct. 26, 1873.

28. George Graham pardon papers.

29. "Prison Pencilings," *FWS*, Mar. 1, 1875.

30. George Graham pardon papers.

31. "City in General," *FWDG*, Aug. 8, 1877; "A Nest Full of Choice Local Matter," *FWDN*, Dec. 27, 1877; "Graham's Gall," *Fort Wayne Weekly Sentinel*, Nov. 26, 1879; George Graham pardon papers.

32. George Graham pardon papers.

33. "The City Localisms," *FWS*, Jan. 4, 1878; "I. O. G. T.," *FWDN*, Apr. 30, 1878; "Indiana Marriages, 1811–2007"; G-M-L, Preliminary Examination, 58–59.

34. "The City," *FWS*, June 18, 1878; "Breese vs. Breese," *FWS*, Nov. 16, 1878.

35. "Happenings," *FWDN*, June 12, 1879; "City in General," *FWDN*, July 18, 1879; "Graham Gobbled," *FWDG*, Oct. 13, 1879; "Graham's Gall," *FWS*, Nov. 20, 1879.

36. "Happenings," *FWS*, Nov. 13, 1879; "Graham's Gall," *FWS*, Nov. 20, 1879; "Happenings," *FWS*, Feb. 17, 1880.

37. "Graham's Goose," *FWDN*, Dec. 1, 1879; "The City," *FWDN*, Dec. 2, 1879; "Local News," *FWDN*, Dec. 24, 1879; "Graham's Punishment," *FWDG*, Dec. 20, 1879.

38. "Emma's Effusion," *FWDN*, Mar. 3, 1886; "Cora's Cause," *SDL*, June 14, 1887.

3. Allowing an Ex-Convict to Manage Her Affairs

1. Pickrell, *Emma Speaks Out*, 38–39; "New Albany," *Cincinnati Enquirer*, Feb. 19, 1880.

2. Pickrell, *Emma Speaks Out*, 39; "Temperance Talk," *Topeka State Journal*, Oct. 28, 1880; "Local Summary," *Boston Post*, Oct. 29, 1880.

3. "Religious Services," *LT*, Apr. 5, 1881; "The City," *Topeka State Journal*, Feb. 12, 1881; "Kansas Legislature," *Topeka State Journal*, Feb. 13, 1881; Pickrell, *Emma Speaks Out*, 39.

4. "Prohibitionists in Council," *Buffalo (NY) Commercial*, Oct. 20, 1881; "Temperance," *Cleveland (TN) Weekly Herald*, Dec. 9, 1881; Coker, *Liquor*, 100.

5. "Emma's Effusion," *FWDN*, Mar. 3, 1886; "Quiet Yesterday," *SDH*, Mar. 6, 1886; "City in Brief," *FWS*, Nov. 12, 1881.

6. "Quiet Yesterday," *SDH*, Mar. 6, 1886; "The Railways," *FWDG*, Mar. 5, 1882.

7. Pickrell, *Emma Speaks Out*, 41.

8. Swanson, "144 Years of Marriage and Divorce"; Goodheart, "Divorce."

9. "Mr. and Mrs. Ed Molloy Divorced," *Goshen Democrat*, May 3, 1882; "Mrs. Emma Molloy, the well-known . . ." [first line; no title], *Columbus (IN) Repub-*

lic, May 12, 1882; "Local Lines," *FWS*, May 11, 1882; "Miss Emma Molloy, well-known in Kansas . . ." [first line; no title], *Junction City (KS) Weekly Union*, June 3, 1882.

10. United States Census, 1870; *The Graham Tragedy*, 110; "The Case Closes," *SDL*, June 21, 1887.

11. "Quiet Yesterday"; G-M-L file, Preliminary Examination, 59–61; "Emma's Effusion"; "Cora Lee's Trial," *SE*, June 17, 1887; Pickrell, *Emma Speaks Out*, 148.

12. "Emma's Escapade," *FWDG*, June 29, 1882.

13. "While the People of Kansas," *Emporia (KS) Daily News*, June 28, 1882; "A Dispatch from Wabash," *Chicago Inter Ocean*, June 27, 1882.

14. "Iowa," *Leavenworth Weekly Times*, July 13, 1882; "Quiet Yesterday"; "Cora Lee's Trial," *SE*, June 17, 1887; Illinois Statewide Marriage Index.

15. "Mrs. Molloy's Address," *Wellington (OH) Enterprise*, Sept. 12, 1883; "Xenia Local News," *Xenia (OH) Daily Gazette*, Sept. 24, 1883; Whitaker, "The Ohio WCTU," 98.

16. "Local News," *Muskogee Indian Journal*, Dec. 20, 1883; "Return of Mrs. Molloy," *Tahlequah Cherokee Advocate*, Jan. 11, 1884; Pickrell, *Emma Speaks Out*, 43–44; "The City," *FWS*, Jan. 15, 1884.

17. "Local Happenings," *Goshen Daily News*, Jan. 21, 1884; "Mrs. Molloy," *Madison (IN) Herald*, Mar. 12, 1884.

18. "During the Revival," *Oskaloosa (KS) Independent*, Apr. 19, 1884; "Subscriptions Are Being Taken," *Washington (KS) Republican*, Apr. 4, 1884.

19. "Local Department," *Goshen Times*, Apr. 10, 1884; "Letter from Rev. M. L. Butler," *Muskogee Our Brother in Red*, Feb. 1, 1884; "Local News," *Tahlequah Cherokee Advocate*, May 2, 1884; "Mrs. Emily Molloy," *Tahlequah Cherokee Advocate*, May 9, 1884; "Tahlequah," *Tahlequah Cherokee Advocate*, May 30, 1884; "Mrs. Emily Molloy Reached Here," *Chetopa (KS) Advance*, May 29, 1884.

20. "Quiet Yesterday"; "Emma's Effusion"; "Morning and Day of Reform," *Washington (KS) Register*, Dec. 6, 1884.

21. "Quiet Yesterday"; "Very Interesting!," *SDH*, Mar. 17, 1886; "Emma's Effusion"; "Morning and Day of Reform," *Washington County Register*, Dec. 6, 1884; "Emma Molloy," *SDL*, June 15, 1887.

22. "Mrs. Emma Molloy," *Chetopa Advance*, June 5, 1884; "Quiet Yesterday"; "Kansas Women," *Manhattan (KS) Mercury*, Oct. 8, 1884.

23. "City News," *FWDG*, July 14, 1884; "In Memoriam," *FWDG*, Aug. 25, 1884.

24. "Quiet Yesterday"; "Although We Have Noted," *Independence (KS) Weekly Star and Kansan*, July 4, 1884.

25. "Sam Clarke Has Sold," *Washington County Register*, June 7, 1884.

26. "The Prohibition Convention," *Topeka Daily Commonwealth*, Sept. 3, 1884.

27. Willard, *Let Something Good Be Said*, xix; "Quiet Yesterday"; "The Press Formerly Used," *Coffeyville (KS) Weekly Journal*, Jan. 10, 1885; "Boy-cotting Mrs. Emma Molloy," *Garnett (KS) Journal*, Jan. 17, 1885; G-M-L, Preliminary Examination, 126.

28. "At Tuesday Night's 'Revival Meeting,'" *Concordia (KS) Blade,* Feb. 13, 1885; "Knight Errentry," *Concordia (KS) Blade,* Feb. 27, 1885; "The Evening Meeting," *Concordia (KS) Blade,* Mar. 20, 1885.

29. "We Received a Pleasant Call," *Concordia Daily Times,* Jan. 17, 1885; "If Rev. Mrs. Molloy Does Not Want," *Concordia Blade,* Feb. 20, 1885.

4. Marriage at Highland Cottage

1. "City Items," *FWDG,* Apr. 6, 1885; "Quiet Yesterday," *SDH,* Mar. 6, 1886; "Mrs. Emma Molloy Was the Guest," *Atchison Daily Globe,* Mar. 28, 1885.

2. "Charley Barrett of the Post," *Washington Republican,* May 8, 1885; "An Evil Easily Cured," *Wichita Beacon,* May 15, 1885; "Whoa Emma!," *Concordia Blade,* June 5, 1885; "Mrs. Molloy's Statement," *SE,* May 14, 1886.

3. "Mrs. Molloy's Statement," *SE,* May 14, 1886.

4. Wood, *Wicked Springfield,* 11–57, for a background on Springfield from its founding to Mrs. Molloy's arrival.

5. "First Congregational Church"; "Our Neighbors," *SLPD,* May 6, 1885; "Our Neighbors," *SLPD,* May 21, 1885; "Our Neighbors," *SLPD,* May 27, 1885; "Our Neighbors," *SLPD,* June 12, 1885; "Mrs. Emma Molloy, the Noted Evangelist," *Washington Republican,* June 5, 1885, quoting the *SDH.* Springfield and North Springfield were separate towns from North Springfield's formation in 1870 until 1887, when they merged as Springfield.

6. "Rev. J. C. Plumb," *SDH,* Feb. 28, 1886; "Quiet Yesterday"; "Emma's Effusion."

7. *Pictorial and Genealogical Record of Greene County, Missouri,* 196–98.

8. "Emma's Effusion."

9. "Emma's Effusion"; "Quiet Yesterday."

10. "The Reasons," *SDH,* Apr. 11, 1886; "Emma's Effusion."

11. "Quiet Yesterday"; "Horrible!," *SE,* Mar. 5, 1886.

12. "Emma's Effusion."

5. The Disappearance of Sarah Graham

1. "Horrible!"; "Cora Lee's Trial," *SE,* June 17, 1887; "Emma's Effusion."

2. "Emma's Effusion"; "Horrible!"

3. "Emma's Effusion"; "The Reasons"; "The Third Day," *SDH,* Mar. 16, 1886; "Personal," *LT,* Sept. 15, 1885.

4. "Horrible!"; "The Reasons," *SDH,* Apr. 11, 1886.

5. "Saturday's Yield to the Grist," *SDH,* Feb. 28, 1886; "Horrible!"

6. "Horrible!"; "Very Interesting!" *SDH,* Mar. 17, 1886; "The Seventh Day," *SDH,* Mar. 20, 1886.

7. "Horrible!"; "Saturday's Yield to the Grist."

8. G-M-L, Preliminary Examination, 281–94.

9. "Horrible!"; "The Seventh Day."

10. "Horrible!"; "The Seventh Day."

11. "The Sixth Day," *SDH,* Mar. 19, 1886.

6. George Graham the Forger

1. "The Reasons."
2. "Murder Will Out!," *SDH*, Feb. 27, 1886; "The Ninth Day," *SDH*, Mar. 23, 1886.
3. "Murder Will Out!"; "The Ninth Day."
4. "The Reasons."
5. "Saturday's Yield to the Grist," *SDH*, Feb. 28, 1886; "The Seventh Day," *SDH*, Mar. 20, 1886.
6. "Murder Will Out!"; G-M-L, Preliminary Examination, 297; "The Talk Commenced," *LT*, Mar. 30, 1886.
7. "Murder Will Out!"
8. "Murder Will Out!"; Preliminary Examination, 297–98.
9. "The Ninth Day."
10. "The Reasons."
11. "The Reasons."
12. "The Ninth Day"; "Horrible!"; "In Morris County," *Council Grove Republican*, Jan. 22, 1886.
13. "The Ninth Day."
14. "Murder Will Out!"; "The Ninth Day."
15. "A Check Forger," *SDH*, Jan. 16, 1886; "Graham Again in Trouble," *SDH*, Jan. 30, 1886.
16. "The Reasons."
17. "The Reasons."
18. "Emma's Effusion."
19. "George Graham, Further Particulars," *SDH*, Jan. 31, 1886.
20. "Emma's Effusion."
21. "The Ninth Day."
22. "Emma's Effusion."
23. "Emma's Effusion"; "The Reasons"; *The Graham Tragedy*, 34.
24. *The Graham Tragedy*, 6.

7. George Graham the Bigamist

1. "Very Interesting!"
2. "Heavily Veiled," *SDH*, Mar. 27, 1886.
3. "George Graham, Further Particulars."
4. "Emma's Effusion"; *The Graham Tragedy*, 34.
5. "Heavily Veiled"; Christian County Circuit Court Case Files, Harwood deposition.
6. "Heavily Veiled."
7. "Heavily Veiled."
8. "Emma's Effusion"; "Saturday's Yield to the Grist."
9. "Emma's Effusion"; "The Graham Murder," *SE*, Mar. 26, 1886.
10. "The Graham Murder."
11. "Emma's Effusion"; "Heavily Veiled."

12. "Heavily Veiled."
13. "The Second Day," *SDH*, Mar. 14, 1886; "The Sixth Day," *SDH*, Mar. 19, 1886; G-M-L, Preliminary Examination, 157.
14. "The Second Day."
15. "The Second Day."
16. "The Second Day."
17. "The Fifth Day," *SDH*, Mar. 18, 1886; "The Sixth Day"; G-M-L, Preliminary Examination, 157.
18. "Cora Lee's Trial."
19. "Very Interesting!"; "The Sixth Day."
20. "Murder Will Out!"; "The Sixth Day"; "The Ninth Day," *SDH*, Mar. 23, 1886.
21. "George Graham," *FWDN*, Jan. 22, 1886; "Very Interesting!"
22. "Murder Will Out!"; "The Ninth Day."
23. "Murder Will Out!"; "The Ninth Day."
24. "The Graham Murder."
25. *The Graham Tragedy*, 7.
26. "George Graham," *FWDN*, Jan. 21, 1886. Graham had indeed served three prison terms, as the *Daily News* said, but only two of them were in the Indiana State Prison North.
27. "George Graham," *FWDN*, January 21, 1886.
28. "George Graham," FWDN, Jan. 21, 1886.
29. "George Graham," FWDN, Jan. 22, 1886.
30. "George Graham," FWDN, Jan. 22, 1886.
31. "George Graham," FWDN, Jan. 22, 1886; "After Graham," *FWDN*, Jan. 27, 1886.
32. "The Reasons."
33. "Graham Again in Trouble," *SDH*, Jan. 30, 1886; "Charged with Bigamy," *SE*, Feb. 5, 1886; "After Graham"; G-M-L, arrest warrant of George E. Graham for bigamy.

8. The Search for Sarah Graham

1. "Charged with Bigamy"; "Graham's Grief," *SDH*, Feb. 5, 1886.
2. "George Graham, Further Particulars," *SDH*, Jan. 31, 1886; G-M-L, Charlie Graham subpoena.
3. "Whoa, Emma," *FWDN*, Jan. 30, 1886.
4. *The Graham Tragedy*, 13.
5. *The Graham Tragedy*, 13; G-M-L, Charlie Graham subpoena and officer's return.
6. "Graham's Gush," *FWDN*, Feb. 8, 1886.
7. "Graham's Gush"; George Graham pardon papers. Graham's claim that Governor Williams pardoned him in 1877 is misleading at best. Actually, the governor refused to pardon him in 1877 but did remit the rest of his sentence, a fine and disenfranchisement, in 1878 after he'd already served his prison term.
8. "Graham's Gush."
9. "Graham's Gush."
10. "Graham's Gush."

11. "This Settles It," *FWDN*, Feb. 9, 1886.
12. "Mrs. Molloy," *FWDN*, Feb. 10, 1886.
13. "Mrs. Molloy."
14. "Mrs. Molloy."
15. "Mrs. Molloy."
16. "Emma Molloy," *FWDN*, Feb. 15, 1886, quoting the *Wabash Courier.*
17. "Arrested for Bigamy," *Concordia Blade*, Feb. 5, 1886.
18. "Graham's Grief"; "Graham's Gush."
19. "Graham's Gush."
20. "Graham's Gush."
21. "Graham Jailed," *SDH*, Feb. 6, 1886.
22. "The Reasons."
23. "The Case Opened," *SDH*, Mar. 13, 1886; "The Second Day," *SDH*, Mar. 14, 1886; "The Reasons."
24. "The Case Opened"; "The Second Day"; "The Reasons."
25. "The Case Opened"; "The Second Day"; "The Reasons."
26. "The Case Opened"; "The Second Day"; "The Reasons."
27. "The Reasons."
28. "The Second Day"; "The Fifth Day"; *SDH*, Mar. 18, 1886; "The Sixth Day." It is not certain that Breese's passing the Molloy farm in the wagon occurred the same day as his earlier visit to the home with Abbie, but if not, it happened very shortly thereafter, probably the next day.
29. "The Second Day."
30. "The Reasons."
31. "The Detectives' Theory," *SDH*, Feb. 27, 1886, quoting the *St. Louis Globe-Democrat*, Feb. 26, 1886.
32. "Breese Back," *FWDN*, Feb. 11, 1886; "A Horrible Story!," *SDH*, Feb. 26, 1886; "Murder Will Out!"; "Very Interesting!"
33. "The Reasons."
34. "Murder Will Out!"
35. "Murder Will Out!"
36. "The Reasons."
37. "The Reasons."
38. "Ah, There," *FWDN*, Feb. 15, 1886.
39. "The Reasons."

9. Mrs. Molloy as "An Object of Suspicion"

1. *The Graham Tragedy*, 13–14.
2. "The City," *FWS*, Feb. 17, 1886; "Emma's Effusion."
3. "Emma's Effusion."
4. "Emma's Effusion."
5. "Emma's Effusion."
6. "Emma's Effusion."
7. *The Graham Tragedy*, 18.

8. "The Reasons."
9. "The Reasons."
10. "The Reasons."
11. "The Reasons."
12. "The Reasons."

10. A Ghastly Discovery

1. "The Case Opened," *SDH,* Mar. 13, 1886.
2. "A Horrible Story!"
3. "A Horrible Story!"; "The Second Day."
4. "A Horrible Story!"
5. "A Horrible Story!"
6. "A Horrible Story!"
7. "A Horrible Story!"
8. "Horrible," *FWDN,* Feb. 26, 1886; "A Horrible Story!"; "Hemp!," *FWS,* Feb. 27, 1886.
9. "A Horrible Story!"
10. "Murder Will Out!"
11. "Murder Will Out!"
12. "Murder Will Out!"
13. "Murder Will Out!"
14. "Murder Will Out!"
15. "Horrible!"
16. "'I Did It,'" *FWDN,* Mar. 1, 1886; "Saturday's Yield to the Grist"; "The Graham Case," *Chicago Tribune,* Feb. 27, 1886.
17. "Saturday's Yield to the Grist."
18. "Saturday's Yield to the Grist."
19. "Saturday's Yield to the Grist."
20. "Saturday's Yield to the Grist."
21. "Saturday's Yield to the Grist."
22. "Saturday's Yield to the Grist."
23. "Saturday's Yield to the Grist."
24. "Saturday's Yield to the Grist."
25. "Saturday's Yield to the Grist."
26. "Saturday's Yield to the Grist."
27. "Saturday's Yield to the Grist"; "Graham Will Be Hung," *FWDG,* Feb. 28, 1886.
28. "Saturday's Yield to the Grist"; *The Graham Tragedy,* 28; G-M-L, arrest warrants.

11. Mrs. Molloy under Arrest

1. "Horrible!"
2. *The Graham Tragedy,* 28.
3. *The Graham Tragedy,* 28–29; "Horrible!"; "Graham Confesses," *Chicago Tribune,* Mar. 2, 1886.
4. *The Graham Tragedy,* 28–29; "Horrible!"

5. *The Graham Tragedy*, 29–30.
6. *The Graham Tragedy*, 30.
7. *The Graham Tragedy*, 30.
8. "Horrible!"; *The Graham Tragedy*, 29.
9. *The Graham Tragedy*, 34; "The Graham Murder," *Alton (IL) Evening Telegraph*, Mar. 1, 1886.
10. "Horrible!"; *The Graham Tragedy*, 29.
11. "Horrible!"

12. George Graham the Murderer

1. "Horrible!"; *The Graham Tragedy*, 31.
2. "Horrible!"
3. "Horrible!"
4. "Horrible!"
5. "Horrible!"
6. "Horrible!"
7. "Horrible!"; "The Second Day."
8. "Horrible!"
9. "Who Fired the Shot?," *LT*, Mar. 17, 1886; "Drawing to a Close," *SDH*, Mar. 30, 1886.
10. "Horrible!"
11. "Horrible!"
12. "Horrible!"
13. "Horrible!"; "Graham," *FWS*, Mar. 1, 1886.

13. Mrs. Molloy behind Bars

1. *The Graham Tragedy*, 35.
2. "Horrible!"
3. "Horrible Discovery," *Kinsley (KS) Mercury*, Mar. 6, 1886, quoting the *Kansas City Times*.
4. "Horrible!"
5. "Horrible!"
6. "Horrible!"; "Graham Confesses."
7. *The Graham Tragedy*, 36; Linden, "Lynchings by State and Race"; Holcombe, *History of Greene County, Missouri*, 535–36; Hernando, *Faces Like Devils*, 77–78.
8. "Horrible!"; Bunting, *Ulysses S. Grant*, 136–38.
9. *The Graham Tragedy*, 46
10. *The Graham Tragedy*, 34.
11. "Horrible!"; *The Graham Tragedy*, 37.
12. "Quiet Yesterday," *SDH*, Mar. 6, 1886.
13. "Her 'Poor Boy!,'" *FWDN*, Mar. 4, 1886.
14. "Horrible!"
15. "Horrible!"

14. Taking Sides

1. "Tragic!," *FWS*, Mar. 2, 1886.
2. "Cora Lee," *FWS*, Mar. 1, 1886; "Mrs. Emma Molloy," *FWS*, Mar. 6, 1886, quoting the *Wabash Courier;* "Murdered in Bed," *FWDG*, Mar. 6, 1886; "The Molloy Gang Again," *Washington (KS) Post*, Feb. 5, 1886; "A Revised Edition of 'The Morning and Day of Reform,'" *Washington (KS) Post*, Mar. 5, 1886; "Mrs. Molloy," *Salina (KS) Saline County Journal*, Mar. 11, 1886, quoting the *Atchison Champion;* "Another Good (?) Woman Gone Wrong," *St. Joseph Gazette-Herald*, Mar. 4, 1886, quoting *LT.*
3. *The Graham Tragedy*, 41.
4. *The Graham Tragedy*, 42; "The Celebrated Case," *SDH*, Mar. 7, 1886; "Two Letters," *SDH*, Mar. 12, 1886.
5. "Two Letters"; "That Letter," *Washington (KS) Post*, Mar. 26, 1886.
6. "Quiet Yesterday."
7. *The Graham Tragedy*, 42.
8. "Two Letters."
9. "The Celebrated Case," *SDH*, Mar. 7, 1886; "Mrs. Molloy," *FWDN*, Mar. 9, 1886.
10. "The Celebrated Case," *SDH*, Mar. 9, 1886.
11. "A Card from Mrs. Molloy," *Council Grove (KS) Republican*, Mar. 12, 1886.
12. "A Card from Mrs. Molloy."
13. "The Celebrated Case," *SDH*, Mar. 7, 1886.
14. "The Celebrated Case."

15. The Preliminary Hearing, Part One

1. "The Case Opened," *SDH*, Mar. 13, 1886; "Exposing Infamy," *SE*, Mar. 19, 1886; "The Graham Murder," *LT*, Mar. 12, 1886.
2. "The Case Opened"; "Exposing Infamy"; "The Graham Murder."
3. "The Case Opened"; "Exposing Infamy"; "The Graham Tragedy," *SLPD*, Mar. 12, 1886.
4. "The Case Opened."
5. "The Second Day."
6. "The Second Day."
7. "The Third Day."
8. "The Third Day."
9. "Graham's Great Crime," *Chicago Inter Ocean*, Mar. 16, 1886; *The Graham Tragedy*, 73.
10. "Graham's Great Crime."
11. "Graham's Great Crime."
12. "Very Interesting!"
13. G-M-L, Preliminary Examination, 78–87; "Charley's Charges," *FWDN*, Mar. 17, 1886.
14. "Emma's Man," *FWS*, Mar. 3, 1886; "Exposing Infamy"; "The Graham Trial," *SLPD*, Mar. 16, 1886.

15. "Very Interesting!"
16. "Very Interesting!"
17. "The Terrible Tragedy," *FWDG*, Mar. 17, 1886.
18. "Emma's Fall," *FWDG*, Mar. 19, 1886.
19. "The Fifth Day."
20. "The Fifth Day"; G-M-L, Preliminary Examination, 117–22.
21. "A Big Find!," *FWDN*, Mar. 18, 1886.
22. "The Sixth Day."
23. "Wrangling!," *FWDN*, Mar. 16, 1886; "The Malloy Trial," *SLPD*, Mar. 18, 1886.
24. "The Seventh Day."
25. "The Seventh Day."
26. "The Eighth Day," *SDH*, Mar. 21, 1886; G-M-L, Preliminary Examination, 213.
27. "A Son of Adam," *Chicago Inter Ocean*, Mar. 21, 1886; "Emma's Escapades," *LT*, Mar. 21, 1886.

16. Graham's Great Story

1. *The Graham Tragedy*, 106; "The Ninth Day"; "The Graham Murder," *SE*, Mar. 26, 1886.
2. "The Ninth Day."
3. "The Ninth Day."
4. "The Ninth Day."
5. "'Tell the Truth,'" *FWDN*, Mar. 22, 1886; "A Poem of Passion," *FWDG*, Mar. 23, 1886; "Emma Is Crushed," *FWDG*, Mar. 24, 1886; "Heavily Veiled," *SDH*, Mar. 27, 1886; *The Graham Tragedy*, 98; "Straight Goods," *SDH*, Mar. 23, 1886.
6. "Graham's Great Story," *Chicago Inter Ocean*, Mar. 22, 1886.
7. "Graham's Great Story."
8. "Graham's Great Story."
9. "Graham's Great Story."
10. "Graham's Great Story." *Poems of Passion* created a controversy when the work was first published in January 1883 because of its supposed immoral content.
11. "Graham's Great Story."
12. "Graham's Great Story."
13. "Graham's Great Story."
14. "Graham's Great Story."
15. "Graham's Great Story."
16. "Graham's Great Story."
17. "Mrs. Molloy Ill," *SDH*, Mar. 24, 1886.
18. "Mrs. Molloy Ill"; "Nearing the Close," *Sabetha (KS) Herald*, Mar. 27, 1886, quoting *Kansas City Times*.
19. "Will and Emma," *FWDN*, Mar. 23, 1886.
20. "Will and Emma."
21. "Mrs. Molloy Continues Ill," *SDH*, Mar. 25, 1886.

22. "Stranger Than Fiction," *Sabetha (KS) Herald*, Feb. 27, 1886; "The papers which assume" [first line; no title], *Atchison Weekly Champion*, Mar. 27, 1886.

23. "There has been much enquiry" [first line; no title], *Goshen Weekly News*, Mar. 26, 1886.

17. The Preliminary Hearing, Part Two

1. "The Graham Murder," *SE*, Mar. 26, 1886.
2. "Heavily Veiled"; "At Last!"
3. "Heavily Veiled."
4. "At Last!"; G-M-L, Preliminary Examination, 294.
5. "Letter from Mrs. Molloy," *FWDN*, Mar. 29, 1886.
6. "Letter from Mrs. Molloy."
7. "Letter from Mrs. Molloy."
8. "At Last!"
9. "Drawing to a Close," *SDH*, Mar. 30, 1886.
10. "Drawing to a Close."
11. "Drawing to a Close."
12. "Drawing to a Close."
13. "Drawing to a Close."
14. "Drawing to a Close."
15. "Coming to a Close," *SDH*, Mar. 31, 1886; "The Talk Commenced," *LT*, Mar. 30, 1886.
16. "Coming to a Close."
17. "Coming to a Close."
18. "Coming to a Close."
19. "Coming to a Close."
20. "Coming to a Close."
21. "Coming to a Close."
22. "Coming to a Close."
23. "Coming to a Close."
24. "Coming to a Close."
25. "Coming to a Close."
26. "At Last!"; "Held to Answer," *LT*, Apr. 1, 1886.
27. "Held to Answer."
28. "Both Held," *Fayetteville (AR) Weekly Democrat*, Apr. 9, 1886.
29. "Democratic Nominations," *LT*, Apr. 1, 1886; "The enemies of temperance" [first line; no title], *Humboldt (KS) Union*, Apr. 3, 1886.
30. "Held to Answer."

18. Mrs. Molloy's Champion Rises to Her Defense

1. "Mrs. Molloy Gives Bond," *SDH*, Apr. 4 1886; "The Molloy-Graham-Lee Murder Case," *Concordia Blade*, Apr. 16, 1886, quoting *SDL*.
2. *The Graham Tragedy*, 106; "Local Intelligence," *Wyandott (KS) Herald*, Apr. 15, 1886.

3. "The Reasons," *SDH*, Apr. 11, 1886.
4. "The Reasons."
5. "The Reasons."
6. "The Reasons."
7. "The Reasons."
8. "The Reasons."
9. "The Reasons."
10. "The Reasons."
11. "The Reasons."
12. "The Reasons."
13. "The Reasons."
14. "The Reasons."
15. "The Molloy-Graham-Lee Murder Case," *Concordia Blade*, Apr. 23, 1886.
16. "A Letter from Mrs. Molloy," *SDL*, Apr. 21, 1886.
17. "A Letter from Mrs. Molloy."
18. "A Letter from Mrs. Molloy."
19. "A Letter from Mrs. Molloy."
20. "Two Letters of a Kind," *SDH*, Apr. 22, 1886.
21. "The Leader is in receipt" [first line; no title], *SDL*, Apr. 23, 1886.
22. "We are informed" [first line; no title], *SDH*, Apr. 17, 1886.
23. "Personal," *SDL*, Apr. 21, 1886; "Cora Lee Bound Over," *SDL*, Apr. 24, 1886; "At Bolivar," *SDH*, Apr. 24, 1886.
24. "The Case in a Nutshell," *SDH*, Apr. 23, 1886.

19. Lynched by "The Three Hundred"

1. "Lynched!," *SDH*, Apr. 27, 1886; "Lynched at Last!," *SE*, Apr. 30, 1886.
2. "Lynched!"; "Lynched at Last!"
3. "Lynched!"; "Lynched at Last!"
4. "Lynched!"; "Lynched at Last!"
5. "Lynched!"; "Lynched at Last!"; "Choked!," *FWS*, Apr. 27, 1886; "Graham Lynched!," *SDL*, Apr. 27, 1886.
6. "Lynched at Last!"; "Lynched!"
7. "Lynched at Last!"; "Lynched!"
8. "Graham Lynched!"; "Lynched!"
9. "Graham Lynched!"
10. "Lynched!"
11. "Lynched!"
12. "Graham Lynched!"
13. "Lynched at Last!"; "Graham Lynched!"
14. "Hangings of the Past," *SDL*, Apr. 28, 1886.
15. "My God!," *FWS*, Apr. 29, 1886.
16. "Graham Lynched!"
17. "Graham Lynched!"; "Hangings of the Past."
18. "Lynched!"

19. "Lynched at Last!"
20. "Not So Slow," *LT*, April 29, 1886.
21. "The Graham Hanging," *LT*, Apr. 28, 1886.
22. "Lynched!"
23. "Graham Lynched!"
24. "Lynched at Last!"
25. "Lynched at Last!"
26. "Lynched at Last!"
27. "Lynched at Last!"
28. "Lynched at Last!"
29. "Lynched at Last!"
30. "Lynched at Last!"
31. "Graham Lynched!"
32. "Graham Lynched!"
33. "Hangings of the Past."
34. "Hangings of the Past"; "Graham Grist," *SDL*, Apr. 29, 1886; *The Graham Tragedy*, 111–23.
35. "The Street Corner," *LT*, May 2, 1886; "Circuit Court Proceedings," *SE*, May 7, 1886.
36. "Graham Lynched!"; "Hangings of the Past."
37. "A Slander Refuted," *FWDN*, July 3, 1886.
38. Pictorial and Genealogical Record, 195–98; Holcombe, *History of Greene County*, 500; United States census, 1870; "Emma's Appeal," *FWS*, Mar. 4, 1886.

20. Mrs. Molloy's Statement

1. "Not So!," *FWS*, Apr. 30, 1886; "Local Laconics," *SDL*, May 3, 1886; "Cora Lee," *SDH*, Apr. 30, 1886.
2. "Mrs. Emma Molloy," *SDH*, May 8, 1886.
3. "Mrs. Emma Molloy."
4. "Mrs. Emma Molloy."
5. "The Molloy-Lee Case," *SLPD*, May 10, 1886; "Mrs. Molloy Makes a Statement," *SDH*, May 11, 1886.
6. "Mrs. Molloy Makes a Statement."
7. "Mrs. Molloy Makes a Statement."
8. "Mrs. Molloy Makes a Statement."
9. "Mrs. Molloy Makes a Statement."
10. "Mrs. Molloy Makes a Statement."
11. "Mrs. Molloy Makes a Statement."
12. "Mrs. Molloy Makes a Statement."
13. "Mrs. Molloy Makes a Statement."
14. "Mrs. Molloy Makes a Statement."
15. "Mrs. Molloy Makes a Statement."
16. "Mrs. Molloy Makes a Statement."
17. "Mrs. Molloy Makes a Statement."
18. "Mrs. Molloy Makes a Statement."

19. "Mrs. Molloy Makes a Statement."
20. "Mrs. Molloy Makes a Statement."
21. "Mrs. Molloy Makes a Statement."
22. "Mrs. Molloy Makes a Statement."
23. "The Molloy-Lee Case."
24. "Mrs. Molloy's Statement," *LT,* May 11, 1886; "Mrs. Emma Molloy," *Manhattan (KS) Nationalist,* May 14, 1886; "Mrs. Emma Molloy has published" [first line; no title], *Wyandotte Gazette,* May 14, 1886.
25. "Mrs. Molloy is out" [first line; no title], *Garnett Journal,* May 15, 1886.
26. "A Little Late, Emma," *LT,* May 11, 1886.
27. "Mrs. Emma Malloy has published" [first line; no title], *Huntington (IN) Daily Democrat,* May 12, 1886.
28. "Mrs. Molloy's Defense," *Atchison Weekly Champion,* May 29, 1886.
29. "Sentimental Charity," *SDL,* May 17, 1886.
30. "Mary to Mrs. Molloy," *SDH,* May 14, 1886.

21. Mrs. Molloy's Desolation

1. G-M-L, Graham-Lee indictment; "Circuit Court," *SDL,* May 12, 1886.
2. "Cora Lee," *SDL,* May 29, 1886.
3. G-M-L, Emma Molloy indictments; "Mrs. Emma Molloy Indicted," *New York Times,* June 13, 1886, quoting the *Chicago Inter Ocean;* "In the case of the State vs." [first line; no title], *SDL,* June 12, 1886; "James Robertson of Springfield," *Ottawa (KS) Daily Republic,* June 18, 1886.
4. G-M-L, motions to quash; "Circuit Court," *SDL,* June 22, 1886.
5. "Miss Francis E. Williard," *SDL,* June 22, 1886.
6. "Happenings," *FWDN,* July 1, 1886.
7. "Wants Damages," *SLPD,* June 29, 1886; "She Means Business," *FWDN,* July 12, 1886, quoting *Peoria Journal.*
8. "Mrs. Molloy Rampant," *SDL,* July 1, 1886.
9. "The City," *FWS,* July 14, 1886.
10. "Drowned at Laporte," *FWS,* July 23, 1886; Pickrell, *Emma Speaks Out,* 47; "Local Lines," *FWDN,* July 24, 1886.
11. "Mrs. Molloy as a Mourner," *SE,* Aug. 27, 1886.
12. "Suicide!," *FWS,* Sept. 4, 1886; "Minor Mention," *Indianapolis News,* Sept. 7, 1886; Pickrell, *Emma Speaks Out,* 47, 150.
13. "Mrs. Molloy's Defense," *St. Joseph Weekly Gazette,* Sept. 23, 1886, quoting *Holton (KS) Signal.*
14. "Determined to Die," *SDH,* Sept. 4, 1886.
15. "Local News," *FWS,* Oct. 15, 1886; "The Battle Creek Idea."
16. "Circuit Court," *SDL,* Nov. 20, 1886; "Emma Molloy Again," *Lawrence (KS) Daily Journal,* Nov. 20, 1886; "Cora Lee Moved to Tears," *Chicago Tribune,* Jan. 8, 1887.
17. "Cora Lee," *SDL,* Dec. 13, 1886; "Our Neighbors," *SLPD,* Jan. 7, 1887.
18. "Cora Lee's Case Continued," *SDL,* Jan. 6, 1887; "Gone West," *SDL,* Jan. 8, 1887; "Cora Lee Moved to Tears."

19. "Cora Lee Gives Bond," *SDL*, Feb. 9, 1887.

20. "Is Mrs. Graham Alive," *Rolla (MO) Herald,* Feb. 10, 1887; "Sarah Graham," *FWDN,* Feb. 10, 1887.

21. "Cora Lee Gives Bond."

22. "Emma Molloy Arrives" *SDL,* Feb. 14, 1887; "Off for the West," *SDL,* Feb. 28, 1887; "Mrs. Molloy's Case," *Rochester (IN) Republican,* Feb. 24, 1887.

23. "Mrs. Emma Molloy," *Portland Morning Oregonian,* Mar. 17, 1887; "Mrs. Emma Molloy," *Portland Morning Oregonian,* Mar. 22, 1887; "Mrs. Emma Molloy," *Portland Morning Oregonian,* Apr. 1, 1887.

24. "Mrs. Molloy in the Northwest," *Argos (IN) Reflector,* Apr. 7, 1887, quoting the *South Bend Register.*

22. Cora Lee's First Trial

1. G-M-L, request for special venire, request for elisor; "Cora Lee, the Difficulties of Getting a Jury," *SDL,* June 8, 1887.

2. G-M-L, plea in abatement; "It Is the Cause," *SE,* June 17, 1887; "Cora Lee, the Celebrated Case Commenced," *SDL,* June 13, 1887.

3. "Cora Lee's Trial," *Springfield Weekly Republican,* June 16, 1887; "Cora Lee's Trial," *Springfield Weekly Republican,* June 23, 1887; "It Is the Cause."

4. "Cora Lee's Trial," *Springfield Weekly Republican,* June 23, 1887.

5. "Cora's Cause!," *SDL,* June 14, 1887; "Emma Molloy Testifies," *SDL,* June 15, 1887.

6. "Emma Molloy Testifies."

7. "It Is the Cause"; "Cora Lee's Trial," *Springfield Weekly Republican,* June 23, 1887.

8. "It Is the Cause."

9. "The Case Closes," *SDL,* June 21, 1887.

10. "The State Rests," *SDL,* June 18, 1887.

11. "The State Rests."

12. "Cora Lee's Trial," *SE,* June 24, 1887; "Cora on the Stand," *SDL,* June 20, 1887.

13. "Cora on the Stand"; "Cora Lee's Trial," *SE,* June 24, 1887.

14. "Cora on the Stand."

15. "Cora on the Stand."

16. "Cora Lee's Trial," *SE,* June 24, 1887.

17. "The Case Closes."

18. "The Case Closes"; "Cora Lee's Trial," *Springfield Weekly Republican,* June 23, 1887.

19. "Cora Lee's Trial," *SE,* June 24, 1887.

20. "Circuit Court Proceedings," *SE,* July 1, 1887; "Mrs. Molloy," *SDL,* June 27, 1887.

21. "Mrs. Molloy"; "Mrs. Molloy Asks for a Change of Venue," *SDL,* June 28, 1887.

22. "Can She Have Justice?," *SDL,* June 29, 1887; "Mrs. Emma Molloy will be tried" [first line; no title], *SDL,* Aug. 19, 1887; G-M-L, Molloy change of venue request.

23. "Mrs. Molloy," *SDL,* June 24, 1887; "Local Laconics," *SDL,* July 1, 1887.

23. Cora Lee's Second Trial

1. "Mrs. Emma Molloy, the celebrated temperance lecturer" [first line; no title], *Wyandott Herald*, Aug. 18, 1887; "Personal," *LT*, Aug. 25, 1887.
2. "The Molloy-Lee Case," *Washington (KS) Register*; "Local Intelligence," *Washington Republican*, Oct. 21, 1887.
3. "The Molloy Case," *SDL*, Aug. 28, 1887.
4. "The Day's Doings," *SDL*, Nov. 17, 1887; "The Day's Doings," *SDL*, Nov. 15, 1887.
5. "Cora Lee Graham," *SDL*, Jan. 10, 1888; "Circuit Court," *SDL*, Jan. 17, 1888; "Newcomers," *SDH*, Jan. 15, 1888.
6. "Cora E. Lee," *SDL*, Jan. 20, 1888; "The Lee Trial," *Springfield Daily Republican*, Jan. 20, 1888.
7. "Cora E. Lee."
8. "Cora E. Lee"; "Hole in the Wall," *SDL*, Jan. 21, 1888.
9. "Charlie Graham," *Springfield Daily Republican*, Jan. 21, 1888.
10. "Hole in the Wall."
11. "Cora E. Lee"; "Hole in the Wall"; "The Veiled Woman," *SDL*, Jan. 23, 1888.
12. "The Veiled Woman."
13. "The Veiled Woman."
14. "The Defense," *SDL*, Jan. 24, 1888.
15. "The Defense."
16. "The Defense."
17. "The Defense."
18. "The Defense"; "Testimony Closed," *SDL*, Jan. 26, 1888.
19. "Hole in the Wall"; "Testimony Closed."
20. "Testimony Closed."
21. "The Arguments," *SDH*, Jan. 28, 1888; "Not Guilty," *SE*, Feb. 3, 1888.
22. G-M-L, instructions to jury; "The Last Accusing Witness," *SDH*, Jan. 24, 1888; "Cora Lee Acquitted," *SDH*, Jan. 29, 1888.
23. "Cora Lee Acquitted."
24. "Not Guilty"; "Cora Lee Acquitted"; "Cora's Case Closed," *SDL*, Jan. 30, 1888.
25. "Not Guilty," *Springfield Weekly Republican*, Feb. 2, 1888; "Cora Lee Acquitted," *SLPD*, Jan. 29, 1888.
26. "Is She Guilty?," *Springfield Daily Republican*, Jan. 26, 1888; "Cora Lee Acquitted"; "Cora's Case Closed."
27. "The verdict reached in the Cora Lee case" [first line; no title], *Springfield Daily Republican*, Jan. 29, 1888.
28. "Cora Lee in Kansas City," *SDL*, Feb. 3, 1888, quoting the *Kansas City Star.*

24. Mrs. Molloy's Redemption

1. "Cora Lee Acquitted," *SLPD*, Jan. 29, 1888; "Court at Ozark," *SDL*, Feb. 27, 1888; "Mrs. Emma Molloy," *SE*, Mar. 9, 1888.
2. "Mrs. Emma Molloy."
3. "Mrs. Emma Molloy."

4. "Mrs. Molloy Again," *SE,* Mar. 16, 1888.

5. "Mrs. Molloy Again."

6. "Mrs. Molloy Again."

7. "Mrs. Emma Molloy recently told a reporter" [first line; no title], *Portland Morning Oregonian,* Mar. 15, 1888.

8. "Territorial News," *Olympia (WA) Standard,* Aug. 3, 1888; Pickrell, *Emma Speaks Out,* 48

9. Pickrell, *Emma Speaks Out,* 48–49.

10. Pickrell, *Emma Speaks Out,* 48, 150.

11. "Noted Revivalist," *Salem (OR) Statesman Journal,* Jan. 8, 1889; "Harrisburg," *Albany (OR) Daily Democrat,* Feb. 4, 1889.

12. Pickrell, *Emma Speaks Out,* 49.

13. Pickrell, *Emma Speaks Out,* 50.

14. Pickrell, *Emma Speaks Out,* 50.

15. Pickrell, *Emma Speaks Out,* 50–51, 151.

16. "Nebraska Marriages"; United States Census, 1900, 1920, 1930; "Cora Elizabeth Lee Juel," *Find a Grave.*

17. United States Census, 1910, 1920.

18. "A Reminiscence," *Great Bend (KS) Barton County Democrat,* Feb. 26, 1891; "Famous Murder Is Recalled," *FWS,* Jan. 17, 1923; "Justice Rides with a Springfield Mob," *SDL,* Aug. 14, 1930.

19. "Last Chapter Written on 1885 Murder Victim's Life," *Springfield News-Leader,* Sept. 26, 2004.

25. Unanswered Questions

1. "The Mistakes of Molloy," *FWS,* Mar. 17, 1886.

2. "Geo. Graham Lynched," *Richmond (IN) Item,* Apr. 28, 1886, quoting *St. Louis Globe Democrat.*

3. "The Reasons," *SDH,* Apr. 11, 1886.

4. "The Reasons."

5. "Her 'Poor Boy!,'" *FWDN,* Mar. 4, 1886.

6. "Xenia Local News," *Xenia Daily Gazette,* Oct. 9, 1883; "Mrs. Molloy, the eloquent temperance advocate" [first line; no title], *Wellington Enterprise,* Nov. 7, 1883; "Mrs. Emma Molloy," *SE,* Mar. 9, 1888; "Mrs. Molloy Makes a Statement," *SDH,* May 11, 1886.

7. "There has been much enquiry" [first line; no title], *Goshen Weekly News,* Mar. 26, 1886.

8. "Ah, There," *FWDN,* Feb. 15, 1886.

9. "The papers which assume" [first line; no title], *Atchison Daily Champion,* Mar. 21, 1886.

10. "Molloy, Graham, Lee," *Concordia Blade,* July 2, 1886.

Epilogue

1. "Brookline Will Get Police, Fire Protection," *Springfield News-Leader,* June 6, 2005.

Bibliography

Anderson and Cooley, comp. *South Bend and the Men Who Have Made It.* South Bend, IN: The Tribune Printing Co., 1901.

"The Battle Creek Idea." *Heritage Battle Creek.* http://www.heritagebattlecreek. org/index. php?option=com_content&view=article&id=95&Itemid=73.

Bunting, Josiah, III. *Ulysses S. Grant.* New York: Henry Holt and Company, 2004.

Christian County Circuit Court Case Files. Microfilm Copies. Christian County Library, Ozark, MO.

Coker, Joe L. *Liquor in the Land of the Lost Cause.* Lexington: Univ. Press of Kentucky, 2007.

Convict Register. Illinois State Penitentiary, Illinois State Archives, Springfield, IL.

Descriptive List of Convicts. Indiana State Prison North, Indiana State Archives, Indianapolis, IN.

Emma Barrett Molloy Collection. Indiana Historical Society, Indianapolis, IN.

Fahey, David M. *Temperance and Racism: John Bull, Johnny Reb, and the Good Templars.* Lexington: Univ. Press of Kentucky, 1996.

Fairbanks, Jonathan, and Clyde Edwin Turk. *Past and Present of Greene County, Missouri.* Vol. 1. Indianapolis: A. W. Bowen and Company, 1915.

Find a Grave. https://www.findagrave.com.

"First Congregational Church." Springfield-Greene County Library. http://thelibrary.org/blogs/article.cfm?aid=636.

Fletcher, Holly Berkley. *Gender and the American Temperance Movement.* New York: Routledge, 2008.

George Graham pardon papers. Indiana State Archives, Indianapolis, IN.

Graham-Molloy-Lee File. Greene County Archives and Records Center, Springfield, MO.

The Graham Tragedy and the Molloy-Lee Examination. 1886. Facsimile of the first edition with an introduction by Robert Neumann. Springfield: Greene County Archives, 2001.

Hernando, Matthew J. *Faces Like Devils: The Bald Knobber Vigilantes in the Ozarks.* Columbia: Univ. of Missouri Press, 2015.

Hiatt, James. *The Ribbon Workers.* Chicago: Goodspeed Publishing, 1878.

Holcombe, R. I., ed. *History of Greene County, Missouri.* St. Louis: Western Historical Company, 1883.

History of St. Joseph County, Indiana. Chicago: Charles C. Chapman and Co., 1880.

Illinois Statewide Marriage Index. Illinois State Archives. http://www.ilsos.gov /isavital/marriagesrch.jsp.

An Illustrated Historical Atlas Map of Greene County, Mo. Philadelphia: Brink, McDonough & Co., 1876.

"Indiana Marriages, 1811–2007." https://familysearch.org.

Linden, Douglas O. "Lynchings by State and Race, 1882–1968." University of Missouri Kansas City School of Law. http://www.famous-trials.com/sheriffshipp /1083-lynchingsstate.

"Nebraska Marriages." www.familysearch.org.

"Ohio Marriages, 1800–1958." https://familysearch.org.

Pacey, Mary Alice, comp. Washington County Newspaper Clippings and Transcriptions. Washington County Historical Society, Washington, KS.

Pickrell, Martha M. *Emma Speaks Out: Life and Writings of Emma Molloy, 1839–1907.* Carmel, IN: Guild Press, 1999.

Pictorial and Genealogical Record of Greene County, Missouri. Chicago: Goodspeed, 1893.

Thornbrough, Emma Lou. *Indiana in the Civil War Era, 1850–1880.* Vol. 3. Indianapolis: Indiana Historical Society, 2016.

United States censuses. https://familysearch.org.

Whitaker, F. M. "The Ohio WCTU and the Prohibition Amendment Campaign of 1883." *Ohio History Journal* 83, no. 2 (Spring 1974): 84–102.

Willard, Frances E. *Let Something Good Be Said: The Speeches and Writings of Frances E. Willard.* Edited by Carolyn De Swarte Gifford and Amy R. Slagell. Urbana: Univ. of Illinois Press, 2007.

Wood, Larry. *Wicked Springfield.* Charleston, SC: The History Press, 2012.

Index

Page numbers in italics refer to illustrations.